LOW-COST CARRIER OPPORTUNITIES, AIR TRANSPORT LIBERALIZATION, AND POST-PANDEMIC RECOVERY IN CAREC

MAY 2024

 Creative Commons Attribution 3.0 IGO license (CC BY 3.0 IGO)

© 2024 Asian Development Bank
6 ADB Avenue, Mandaluyong City, 1550 Metro Manila, Philippines
Tel +63 2 8632 4444; Fax +63 2 8636 2444
www.adb.org

Some rights reserved. Published in 2024.

ISBN 978-92-9270-706-4 (print); 978-92-9270-707-1 (PDF); 978-92-9270-708-8 (e-book)
Publication Stock No. SPR240273-2
DOI: http://dx.doi.org/10.22617/SPR240273-2

The views expressed in this publication are those of the authors and do not necessarily reflect the views and policies of the Asian Development Bank (ADB) or its Board of Governors or the governments they represent.

ADB does not guarantee the accuracy of the data included in this publication and accepts no responsibility for any consequence of their use. The mention of specific companies or products of manufacturers does not imply that they are endorsed or recommended by ADB in preference to others of a similar nature that are not mentioned.

By making any designation of or reference to a particular territory or geographic area in this document, ADB does not intend to make any judgments as to the legal or other status of any territory or area.

This publication is available under the Creative Commons Attribution 3.0 IGO license (CC BY 3.0 IGO) https://creativecommons.org/licenses/by/3.0/igo/. By using the content of this publication, you agree to be bound by the terms of this license. For attribution, translations, adaptations, and permissions, please read the provisions and terms of use at https://www.adb.org/terms-use#openaccess.

This CC license does not apply to non-ADB copyright materials in this publication. If the material is attributed to another source, please contact the copyright owner or publisher of that source for permission to reproduce it. ADB cannot be held liable for any claims that arise as a result of your use of the material.

Please contact pubsmarketing@adb.org if you have questions or comments with respect to content, or if you wish to obtain copyright permission for your intended use that does not fall within these terms, or for permission to use the ADB logo.

Corrigenda to ADB publications may be found at http://www.adb.org/publications/corrigenda.

Notes:
In this publication, "$" refers to United States dollars.

ADB recognizes "China" as the People's Republic of China, "Korea" as the Republic of Korea, "Kyrgyzstan" as the Kyrgyz Republic, and "Russia" as the Russian Federation.

ADB placed its regular assistance to Afghanistan on hold effective 15 August 2021.

Cover design by Jasper Lauzon.

Contents

Tables and Figures	iv
Preface	vi
Acknowledgments	x
Abbreviations	xi
Executive Summary and Recommendations	xii
Background and Introduction	1
Overview of Low-Cost Carriers in CAREC	6
Overview of Market Recovery in CAREC	12
Opportunities: Intra-CAREC Market	16
Opportunities: Domestic Market	24
Opportunities: International Market (Excluding Intra-CAREC)	27
Opportunities: Airport Infrastructure Focused on Low-Cost Carriers	30
CASE STUDY 1: Azerbaijan and Buta Airways	31
CASE STUDY 2: Georgia and Kutaisi Airport (Wizz Air Base)	39
CASE STUDY 3: Kazakhstan and FlyArystan	53
CASE STUDY 4: Kyrgyz Republic and Air Manas	71
CASE STUDY 5: Mongolia and Eznis Airways	83
CASE STUDY 6: Uzbekistan and Uzbekistan Express	102

Tables and Figures

Tables

1	CAREC International Seat Capacity Recovery Rate by Country (First 3 Quarters of 2023)	ix
2	International Seat Capacity Recovery Rate by Market (First 3 Quarters of 2023)	ix
3	CAREC Scheduled International Seat Capacity Share by Country	2
4	Top Four CAREC Airline Groups Based on Capacity Share	4
5	Local Low-Cost Carriers in CAREC Ranked by Start Date with Fleet Size, as of end of 2022	5
6	CAREC Low-Cost Carrier Penetration Rate by Country, 2019	6
7	Low-Cost Carrier Penetration Rate by Region, 2019	7
8	CAREC Low-Cost Carrier Penetration Rate by Country, 2022	8
9	Low-Cost Carrier Penetration Rate by Region, 2022	8
10	Seat Capacity for Local CAREC Low-Cost Carriers, 2022 versus 2019	9
11	Seat Capacity for Foreign Low-Cost Carriers in CAREC, 2022 versus 2019	10
12	Number of Foreign Low-Cost Carriers Serving CAREC by Country, 2022 versus 2019	11
13	Scheduled Seat Capacity Recovery Rates by Country, 2022 versus 2019	12
14	Scheduled International Seat Capacity Recovery Rates by Country, 2022 versus 2019	13
15	Seat Capacity Recovery Rate by Region, 2022 versus 2019	14
16	Scheduled Seat Capacity Recovery Rates by Country, January 2023 versus January 2020	15
17	New Intra-CAREC Routes, 2021 and 2022	17
18	Intra-CAREC Routes That Operated Pre-pandemic and Resumed by end of 2022	19
19	Intra-CAREC Capacity Share by Airline, 2022 and 2019	20
20	Intra-Regional Portion of Total International Seat Capacity by Region, 2022 and 2019	21
21	Intra-CAREC Portion of Total International Seat Capacity by Country, 2022 and 2019	21
22	Top Five International Markets for CAREC Based on Share of Seat Capacity, 2022 and 2019	27
23	Low-Cost Carriers in Azerbaijan Ranked by Seat Capacity Share, 2022 versus 2019	33
24	Top 10 Airlines in Georgia Based on Passenger Traffic, 2019 and 2022	42
25	Kazakhstan Airports Ranked by Domestic Seat Capacity	56

26	International Low-Cost Carrier Seat Capacity in Kazakhstan Ranked by Airline, 2022 versus 2019	61
27	Kyrgyz Republic International Capacity Share by Airline, Excluding Russian Federation	73
28	Top 10 International Routes from Mongolia Based on Passenger Traffic	85
29	Top 10 Domestic Routes in Mongolia Based on Passenger Traffic	97
30	Low-Cost Carrier Routes in Uzbekistan Ranked by Weekly Frequency, January 2023	104
31	Domestic routes in Uzbekistan Ranked by Weekly Frequency (Prior to Silk Avia Launch)	114

Figures

1	Nine Freedoms of the Air	23
2	Kutaisi Airport Annual Passenger Traffic, 2012–2023	41
3	Tbilisi Airport Annual Passenger Traffic, 2005–2022	43
4	Batumi Airport Annual Passenger Traffic, 2008–2022	44
5	Almaty Airport Annual Domestic Passenger Traffic, 2018–2022	55
6	Bishkek Manas International Airport Annual Passenger Traffic, 2013–2022	74
7	Osh Airport Annual Passenger Traffic, 2013–2022	75
8	Mongolia International Passenger Traffic, 2009–2022	86

Preface

The initial research for this study began in the second half of 2022 and the study was written in early 2023. Data from 2022 and January 2023 were used as well as data from 2019 and January 2020, which provide a baseline for pre-pandemic comparisons. The initial pre-publication draft was completed in March 2023 and shared with Central Asia Regional Economic Cooperation (CAREC) aviation industry stakeholders in April 2023.

The CAREC aviation market has since been continuing to develop at a rapid pace. There has been rapid growth observed in the summer of 2023, with scheduled international seat capacity in CAREC, excluding Afghanistan and the People's Republic of China (PRC), up by about 20% compared to the same period in 2019. Low-cost carriers (LCCs) have continued to expand in the CAREC region—continuing the trend which started during the pandemic and that is discussed extensively in this study. Most full-service carriers (FSCs) in CAREC are also now fully recovered and are showing signs of growth.

Latest scheduled seat capacity data (as shown in the two succeeding tables) highlight how the overall market is enjoying rapid growth in 2023. Total international seat capacity in CAREC, excluding Afghanistan and the PRC, reached pre-coronavirus disease (COVID-19) levels for the first time in September 2022, and the market was up a modest 4% in the fourth quarter of 2022 (Q4 2022) compared to Q4 2019, based on scheduled seat capacity data from OAG. Only four of the nine CAREC member countries had fully recovered international seat capacity in Q4 2022—Azerbaijan, the Kyrgyz Republic, Tajikistan, and Uzbekistan.

In Q1 2023, international seat capacity in Kazakhstan, Mongolia, and Pakistan was also fully recovered, while Georgia achieved full recovery in Q2 2023. Overall, international seat capacity in CAREC (excluding Afghanistan and the PRC) reached 112% of 2019 levels in Q1 2023, after reaching 104% of 2019 levels in Q4 2022 and 94% of 2019 levels for the full year in 2022. Scheduled international seat capacity in CAREC reached 116% of 2019 levels in Q2 2023 and 122% in Q3 2023. All these recovery figures are based on seats—both filled and unfilled—with 2019 as the baseline period.

Table 1 summarizes the international seat capacity recovery rates by country for the first 3 quarters of 2023. The global average for international seat capacity is also provided, highlighting how CAREC continues to track well above the global average. For 2023, CAREC is on pace to achieve an international recovery rate of about 30 percentage points above the global average, after achieving a rate of 25 percentage points above the global average in 2022.

In Q3 2023, scheduled international seat capacity for LCCs is about double 2019 levels, while scheduled international seat capacity for FSCs is up by about 7%. LCCs are on pace to achieve for the full year in 2023 a 26%–27% share of the CAREC international market. While LCCs continue to gain market share after reaching a 25% share of international seat capacity in 2022, the rate of the gains is moderating, which is typical once LCCs start to reach higher levels of capacity in a market. However, LCCs in the CAREC region are still growing rapidly alongside rapid growth in the overall market.

Table 2 shows the LCC and FSC seat capacity recovery rates in the overall CAREC international market for the first 3 quarters of 2023, as well as recovery rates in key markets.

Table 1: CAREC International Seat Capacity Recovery Rate by Country (First 3 Quarters of 2023)

Rank	Country	Q1 2023	Q2 2023	Q3 2023	9M 2023
1	Tajikistan	157%	207%	186%	181%
2	Kyrgyz Republic	159%	166%	176%	167%
3	Uzbekistan	138%	140%	149%	142%
4	Azerbaijan	121%	113%	116%	116%
5	Kazakhstan	104%	109%	112%	109%
6	Mongolia	101%	108%	113%	108%
7	Pakistan	102%	103%	114%	106%
8	Georgia	94%	103%	114%	105%
9	Turkmenistan	29%	56%	46%	43%
	Central Asia subtotal	**124%**	**135%**	**135%**	**132%**
	Global average	82%	89%	93%	88%
	CAREC Total	**112%**	**116%**	**122%**	**117%**

CAREC = Central Asia Regional Economic Cooperation.

Notes: CAREC total excludes Afghanistan and the People's Republic of China. Central Asia includes Kazakhstan, the Kyrgyz Republic, Tajikistan, Turkmenistan, and Uzbekistan. Recovery rate is calculated using the same quarter of 2019 as a baseline. Ranking is based on recovery rate of international seat capacity for the first 9 months of 2023 (9M 2023).

Source: Author, based on data from the OAG schedules database (as of mid-July 2023).

Table 2: International Seat Capacity Recovery Rate by Market (First 3 Quarters of 2023)

Market/Segment	Q1 2023	Q2 2023	Q3 2023	9M 2023	% of Total 9M 2023
Russian Federation	110%	115%	122%	116%	24%
GCC	120%	116%	133%	123%	38%
Türkiye	144%	149%	151%	149%	14%
Europe	92%	103%	99%	99%	10%
Intra-CAREC	128%	133%	142%	136%	7%
PRC	36%	68%	69%	59%	2%
Others	85%	104%	90%	93%	5%
Total	**112%**	**116%**	**122%**	**117%**	
Full-service carriers	**99%**	**104%**	**107%**	**103%**	**74%**
Low-cost carriers	**179%**	**184%**	**199%**	**188%**	**26%**

CAREC = Central Asia Regional Economic Cooperation, GCC = Gulf Cooperation Council, PRC = People's Republic of China.

Note: Intra-CAREC excludes Afghanistan and the PRC; The PRC is listed separately. Europe excludes the Russian Federation and Türkiye, which are listed separately. GCC includes Bahrain, Kuwait, Oman, Qatar, Saudi Arabia, and the United Arab Emirates. Recovery rate is calculated using the same quarter of 2019 as a baseline.

Source: Author, based on data from the OAG schedules database (as of mid-July 2023).

The Russian Federation is the largest individual market, accounting for about 24% of total international seat capacity from CAREC, and it has continued to grow in 2023. However, the Russian Federation growth rate is slower than the overall growth rate despite CAREC countries benefiting from the lack of direct flights from other regions to the Russian Federation due to Russia's war in Ukraine.

The Gulf Cooperation Council (GCC) and Türkiye markets have grown faster than the Russian Federation. The 5 GCC countries combined account for about 38% of international seat capacity in CAREC, led by the United Arab Emirates (UAE) with 19% and Saudi Arabia with 11%. Türkiye is the third-largest individual market (after the Russian Federation and the UAE), accounting for a 14% share of CAREC international seat capacity in the first 9 months of 2023.

The regional market within CAREC (international flights between the CAREC countries excluding Afghanistan and the PRC) has also grown faster than the Russian Federation market. But this remains a very small and underserved market, accounting for only 7% of total international seat capacity in the first 9 months of 2023.

Not surprisingly, the PRC market (flights from the nine CAREC countries included in this study to the PRC) is still not fully recovered as the PRC only reopened its borders in early 2023. However, CAREC–PRC capacity was almost 70% recovered in Q2 2023. Flights from Inner Mongolia and Xinjiang (parts of the PRC that are covered by CAREC) to other CAREC countries account for about one-third of the total CAREC–PRC capacity. The recovery rate on these flights is similar to the recovery rate of flights from other regions of the PRC to CAREC countries.

Urumqi in Xinjiang was connected to 10 destinations in other CAREC countries in the summer of 2023, compared to 11 destinations in 2019, but seat capacity was still down by about 35%. The Inner Mongolia–CAREC market is very small, consisting of three routes from cities in Inner Mongolia to Mongolia in both summer of 2019 and 2023.

Overall, there were 59 intra-CAREC routes in the summer of 2023, including the 13 routes from the CAREC regions of the PRC and 46 routes connecting the nine CAREC countries which are included in this study. However, 10 of these routes had very limited services (less than one weekly flight on average for the summer season).

In the summer of 2019, there were 41 intra-CAREC routes, including 14 from the CAREC regions of the PRC and 27 connecting the nine CAREC countries included in this study. There were two routes which had very limited services (less than one weekly flight on average).

There has been a surge of new intra-CAREC routes both in 2022 (which is discussed in one of the main sections of this study) and again in 2023. While the improvement in intra-CAREC connectivity is encouraging, most of the new routes are not served year-round and some have already been suspended.

Of the 59 intra-CAREC routes that were operated in summer of 2023, only six were served daily (at least seven weekly frequencies). The average number of weekly frequencies for these 59 routes is only three. The need for more regular services on more intra-CAREC routes—and the potential role of LCCs in driving an increase in intra-CAREC flights—is discussed in the study.

In the non-regional international market (connecting CAREC countries with countries in other regions), there also has been another surge of new routes in 2023, launched by both FSCs and LCCs. Perhaps the most significant network development in 2023 is the launch of services to CAREC by India's leading LCC, IndiGo. In June 2023, IndiGo announced plans to serve four CAREC destinations—Almaty, Baku, Tashkent, and Tbilisi—with flights from Delhi starting in August and September 2023. In September 2023, CAREC–India capacity was more than double September 2022 levels driven by IndiGo as well as the launch of Kazakhstan–India services by FlyArystan, CAREC's largest LCC.

India is still a tiny market for CAREC, accounting for less than 1% of CAREC's total international seat capacity. There is a massive opportunity for further CAREC–India growth. This study identifies India, among others, as a major potential growth market for CAREC, particularly for LCCs.

There are also opportunities in CAREC's domestic market, although only Kazakhstan and Pakistan have sizable domestic markets. In the summer of 2023, Kazakhstan's scheduled domestic seat capacity was up by about 50% compared to 2019, while Pakistan's domestic seat capacity was roughly flat. Most of the growth in the Kazakhstan domestic market was already achieved in 2022 and is analyzed in detail in the main sections of this study.

Pakistan has experienced an increase in domestic LCC capacity since the launch of Fly Jinnah in November 2022, but the overall domestic market has not grown. Fly Jinnah also did not pursue expansion in the first half of 2023, and by July 2023, it was operating only a slightly higher number of flights compared to the start of the year.

FlyArystan, which commenced operations in May 2019, also did not expand in the first half of 2023. But it resumed expansion in the second half of 2023 and already drove the rapid domestic growth Kazakhstan experienced from 2019 to 2022.

The other seven CAREC countries that are included in this study have very small domestic markets, but there have been noteworthy developments in 2023. In April 2023, Silk Avia, a new domestic LCC that was established by Uzbekistan Airports, was launched. At the end of June 2023, full-service flag carrier MIAT Mongolian Airlines relaunched scheduled domestic services for the first time since 2008. In July 2023, full-service flag carrier Uzbekistan Airways expanded in the domestic market after taking delivery of a small turboprop aircraft, marking the first time it has operated turboprops since 2018. A new domestic airline is also planned in the Kyrgyz Republic and established by Manas International Airport OJSC. In Georgia, the government is planning to select a new airline to take over subsidized domestic services from AK Air.

While there is a need to improve domestic services in CAREC, governments using airport companies to launch domestic airlines is a concerning trend. CAREC would benefit from a review of domestic air transport policies—both in the smaller markets as well as the two larger markets—to ensure global best practices are followed.

Acknowledgments

The study was prepared by the Asian Development Bank (ADB) under the technical assistance (TA) project TA 9754-REG: Central Asia Regional Economic Cooperation (CAREC): Knowledge Sharing and Services in Transport and Transport Facilitation (Phase 2). The Central and West Asia Department led the study under the guidance and supervision of Ganesh Kailasam. All chapters were written by Brendan Sobie of Sobie Aviation, also acting as senior aviation specialist and consultant for CAREC.

Much appreciation is expressed to the governments of Azerbaijan, Georgia, Kazakhstan, the Kyrgyz Republic, Mongolia, and Uzbekistan for supporting missions to their respective countries during the research phase of this study. Much appreciation is also expressed to the over 20 companies from these six countries that supported the research phase of this study.

Abbreviations

ADB	Asian Development Bank
AOC	air operator certificate
CAREC	Central Asia Regional Economic Cooperation
CAAM	Civil Aviation Authority of Mongolia
COVID-19	coronavirus disease
EASA	European Union Aviation Safety Agency
ECAA	European Common Aviation Area
EU	European Union
FAA	Federal Aviation Administration (United States)
FSC	full-service carrier
GCC	Gulf Cooperation Council
GDP	gross domestic product
GNTA	Georgian National Tourism Administration
IATA	International Air Transport Association
LCC	low-cost carrier
PPP	public–private partnership
PRC	People's Republic of China
TA	technical assistance
UAG	United Airports of Georgia
US	United States

Executive Summary and Recommendations

Executive Summary

In announcing record financial results for 2022, Air Astana Group president and chief executive officer Peter Foster pointed out that its low-cost carrier (LCC) subsidiary FlyArystan "has grown by 366% since its inaugural year of 2019. It has a great future, as this region probably has the fastest growing low-cost travel market in the world today."

FlyArystan flew 700,000 passengers in 2019 and 3.26 million passengers in 2022, equivalent to 366% growth. In 2022, FlyArystan was the third-largest airline in Central Asia and the fourth-largest airline in the Central Asia Regional Economic Cooperation (CAREC) region, excluding the People's Republic of China (PRC). Only its full-service parent Air Astana, and Pakistan International Airlines and Uzbekistan Airways, were larger.

FlyArystan provides the best example of how fast LCCs grew in Central Asia and the CAREC region during the COVID-19 pandemic. But it is not the only example as the overall LCC market in Central Asia more than tripled in size from 2019 to 2022, making it indeed the fastest-growing low-cost travel market in the world. FlyArystan accounted for nearly 70% of this growth, with Uzbekistan Airways' LCC subsidiary, Uzbekistan Express, accounting for about 15% and foreign LCCs accounting for the remaining 15%.

In the wider CAREC region, the LCC market grew by 60% from 2019 to 2022, with FlyArystan accounting for nearly half of this growth. FlyArystan is now the largest LCC in CAREC, capturing about a 23% share of the region's LCC seat capacity in 2022. Pakistan's airblue is the second-largest CAREC-based LCC with about a 13% share of total LCC capacity in CAREC, followed by Uzbekistan Express with 4% and AZAL Azerbaijan Airlines' LCC subsidiary, Buta Airways, with 4%. Over half the market is controlled by foreign LCCs, led by flydubai with about a 17% share and Air Arabia with a 10% share.

Foreign LCCs have grown rapidly in CAREC and have accounted for most of the recent LCC growth in the international air transport market. In 2022, LCCs accounted for 15% of international seat capacity in Central Asia and 25% in CAREC. In 2019, LCCs accounted for only a 5% share of international seat capacity in Central Asia and a 17% share in CAREC. When including the domestic market, the LCC share of total seat capacity increased from 7% to 20% in Central Asia and from 15% to 25% in CAREC.

The rapid LCC growth during the pandemic has helped drive a quick recovery of the CAREC air transport market. Total seat capacity in the CAREC region was 98% recovered in 2022, while Central Asia was 106% recovered. Central Asia was the only region in the world with seat capacity above 2019 levels in 2022. LCC capacity was 318% recovered in Central Asia and 161% recovered in CAREC, while full-service carrier (FSC) capacity was 91% recovered in Central Asia and 86% recovered in CAREC.

The CAREC region includes the five Central Asian countries—Kazakhstan, the Kyrgyz Republic, Tajikistan, Turkmenistan, and Uzbekistan—as well as Azerbaijan, Georgia, Mongolia, and Pakistan. (The Inner Mongolia and Xinjiang regions of the PRC are also part of CAREC, but are not included in this study.)

Azerbaijan and Georgia had the highest LCC market shares in CAREC (both before and after the pandemic), while Kazakhstan and Uzbekistan had the biggest growth in LCC market share during the pandemic.

However, Georgia was the only CAREC country with an LCC share capacity that was above the global average in 2022. This highlights the opportunity for further LCC growth in virtually every CAREC country.

Rapid LCC growth over the remainder of this decade is critical for CAREC to achieve aspirations to improve connectivity—within and outside the region—and further grow tourism in the region. LCCs generate massive economic benefits as lower fares make air travel more affordable, stimulating demand in both the domestic and international markets. With higher volumes of traffic, there are more tourists staying in hotels, eating out, and visiting local attractions. More passenger traffic also supports expansion of airports and the overall aviation ecosystem, creating jobs.

However, LCCs cannot proliferate and thrive without a supportive regulatory environment. Several CAREC countries have adopted more liberal aviation policies over the last several years, facilitating the recent wave of LCC growth. However, the principal finding of this study is that further liberalization is needed for further growth and for LCCs to reach their full potential in the CAREC region.

True "open skies" are uncommon in CAREC, as most CAREC countries have not yet adopted any open skies policy or have adopted open skies policies with significant limitations. Traffic rights are not always available, making it impossible on some routes to attract new LCC competition and therefore reduce airfares. More liberal open skies policies, which are common in other regions, would ensure airlines are always able to operate between their home country and another country (third and fourth freedoms). Liberal policies could also permit airlines to operate between two countries, neither of which is their home country (fifth and seventh freedoms).

High airport costs are another major impediment to LCC growth in CAREC, which is highlighted in several sections of this study. Most CAREC airports have charges, fees, and taxes for international flights that are well above global averages. There is a lack of sufficient regulation, resulting in exorbitant charges from monopoly service providers. While LCCs have expanded in recent years despite high airport costs, their ability to stimulate the market is limited as they need to pass on these costs to passengers.

Lower airport costs would enable lower fares, leading to higher volumes of traffic, and help attract more LCCs. This study recommends a re-examination of airport pricing structures to facilitate LCC growth as well as the introduction of new programs to incentivize LCC route development.

It was not possible in this study to publish a table comparing airport charges and fees in CAREC with other regions due to a lack of disclosure and transparency. However, interviews with several airlines highlight how much more they are paying in charges and fees at most CAREC airports compared to airports in other regions. In some CAREC countries, airport charges and fees are higher for foreign airlines than local airlines, creating an unlevel playing field and making it harder for these countries to attract foreign LCCs.

There are four sets of CAREC recommendations aimed at three market segments—intra-CAREC (air travel between CAREC countries), domestic, and international (air travel connecting CAREC with the rest of the world)—and at airport infrastructure. The 12 CAREC recommendations across these four categories are included in the summary of recommendations and are explained in the four "opportunities" sections of this study (pages 35 to 51). There are also specific recommendations for each of the six CAREC countries that are included in the case studies. These recommendations can be found at the conclusion of each case study (pages 53 to 145).

Summary of Recommendations

Intra-CAREC

1. CAREC countries should consider providing fifth and seventh freedom rights for intra-CAREC routes, enabling local as well as foreign airlines to launch more intra-CAREC routes and facilitating the development of the intra-CAREC market, including LCC development.

2. CAREC countries should consider adopting a universal visa-free policy for all CAREC countries, which would facilitate cross-CAREC tourism and drive improved connectivity within CAREC, as well as boost the CAREC aviation and tourism sectors.

3. CAREC countries should consider reducing taxes, fees, and charges for intra-CAREC flights to help facilitate the development of more flights within CAREC, and improve intra-CAREC connectivity.

4. CAREC countries should consider establishing programs to incentivize and support new intra-CAREC routes.

Domestic

1. CAREC countries should consider policies and programs to facilitate the development of domestic air transport, particularly LCC development.

2. CAREC countries subsidizing domestic air travel and/or regulating domestic airfares should examine new options or funding mechanisms for both airports and airlines.

3. CAREC should consider a separate study on the opportunities for domestic LCC development in Pakistan, as the scale of the opportunities in Pakistan and the market characteristic are very different than in other CAREC countries.

International

1. CAREC airports should re-examine their structure of prices and charges to ensure they are not dissuading airlines from new markets from launching services, particularly LCCs.

2. CAREC countries should consider programs, policies, and strategies to tackle high international airfares, which have become the largest impediment to tourism growth.

3. CAREC countries should introduce new policies and strategies that facilitate a diversification of their international air transport markets by reducing their reliance on the Russian Federation, the GCC, and Türkiye.

Airport Infrastructure

1. CAREC countries should consider public–private partnerships and other options for facilitating development of airport infrastructure and for improving airport efficiency levels.

2. CAREC airports should consider developing LCC terminals and focusing more on LCCs as they upgrade their infrastructure.

(There are also six sets of specific recommendations for six CAREC member countries; these are included in the case studies.)

Background and Introduction

CAREC Aviation Program Background

The Central Asia Regional Economic Cooperation (CAREC) launched an aviation program in 2017, following a recommendation by the Prime Minister of Pakistan at CAREC's 15th Ministerial Conference in October 2016. An initial workshop on the aviation sector was held in Singapore in April 2017, and an initial scoping study on aviation and the role of CAREC was published in September 2018. A subsequent study on the impact of the coronavirus disease (COVID-19) pandemic on CAREC aviation and tourism was published in February 2021.

Related links:

CAREC Aviation Consultation Workshop. https://www.carecprogram.org/?event=carec-aviation-consultation-workshop-apr-2017.

ADB. 2018. Aviation and the Role of CAREC: A Scoping Study. https://www.adb.org/publications/aviation-role-carec-study.

ADB. 2021. Impact of COVID-19 on CAREC Aviation and Tourism. https://www.adb.org/publications/impact-covid-19-carec-aviation-tourism.

In the second half of 2020, videoconferences were held with several member countries to discuss the initial draft of the CAREC aviation and tourism study, and the CAREC air pass proposal/study was shared with member countries, including airlines. A series of three CAREC aviation webinars were held in Q1 2021, focusing on the impact of COVID-19, the CAREC air pass proposal, and low-cost carrier (LCC) opportunities. The idea of a study looking at LCC opportunities was endorsed by the CAREC aviation community at the third webinar.

Related links:

CAREC. 2020. Silk Road Air Pass: A CAREC Proposal. https://www.carecprogram.org/uploads/REVISED_AirPass_CARECProposal.pdf.

CAREC Webinar Series – Aviation and Tourism. https://www.carecprogram.org/?event=carec-transport-webinar-series-aviation-and-tourism.

This is the third CAREC aviation study to be published under the technical assistance on Knowledge Sharing and Services in Transport and Transport Facilitation, which is an umbrella TA covering several modes of transport. This TA also has been used to assist four CAREC member countries in assessing specific aviation opportunities—Georgia, Kazakhstan, the Kyrgyz Republic, and Mongolia. The CAREC aviation program continues to support projects in member countries, in addition to continuing its series of regional knowledge products. More webinars and a second aviation workshop are planned.

Aviation is now a pillar under the CAREC Transport Strategy 2030, which was signed at the 18th CAREC Ministerial Conference in November 2019. The CAREC aviation program strives to facilitate development of the aviation sector and welcomes feedback, suggestions, and requests.

CAREC Aviation Sector Background and Description of the Study Area

This study analyzes the air transport market in CAREC, excluding Afghanistan and the People's Republic of China (PRC). The PRC's Xinjiang Uygur and Inner Mongolia autonomous regions are part of CAREC, but the PRC market is very different, and including the PRC would distort the overall data. Afghanistan has been excluded from all CAREC studies since 2021.[1]

The data examined in this study includes nine CAREC countries—Azerbaijan, Georgia, Kazakhstan, the Kyrgyz Republic, Mongolia, Pakistan, Tajikistan, Turkmenistan, and Uzbekistan. There are case studies on six CAREC countries—Azerbaijan, Georgia, Kazakhstan, the Kyrgyz Republic, Mongolia, and Uzbekistan. Missions to these countries were conducted in September and October 2022 as part of the research phase of this study. Pakistan is a larger market with different characteristics compared to the other eight countries and has limited connectivity to Central Asia. LCC development and opportunities in Pakistan could be examined in a separate study in the future. Tajikistan and Turkmenistan are small markets without any LCCs. The other seven countries now have LCCs based in their markets.

The overall CAREC air transport market, excluding Afghanistan and the PRC, consists of more than 50 million passengers per annum. The 50-million-passenger milestone was reached prior to the pandemic, resulting in CAREC (excluding Afghanistan and the PRC) accounting for about 1.2% of the 4.5 billion scheduled passengers (based on International Civil Aviation Organization data) that were transported globally in 2019. CAREC (excluding Afghanistan and the PRC) again reached 50 million passengers in 2022 as the overall CAREC aviation market essentially fully recovered from the pandemic, although not all CAREC countries fully recovered in 2022.

Scheduled airline capacity for the nine countries combined was nearly 70 million seats in both 2019 and 2022 (Table 3). Scheduled seats are higher than passenger numbers as seats include both seats filled and unfilled. Scheduled seats are the primary metric used in this study as passenger traffic data is not available for all markets and market segments.

Table 3: CAREC Scheduled International Seat Capacity Share by Country (% of total seats)

Rank	Country	Capacity Share 2019	Capacity Share 2022	Population 2021	GDP per Capita 2021
1	Pakistan	34%	34%	225 million	$1,538
2	Kazakhstan	21%	22%	19 million	$10,042
3	Uzbekistan	11%	12%	35 million	$1,983
4	Georgia	10%	8%	4 million	$5,042
5	Azerbaijan	10%	9%	10 million	$5,384
6	Kyrgyz Republic	5%	7%	7 million	$1,276
7	Turkmenistan	5%	2%	6 million	$7,612
8	Tajikistan	4%	6%	10 million	$897
9	Mongolia	2%	1%	3 million	$4,535

CAREC = Central Asia Regional Economic Cooperation, GDP = gross domestic product.
Notes: Excludes Afghanistan and the People's Republic of China. Rank is based on 2019 seat capacity. Population and GDP per capita figures based on World Bank data for 2021, except for Turkmenistan GDP which is based on 2019 data. Capacity share figures have been rounded to the nearest 1%.
Source: Author, using data from OAG and other sources including interviews.

---

[1] ADB placed its regular assistance to Afghanistan on hold effective 15 August 2021.

Pakistan is by far the largest market, accounting for 34% of the total scheduled airline seat capacity in CAREC in both 2019 and 2022. Kazakhstan is second largest, accounting for 21% in 2019 and 22% in 2022. The third-largest market, Uzbekistan, accounted for 11% and 12%, respectively. Kazakhstan and Uzbekistan had higher shares in 2022 than 2019 as these markets, along with the Kyrgyz Republic and Tajikistan, have grown, while the four other markets (Azerbaijan, Georgia, Mongolia, and Turkmenistan) had lower shares in 2022 as they did not yet fully recover.

Georgia and Kazakhstan are the most developed markets with much higher passenger traffic per capita than other CAREC countries. This is due to Georgia having by far the strongest inbound market in CAREC with visitors from outside the region accounting for most of its passenger traffic, while Kazakhstan has the highest gross domestic product (GDP) per capita. Kazakhstan also has the largest domestic air transport market in CAREC as it the largest CAREC country (excluding the PRC) in terms of geographic size.

Kazakhstan and Pakistan are the only CAREC countries with significant domestic markets in CAREC. In 2022, Kazakhstan and Pakistan accounted for about 55% and 23% of total scheduled domestic seat capacity in CAREC, respectively. Azerbaijan, the Kyrgyz Republic, Turkmenistan, and Uzbekistan all have small domestic markets, with each accounting for 5% or 6% of total domestic seat capacity in CAREC. Georgia and Tajikistan have very limited domestic services, while the scheduled domestic passenger traffic volumes in Mongolia are also relatively insignificant (Mongolia has more significant domestic charter traffic due to the need to shuttle workers to remote mines, but charter traffic is not included in any of the CAREC overall data highlighted in this study.)

Domestic accounted for 22% of total scheduled seat capacity in CAREC (excluding Afghanistan and PRC) in 2019 and 24% in 2022. This increase is due primarily to Kazakhstan's LCC-driven rapid domestic growth. International accounted for the remaining 78% and 76%, respectively. Foreign airlines accounted for about two-thirds of this capacity, with airlines based in the nine CAREC countries accounting for only about one-third of the overall international market. There are currently about 20 airlines from these nine countries operating scheduled international services, while about 100 foreign airlines serve CAREC.

Intra-CAREC (flights between the nine countries) is a very small segment of the international market. There were only about 1.7 million seats connecting the nine countries in both 2019 and 2022, which represents only slightly more than 3% of CAREC's overall international market. The lack of connectivity within CAREC was highlighted in the two earlier CAREC aviation studies and improving intra-CAREC connectivity is one of the main objectives of the CAREC aviation program. This study highlights the opportunity for LCCs to drive growth in this critical market segment, facilitating the development of economic ties and tourism between CAREC countries.

The pre-pandemic market and the initial impact of the pandemic were analyzed in the *Impact of COVID-19 on CAREC Aviation and Tourism* study, which was published by the Asian Development Bank (ADB) in February 2021. This study examines how the market has recovered since the pandemic and focuses on the opportunities for post-pandemic growth, particularly in the LCC sector.

Scope of the Study

LCCs have grown significantly in CAREC since 2019, helping fuel a recovery in the overall market. However, the LCC penetration rate in CAREC is still low compared to other regions (LCC penetration rate is calculated using scheduled seats for LCCs compared to scheduled seats for all airlines; scheduled seats include seats that are both sold and unsold).

LCCs typically offer substantially lower fares compared to full-service carriers (FSCs), thus making air travel more affordable to a large segment of the population. Higher penetration of LCCs in an aviation market can create substantial economic benefits, including trade and tourism growth. Higher penetration of LCCs also results in more competition, which benefits consumers in terms of lower airfares, wider airline choices, more mobility, and improved connectivity.

More LCC flights in CAREC would help CAREC countries attract more international visitors from both outside the region and within CAREC (the inbound leisure segment of the air transport market). It would enable CAREC residents to travel overseas more frequently (the outbound leisure segment) and enable citizens of CAREC countries who work overseas to travel home more frequently (the migrant worker segment). These are the three largest segments of CAREC's air transport market, and all are highly price sensitive—and therefore could experience rapid growth if more LCC flights result in lower fares, stimulating demand. Business travel is also important and could also benefit from more LCC flights, but this is a smaller segment of CAREC's air transport market and is generally not as price sensitive.

Within this context, this study provides an overview of the current state of LCC operations in the CAREC region, assesses opportunities and impediments to further LCC growth, and outlines recommendations to help LCCs flourish and strengthen their presence in the CAREC aviation sector. The report includes detailed case studies on six CAREC countries with specific recommendations as well as CAREC overall recommendations that are aimed at facilitating overall air transport development, including LCCs.

While there has been significant progress in market liberalization, which has helped facilitate some of the recent LCC growth, CAREC could benefit from further air transport liberalization. Regulatory obstacles are common and until these and other challenges impeding LCC growth are resolved, the air transport market will not be able to reach its full potential. This study intends to identify these obstacles and challenges, as well as the opportunities. The objective of this study is to raise awareness of these obstacles, challenges, and opportunities, and provide some high-level recommendations. With this knowledge product, the CAREC aviation program aims to facilitate a dialogue in the region's aviation community and provide a platform so that countries can learn from each other and discuss best next steps in developing their aviation sectors.

This study is focused primarily on LCCs, as LCC penetration rates that are higher—and closer to global norms—would be able to stimulate the market by offering low fares and accelerate growth. This would help the tourism sector bring in more visitors and facilitate faster overall economic growth in CAREC. It would also result in improved connectivity within CAREC, which has been an impediment to economic development and closer economic ties between CAREC countries.

LCCs typically do not take away traffic from FSCs, but instead grow the overall market. As a market liberalizes, FSCs often also grow, albeit at a much more modest rate. In addition, FSCs often benefit from LCC growth as they have subsidiary companies or divisions that are LCCs.

Three of the largest FSCs in CAREC now have LCCs or LCC brands—Air Astana, AZAL Azerbaijan Airlines, and Uzbekistan Airways. These, along with Pakistan International Airlines, are the four largest airlines in CAREC. Combined, these four airlines (including their LCC brands) accounted for 63% of total scheduled seats flown by CAREC airlines in 2019 and 66% in 2022 (Table 4). All are government-owned—or partially government-owned—and have flag carrier status.

Table 4: Top Four CAREC Airline Groups Based on Capacity Share (% of total seats[a])

	Airline Group	2019 Share	2022 Share	LCC Brand (2022 Share)
1	Air Astana	21%	26%	FlyArystan (12%)
2	Pakistan International Airlines	20%	18%	N/A
3	Uzbekistan Airways	14%	14%	Uzbekistan Express (2%)
4	AZAL Azerbaijan Airlines	8%	8%	Buta Airways (2%)
	Total	**63%**	**66%**	**16%**

CAREC = Central Asia Regional Economic Cooperation, LCC = low-cost carrier, N/A = not applicable.
[a] Total seats for all CAREC airlines combined. Excludes Afghanistan and the People's Republic of China.
Notes: Rank is based on 2019 seat capacity. Capacity share figures have been rounded to the nearest 1%.
Source: Author, using data from OAG and other sources including interviews.

The three low-cost brands—FlyArystan, Buta Airways, and Uzbekistan Express—accounted for slightly over 15% of total scheduled seats flown by CAREC airlines in 2022, but only 2% in 2019. Buta, FlyArystan, and Uzbekistan Express are featured in the case studies on Azerbaijan, Kazakhstan, and Uzbekistan.

These three brands are considered LCCs in this study although they are technically not separate airlines as their flights are operated using the air operator certificates (AOCs) and International Air Transport Association (IATA) airline designator codes of their parent brands. Almost all LCCs that are owned by FSCs in other regions have their own AOCs and IATA designator codes, making them separate entities from a regulatory perspective. However, there are some exceptions, for example, AnadoluJet, the low-cost brand of Turkish Airlines that also now has a significant presence in CAREC. Low-cost brands typically follow some components of the LCC model and therefore are considered LCCs in this study.

The other LCCs based in CAREC are privately owned independent airlines and therefore have their own AOCs along with IATA airline designator codes. They include Air Manas from the Kyrgyz Republic, Eznis Airways from Mongolia, and airblue and Fly Jinnah in Pakistan. Air Manas and Eznis are included in the case studies on the Kyrgyz Republic and Mongolia.

Fly Jinnah launched operations on 1 November 2022, becoming the seventh CAREC-based LCC. However, two of the local LCCs included in this study are currently not operating scheduled services (as of summer 2023). Eznis is currently (as of July 2023) operating wet-lease flights in Africa, but plans to resume scheduled flights in future. Air Manas temporarily had to suspend operations in 2022 due to Russia's war in Ukraine, as its fleet was sourced from a Russian aircraft leasing company, but aimed to resume operations by the end of 2023.

There are also two new LCCs in Uzbekistan that launched in the first few months of 2023, Centrum Air and Silk Avia, which increased the number of LCCs based in CAREC to nine. Centrum Air began operations in February 2023 and Silk Avia in April 2023. As of July 2023, Centrum had three A320s, but two of these aircraft were operating wet-lease flights in the Middle East, while Silk Avia had three ATR 72-600s.

Georgia is the only other CAREC country that has an LCC base, but this base is operated by a foreign airline, Hungary-based Wizz Air. The Wizz base at Kutaisi, which is the only airport in CAREC that has been developed for LCCs, is analyzed in the Georgia case study.

Wizz is one of about 20 foreign LCCs now serving CAREC (excluding Afghanistan and the PRC). Foreign LCCs have also recently grown their presence in CAREC, helping fuel the recovery of the overall market and an increase in LCC market share or LCC penetration rate, a metric used frequently in this study.

Table 5: Local Low-Cost Carriers in CAREC Ranked by Start Date with Fleet Size, as of end of 2022

Rank	LCC	IATA Code	Country	Launch Year	Fleet Size
1	Airblue	PA	Pakistan	2004	12
2	Air Manas	ZM	Kyrgyz Republic	2013	1
3	Buta Airways	J2	Azerbaijan	2017	8
4	FlyArystan	KC	Kazakhstan	2019	14
5	Eznis Airways	MG	Mongolia	2019	3
6	Uzbekistan Express	HY	Uzbekistan	2021	4
7	Fly Jinnah	9P	Pakistan	2022	3
8	Centrum Air	C6	Uzbekistan	2023	0
9	Silk Avia	US	Uzbekistan	2023	0

CAREC = Central Asia Regional Economic Cooperation, IATA = International Air Transport Association, LCC = low-cost carrier.
Notes: Air Manas' aircraft has been grounded since May 2022, but plans to relaunch operations in 2023. Eznis has not operated any scheduled services since March 2020, but plans to relaunch scheduled services in 2023. Silk Avia and Centrum Air did not take delivery of any aircraft until 2023. FlyArystan uses Air Astana's KC code, Uzbekistan Express uses Uzbekistan Airways' HY code, and Buta uses AZAL's J2 code.
Source: Author, using data from several other sources and interviews.

Overview of Low-Cost Carriers in CAREC

Central Asia in many respects is the last frontier for LCCs. In 2019, LCCs accounted for only 7% of total scheduled seat capacity in Central Asia. Of the five Central Asian countries (Kazakhstan, the Kyrgyz Republic, Tajikistan, Turkmenistan, and Uzbekistan), only the Kyrgyz Republic had an LCC penetration rate above 10% in 2019.

At the beginning of 2019, the Kyrgyz Republic was also the only Central Asian country with a local LCC. However, Air Manas was tiny, operating just one aircraft and one route.

FlyArystan launched in May 2019, becoming only the second Central Asian LCC. FlyArystan has expanded rapidly, but was still relatively small prior to the pandemic, flying about 700,000 passengers in 2019, while Air Manas flew fewer than 300,000 passengers.

In CAREC, the overall LCC penetration rate was only 15% in 2019 (excluding Afghanistan and the PRC). The only country with an LCC penetration rate above the global average was Georgia. While LCCs were starting to expand their presence in CAREC in the few years prior to the pandemic, the market was still significantly underpenetrated by LCCs.

The 15% overall penetration rate for CAREC prior to the pandemic was half the global average (Table 6). In 2019, LCCs accounted for about 30% of seat capacity globally. South Asia and Southeast Asia had the highest LCC penetration rates. Central Asia had the lowest LCC penetration rate among all regions.

In 2022, the LCC penetration rate reached 20% in Central Asia and 25% in the overall CAREC region (excluding the PRC) (Table 7). FlyArystan was the

Table 6: CAREC Low-Cost Carrier Penetration Rate by Country, 2019 (% of total seats flown)

Country	Total Market	Domestic	International
Kazakhstan	8	11	6
Kyrgyz Republic	19	40	13
Tajikistan	2	0	2
Turkmenistan	2	0	5
Uzbekistan	1	0	1
Central Asia subtotal	**7**	**10**	**5**
Azerbaijan	25	0	22
Georgia	37	0	37
Mongolia	5	0	5
Pakistan	19	9	21
CAREC total[a]	**15**	**9**	**17**

CAREC = Central Asia Regional Economic Cooperation.
[a] Excludes Afghanistan and the People's Republic of China.
Source: Author, based on data from the OAG schedules database and other sources.

Table 7: Low-Cost Carrier Penetration Rate by Region, 2019 (% of total seats flown)

Rank	Region	Total Market	Domestic	International
1	South Asia	53	72	24
2	Southeast Asia	45	58	34
3	Southwest Pacific	36	46	20
4	Latin America	35	46	21
5	Europe	33	31	33
6	North America	27	31	14
7	Middle East	17	21	16
8	Northeast Asia	13	9	20
9	Africa	12	12	12
10	Central Asia	7	10	5
	Global average	30	31	28
	CAREC total[a]	**15**	**9**	**17**

CAREC = Central Asia Regional Economic Cooperation.
[a] Excludes Afghanistan and the People's Republic of China.
Notes: Regions ranked by overall LCC penetration rate (domestic and international combined). Kazakhstan, the Kyrgyz Republic, Tajikistan, Turkmenistan and Uzbekistan are counted under Central Asia and CAREC. Azerbaijan and Georgia are counted under Europe and CAREC. Pakistan is counted under South Asia and CAREC. Mongolia is counted under Northeast Asia and CAREC. Latin America includes South America, Central America, and the Caribbean.
Source: Author, based on data from the OAG schedules database and other sources.

biggest driver of the increase compared to 2019, as Kazakhstan's overall LCC penetration rate increased from 8% in 2019 to 30% in 2022. In 2018, before FlyArystan's launch, Kazakhstan's LCC penetration rate was only 3%.

There was a similar increase in the LCC penetration rate in Uzbekistan, but from a smaller base. LCCs accounted for 14% of total seat capacity in Uzbekistan in 2022 compared to only 1% in 2019. Uzbekistan Express, which launched in August 2021, was the biggest driver of this increase, along with the launch of service to Uzbekistan by several foreign LCCs..

Georgia and Azerbaijan, which already had relatively high LCC penetration rates prior to the pandemic, also had significant increases (Table 8). Georgia's LCC penetration rate reached 55% in 2022, compared to an already relatively high 37% in 2019 as foreign LCCs resumed expansion. Azerbaijan's LCC penetration rate increased from 25% to 32%, which was also driven by foreign LCC expansion as Buta Airways contracted slightly.

Mongolia had a slight increase in LCC penetration rate driven by foreign LCCs. It is a much smaller market and is currently only served by LCCs from the Republic of Korea. Pakistan also had a slight increase in LCC penetration rates, but a more significant increase is expected in 2023 as Fly Jinnah only launched in late 2022. Tajikistan and Turkmenistan had a slight decline, but did not impact the total figures as it already had very low LCC penetration rates prior to the pandemic.

Central Asia and CAREC were still below the global average LCC penetration, which increased to 33% in 2022 (Table 9). Nearly every region had a higher LCC penetration rate in 2022 compared to 2019 as, generally, LCCs recovered faster than FSCs. However, the gap between CAREC and the rest of the world has narrowed, and Central Asia no longer has the lowest penetration rate among all regions.

Total LCC capacity in Central Asia more than tripled from about 2 million seats in 2019 to over 6 million in 2022. In CAREC, there was an overall increase of

Table 8: CAREC Low-Cost Carrier Penetration Rate by Country, 2022 (% of total seats flown)

Country	Total Market	Domestic	International
Kazakhstan	30	36	21
Kyrgyz Republic	16	1	19
Tajikistan	1	0	1
Turkmenistan	0	0	0
Uzbekistan	14	0	16
Central Asia subtotal	**20**	**28**	**15**
Azerbaijan	32	0	37
Georgia	55	0	56
Mongolia	7	0	8
Pakistan	23	19	24
CAREC total[a]	**25**	**24**	**25**

CAREC = Central Asia Regional Economic Cooperation.
[a] Excludes Afghanistan and the People's Republic of China.
Source: Author, based on data from the OAG schedules database and other sources.

Table 9: Low-Cost Carrier Penetration Rate by Region, 2022 (% of total seats flown)

Rank	Region	Total Market	Domestic	International
1	South Asia	57	73	30
2	Southeast Asia	50	61	29
3	Europe	38	35	39
4	Latin America	37	46	21
5	Southwest Pacific	36	43	16
6	North America	30	47	24
7	Middle East	24	29	23
8	Central Asia	20	28	15
9	Africa	13	3	16
10	Northeast Asia	11	10	14
	Global average	33	33	33
	CAREC total[a]	**25**	**24**	**25**

CAREC = Central Asia Regional Economic Cooperation.
[a] Excludes Afghanistan and the People's Republic of China.
Notes: Regions ranked by overall LCC penetration rate (domestic and international combined). Kazakhstan, the Kyrgyz Republic, Tajikistan, Turkmenistan, and Uzbekistan are counted under Central Asia and CAREC. Azerbaijan and Georgia are counted under Europe and CAREC. Pakistan is counted under South Asia and CAREC. Mongolia is counted under Northeast Asia and CAREC. Latin America includes South America, Central America, and the Caribbean.
Source: Author, based on data from the OAG schedules database and other sources.

over 60%, from about 10 million seats in 2019 to over 16 million in 2022.

Local LCCs accounted for only 35% of the 10 million LCC seats in 2019, but their share increased to 46% in 2022 as they more than doubled their capacity. FlyArystan has become the largest LCC in CAREC with 3.7 million seats in 2022. This equates to about a 50% share of all seats from local LCCs or about a 23% share of total LCC seat capacity in CAREC when also including foreign LCCs. Over half of local LCC capacity was in the domestic market (Table 10), with domestic services accounting for 87% of FlyArystan's capacity.

Foreign LCCs accounted for 54% of total LCC capacity in CAREC in 2022, but their share of international LCC capacity in 2022 was 73%. This is a better indication of market share as foreign airlines are unable to compete in the domestic market, and highlights how local LCCs are still very small in the international market. Local LCCs flew slightly over 3 million scheduled international seats in 2022, with airblue accounting for nearly half of this total.

Foreign LCCs had nearly 9 million scheduled international seats in CAREC in 2022, compared to about 6.6 million seats in 2019. flydubai is the largest foreign LCC in CAREC based on capacity share and number of destinations. It accounted for 22% of international LCC seat capacity in 2022 and 26% in 2019. While flydubai expanded its CAREC operation by over 20%, its market share declined as several LCCs entered the market or expanded more rapidly.

In 2022, flydubai had 16 destinations in CAREC across six countries. In 2019, it had 14 destinations in seven countries, including Turkmenistan (flydubai did not operate any services to Turkmenistan in 2022, as Turkmenistan borders remained closed).

Sharjah-based Air Arabia is the second-largest foreign LCC in CAREC and had 15 destinations in 2022 across six countries. It accounted for 12% of international LCC seat capacity in 2022 and 18% in 2019. When including its joint venture in Abu Dhabi, Air Arabia Abu Dhabi, the Air Arabia brand had a 13% share in 2022.

Türkiye's Pegasus was the third-largest foreign LCC in 2022 with a 9% share. Wizz also had a 9% share in 2022 when including Hungary-based Wizz Air as well as Wizz Air Abu Dhabi. Most of the flights flown by the Hungarian carrier are operated with aircraft based in Georgia.

The top 10 LCCs (Table 11) accounted for over 95% of the total foreign LCC capacity in 2022. Overall, there were 21 LCCs operating scheduled services to CAREC in 2022 (Table 12). However, the other 11 LCCs were small and generally only served one CAREC country. All of them accounted for less than a 1% share of total LCC capacity in CAREC in 2022.

Table 10: Seat Capacity for Local CAREC Low-Cost Carriers, 2022 versus 2019 (million)

Rank	LCC	2022	2019	Domestic % 2022	Domestic % 2019
1	FlyArystan	3.7	0.7	87%	99%
2	airblue	2.1	1.7	20%	29%
3	Uzbekistan Express	0.7	0	2%	N/A
4	Buta Airways	0.6	0.7	0%	0%
5	Fly Jinnah	0.1	0	100%	N/A
6	Air Manas	<0.1	0.3	27%	93%
7	Eznis Airways	0	<0.1	N/A	0%
	TOTAL	**7.3**	**3.5**	**55%**	**40%**

CAREC = Central Asia Regional Economic Cooperation, LCC = low-cost carrier, N/A = not applicable.
Notes: Ranking based on 2022 capacity. Seat capacity is rounded to the nearest 100,000. CAREC excludes Afghanistan and the People's Republic of China.
Source: Author, based on data from the OAG schedules database, other sources, and interviews.

Georgia is served by the most foreign LCCs, followed by Azerbaijan. Uzbekistan has had the biggest increase, attracting nine additional foreign LCCs and had the third-highest total in 2022. Some of the other CAREC countries still do not have many foreign LCCs, although the number has been increasing.

LCCs vary in terms of their business model, with some following a pure low-cost model and others following more of a hybrid model. Pure LCCs typically charge extra for bags, food, and drinks and only offer economy class seats. Several of the foreign LCCs serving CAREC follow hybrid rather than pure LCC models, including flydubai and Jazeera.

Some of the local LCCs, such as Buta and Uzbekistan Express, also follow hybrid models. As explained in the scope of this study, some of the local LCCs do not meet the strict definition of LCCs as they are divisions or brands rather than subsidiaries of full-service airlines, and therefore use the same IATA airline designator codes and AOCs of their parent brands. AnadoluJet, for example, is not a subsidiary of Turkish Airlines but uses the latter's designator code and AOC. Low-cost brands or divisions are counted under their full-service parent in airline schedule databases because they use their parent's designator code, but this study has been able to include all of them in the LCC data by separating out their flights based on flight numbers. Some of these are pure LCCs from a product perspective, such as FlyArystan.

While this study uses a loose definition of LCC, all the airlines counted under LCC do follow several components of the LCC model. These airlines are all able to stimulate demand by offering generally lower fares than full-service airlines and therefore drive growth (although not all their fares are low).

Table 11: Seat Capacity for Foreign Low-Cost Carriers in CAREC, 2022 versus 2019 (million)

Rank	LCC (country)	Seats 2022	Seats 2019	Number of Destinations 2022	Number of Destinations 2019
1	flydubai (UAE)	2.7	2.3	16	14
2	Air Arabia (UAE)	1.6	1.6	15	12
3	Pegasus (Türkiye)	1.1	0.4	9	4
4	Wizz Air (Hungary)	0.8	1.0	4	3
5	flynas (Saudi Arabia)	0.7	0.3	8	6
6	Jazeera (Kuwait)	0.5	0.2	10	5
7	AnadoluJet (Türkiye)	0.4	0	5	0
8	Wizz Air Abu Dhabi (UAE)	0.3	0	6	0
9	SalamAir (Oman)	0.2	0.2	8	3
10	Air Arabia Abu Dhabi (UAE)	0.1	0	5	0
	Other foreign LCCs	0.3	0.4		
	TOTAL	**8.7**	**6.6**		

CAREC = Central Asia Regional Economic Cooperation, LCC = low-cost carrier, UAE = United Arab Emirates.
Notes: Ranking based on 2022 capacity. Seat capacity is rounded to the nearest 100,000. Airlines with fewer than 100,000 seats in 2022 are included under other foreign LCCs.
Source: Author, based on data from the OAG schedules database and other sources.

Table 12: Number of Foreign Low-Cost Carriers Serving CAREC by Country, 2022 versus 2019

Rank	Country	2022	2019
1	Georgia	14	12
2	Azerbaijan	12	7
3	Uzbekistan	10	1
4	Pakistan	8	5
5	Kazakhstan	7	5
6	Kyrgyz Republic	6	4
7	Mongolia	3	2
8	Tajikistan	2	1
9	Turkmenistan	0	1
	CAREC Total	**21**	**15**

CAREC = Central Asia Regional Economic Cooperation, LCC = low-cost carrier.
Notes: Only LCCs from outside CAREC are included; LCCs from other CAREC countries are excluded. Only LCCs operating regularly scheduled services to CAREC are included. Charter flights and flights using CAREC countries as technical fuel stops (no passengers get on or off) are excluded.
Source: Author, based on data from the OAG schedules database and other sources.

Air Arabia is the second-largest foreign low-cost carrier in CAREC with 15 destinations in six CAREC countries from Sharjah, as well as four CAREC destinations in three countries from Abu Dhabi in the summer of 2023 (photo by Air Arabia).

Overview of Market Recovery in CAREC

The rapid expansion of LCCs in 2022 helped drive a recovery of the overall market. In 2022, seat capacity in CAREC, excluding Afghanistan and the PRC, was at 98% of 2019 levels (Table 13). While LCC capacity increased by 61%, FSC capacity declined by 14%.

The overall 98% recovery was 16 percentage points above the global average, with the FSC recovery rate also 8 percentage points above the global average. CAREC would have still achieved a faster-than-average recovery rate without the expansion of LCCs. However, the LCC expansion played an important role in enabling CAREC to achieve a quick recovery.

In 2022, a full recovery was achieved in four of the nine countries—Kazakhstan, the Kyrgyz Republic, Tajikistan, and Uzbekistan. LCCs drove recovery in Kazakhstan and Uzbekistan as FSC capacity declined. In the Kyrgyz Republic, both FSC and LCC capacity increased significantly. In smaller Tajikistan, FSCs drove the recovery as the country has very little LCC penetration.

Three of the other CAREC countries had recovery rates that fell short of a full recovery, but were still at least 80%—Azerbaijan, Georgia and Pakistan. LCC expansion contributed to the relatively high recovery rates in these countries.

Turkmenistan and Mongolia are exceptions as Turkmenistan borders remained closed for all of 2022 while Mongolia relies heavily on the PRC, which remained closed for all of 2022. Mongolia still was able to recover most of its LCC capacity, albeit on a small base, while the only LCC in the Turkmenistan market prior to the pandemic, flydubai, did not resume its Turkmenistan service until January 2023.

Table 13: Scheduled Seat Capacity Recovery Rates by Country, 2022 versus 2019

Rank	Country	Overall Recovery	LCC Recovery	FSC Recovery
1	Tajikistan	143	92	144
2	Kyrgyz Republic	136	117	140
3	Kazakhstan	107	393	81
4	Uzbekistan	106	1428	92
5	Pakistan	98	120	92
6	Azerbaijan	89	131	77
7	Georgia	80	121	57
8	Mongolia	52	82	50
9	Turkmenistan	33	0	34
	Central Asia subtotal	**106**	**318**	**91**
	Global average	82	91	78
	CAREC Total[a]	**98**	**161**	**86**

CAREC = Central Asia Regional Economic Cooperation, FSC = full-service carrier, LCC = low-cost carrier.
[a] Total excludes Afghanistan and the People's Republic of China.
Notes: Rank based on recovery rate of total seat capacity (domestic and international combined)
Source: Author, based on data from the OAG schedules database and other sources.

The exceptionally high recovery rates for Tajikistan and the Kyrgyz Republic are partially due to their ability to continue attracting Russian airlines, including western aircraft operated by Russian airlines, following the start of Russia's war in Ukraine. Azerbaijan, Kazakhstan, and Uzbekistan also continue to be served by Russian carriers, but they have been impacted by limitations on which aircraft they can use to serve these countries.

The Russian Federation overall is a massive market for CAREC, accounting for 24% of total international seats in 2019. In 2022, the Russian Federation again accounted for 24% of total international seats in CAREC. Therefore, the overall recovery of the CAREC market was not due to the ability of CAREC countries to continue handling flights from the Russian Federation (both Russian carriers and CAREC carriers, as most CAREC carriers have continued to serve the Russian Federation). However, some CAREC countries have experienced rapid growth in handling Russian Federation capacity, while others have experienced a decline.

Table 14 shows the recovery rate for the international market, with a breakdown specific to the Russian Federation. While the Kyrgyz Republic and Tajikistan have experienced the largest increases in Russian Federation capacity, the Kyrgyz Republic also had the biggest increase in non-Russian Federation capacity. The Kyrgyz Republic and Tajikistan already had the highest reliance on the Russian Federation before the pandemic, with the Russian Federation accounting for 64% of international seat capacity in the Kyrgyz Republic and 82% in Tajikistan in 2019. Uzbekistan is the only other country relying on the Russian Federation for at least half of its international seat capacity (both before and after the pandemic).

Georgia experienced the largest decline in Russian Federation capacity, but this is due to a ban on direct flights to Georgia that was imposed by the Russian government from July 2019 to May 2023. Almost all the Georgia–Russian Federation capacity from 2019 was flown in the first half of the year.

Table 14: Scheduled International Seat Capacity Recovery Rates by Country, 2022 versus 2019

Rank	Country	Overall Recovery	Recovery excluding Russian Federation	Russian Federation recovery	Russian Federation capacity share, 2019	Russian Federation capacity share, 2022
1	Tajikistan	143	84	155	82	89
2	Kyrgyz Republic	140	130	145	64	66
3	Uzbekistan	106	106	106	52	52
4	Pakistan	98	98	N/A	0	0
5	Azerbaijan	87	85	93	23	25
6	Kazakhstan	82	96	53	33	21
7	Georgia	80	98	N/A	18	N/A
8	Mongolia	52	57	14	12	3
9	Turkmenistan	12	11	18	19	29
	Central Asia	106	93	109	49	52
	Global average	69	70	40	4	2
	CAREC Total[a]	**94**	**94**	**96**	**24**	**24**

CAREC = Central Asia Regional Economic Cooperation, N/A = not applicable.
[a] Total excludes Afghanistan and the People's Republic of China.
Notes: Rank based on recovery rate of international seat capacity (including capacity to/from the Russian Federation).
Source: Author, based on data from the OAG schedules database.

Georgia almost achieved a full recovery in 2022 when excluding the Russian Federation, as international seat capacity reached 98% of 2019 levels. A full recovery was achieved when also excluding Ukraine, which accounted for 7% of total international seat capacity in Georgia in 2019.

Georgia had the highest reliance on Ukraine among all CAREC countries. Overall, Ukraine, accounted for only 1% of international seat capacity in CAREC prior to the Russian invasion. Only three CAREC countries had regularly scheduled services to Ukraine prior to the pandemic. The other two were Azerbaijan and Kazakhstan, which had 4% and 3% exposure, respectively, to Ukraine in 2019.

Kazakhstan had almost a full recovery in international seat capacity when excluding the Russian Federation and Ukraine. Kazakhstan's Russian Federation capacity dropped significantly as Air Astana has not been serving the Russian Federation (or overflying the Russian Federation) since the start of the invasion, although the Kazakhstan–Russian Federation market continues to be served by two other Kazakhstan carriers, SCAT Airlines and Qazaq Air, and Russian carriers. Kazakhstan ranked third in the overall recovery rate (Table 13) due to rapid growth in the domestic market. Kazakhstan ranked sixth in terms of international recovery (Table 14), but ranked fourth based on international capacity recovery rate excluding the Russian Federation.

The overall 94% CAREC recovery rate for international seat capacity in 2022 was well above the global average of 69% (Table 15). Central Asia had the highest international and overall recovery rates among all regions. While lower than Central Asia, the overall CAREC recovery rate was also higher than all other regions.

Northeast Asia had the lowest international recovery rates in 2022. This is due to the PRC, which remained closed all year, as well as a slow reopening in other Northeast Asian countries and territories.

While CAREC's aviation sector was impacted by the long closure of the PRC, which only reopened in early 2023, the impact was relatively small. In 2019, only 3% of international seat capacity from CAREC (the nine countries excluding the PRC and Afghanistan) were on

Table 15: Seat Capacity Recovery Rate by Region, 2022 versus 2019

Rank	Region	Overall	International	Domestic
1	Central Asia	106%	101%	115%
2	Latin America	97%	91%	101%
3	South Asia	92%	84%	98%
4	North America	91%	83%	93%
5	Africa	89%	86%	94%
6	Middle East	85%	84%	87%
7	Europe	82%	80%	87%
8	Southwest Pacific	70%	46%	86%
9	Northeast Asia	67%	20%	91%
10	Southeast Asia	58%	37%	83%
	Global average	82%	69%	91%
	CAREC total	**98%**	**94%**	**109%**

CAREC = Central Asia Regional Economic Cooperation.
Notes: Kazakhstan, the Kyrgyz Republic, Tajikistan, Turkmenistan, and Uzbekistan are included in Central Asia and CAREC. Mongolia is included in Northeast Asia and CAREC. Azerbaijan and Georgia are included in Europe and CAREC. Pakistan is included in South Asia and CAREC. Latin America includes South America, Central America, and the Caribbean.
Source: Author, based on data from the OAG schedules database.

routes to the PRC (all parts of the PRC). Only Mongolia is highly exposed to the PRC, which accounted for 26% of total international seat capacity to Mongolia in 2019. Kazakhstan has the second-highest exposure rate to the PRC, but the PRC accounted for only 6% of total international seat capacity in Kazakhstan in 2019. For all the other countries, the exposure rate was less than 4%. Seat capacity between CAREC and the PRC in 2022 was at only 5% of 2019 levels.

While the CAREC recovery rate was just shy of 100% for the full year in 2022, a full recovery was achieved in the second half of the year after a slower first half. In the early part of 2022, air travel was still impacted by COVID-19-related restrictions and requirements. Most of these restrictions were lifted by summer of 2022.

In January 2023, the scheduled seat capacity recovery rate in CAREC reached 112%, with total seat capacity above January 2020 levels in seven of the nine countries (Tajikistan, the Kyrgyz Republic, Uzbekistan, Kazakhstan, Georgia, Azerbaijan, and Pakistan) (Table 16). International seat capacity was also 112% above January 2020 levels with the same seven countries fully recovered.

As of early 2023, only Mongolia and Turkmenistan were not yet recovered in terms of scheduled seat capacity. However, Mongolia was able to achieve a full recovery by spring of 2023. Turkmenistan could see a full recovery by the end of 2023 as its borders finally reopened in March 2023 and flights have since been gradually resuming.

When excluding the Russian Federation, the international recovery rate in January 2023 for CAREC was 107%, with six of the countries fully recovered. The January 2023 recovery figures are calculated using January 2020, the last "normal" month before the pandemic, as a baseline.

Data for early 2023 were encouraging and indicate a bright outlook for the entire year. Passenger traffic in CAREC will likely grow by at least 15% (compared to 2019) for the full year, driven once again by LCC expansion, while FSCs are also again growing in 2023.

With the resumption of growth comes plenty of opportunities. However, there are also numerous challenges. Only with the right strategies and policies can rapid passenger traffic growth be achieved over the next several years.

Table 16: Scheduled Seat Capacity Recovery Rates by Country, January 2023 versus January 2020

Rank	Country	Overall Recovery	International Recovery	International Recovery Excluding the Russian Federation	Russian Federation Recovery
1	Tajikistan	175%	175%	81%	201%
2	Kyrgyz Republic	166%	175%	170%	177%
3	Uzbekistan	133%	133%	153%	114%
4	Kazakhstan	120%	110%	126%	76%
5	Georgia	109%	109%	112%	0%
6	Azerbaijan	107%	107%	100%	128%
7	Pakistan	102%	100%	100%	N/A
8	Mongolia	77%	80%	86%	20%
9	Turkmenistan	38%	23%	26%	14%
	Central Asia subtotal	**124%**	**128%**	**125%**	**132%**
	Global average	91%	79%	80%	47%
	CAREC Total	**112%**	**112%**	**107%**	**129%**

CAREC = Central Asia Regional Economic Cooperation.
Notes: CAREC total excludes Afghanistan and the People's Republic of China. Overall recovery includes domestic and international combined. Rank based on recovery rate of total seat capacity (including domestic and international, with the Russian Federation included in international).
Source: Author, based on data from OAG and other sources.

Opportunities: Intra-CAREC Market

There are opportunities to develop the regional market within CAREC and use LCCs to boost connectivity between CAREC countries.

The lack of connectivity between CAREC countries was highlighted in the earlier CAREC aviation studies. Recommendations from the earlier studies included removing visa requirements within CAREC to facilitate travel between countries, establishing programs to incentivize the launch of new routes between countries, and reducing taxes on international flights to make intra-CAREC travel more affordable.

All these recommendations are still relevant. Taxes, fees, and charges imposed by CAREC airports for international flights are still much higher than the global average. While this impacts the ability to develop international air services, there is particularly an impact on the intra-CAREC market as flights within the region are short and therefore taxes are a very high portion of the total airfare.

CAREC countries should consider introducing a tiered system that provides lower airport charges for routes between CAREC countries. In other regions, some airports have a lower tax or charge for a regional or short-haul international flight. For example, Malaysia Airports, which operates all airports in Malaysia including Kuala Lumpur International, has a passenger facility charge for routes to other countries in the Association of Southeast Asian Nations that is less than half the charge for routes outside the association's member states. In the United Kingdom, the air passenger duty for a short-haul international flight of up to 2,000 miles is several times less than for a longer flight.

CAREC countries continue to do very little to promote intra-CAREC air travel. There are virtually no incentive programs to support new intra-CAREC routes and there is limited marketing assistance to airlines that launch new intra-CAREC routes.

Visa requirements are also still an impediment in developing intra-CAREC routes and improving connectivity. This is particularly an issue with Pakistan as all CAREC countries (except the PRC) require visas for Pakistani citizens. There are currently very limited flights between Pakistan and other CAREC countries, and this market can only be developed under a more liberal visa policy.

Georgia and the Kyrgyz Republic have the most liberal visa policies among CAREC countries, but both countries still exclude Pakistan (as well as the PRC) from their visa-free lists. Georgia also excludes Mongolia.

Azerbaijan, Kazakhstan, Tajikistan, and Uzbekistan have adopted relatively liberal visa policies in recent years. But Azerbaijan, Tajikistan, and Uzbekistan still do not include Mongolia, Pakistan, and Turkmenistan on their visa-free entry lists, while Kazakhstan does not include Pakistan and Turkmenistan (Azerbaijan and Tajikistan also still exclude the PRC). Mongolia in early 2023 expanded its visa-free list to 61 countries, but still only allows visa-free travel from just three CAREC countries—Kazakhstan, the Kyrgyz Republic, and Uzbekistan.

Turkmenistan and Pakistan have the strictest visa policies among CAREC countries. Pakistan only permits visa-free travel from about 10 countries, with the PRC the only CAREC country on the visa-free list, while Turkmenistan does not provide any exemptions.

While some CAREC countries permit e-visas for countries that are not visa-free, the cost and hassle of an e-visa dissuades some potential travelers. Visa requirements, including e-visas, can be a major impediment, with CAREC residents often deciding to spend holidays outside the region in countries which are visa-free. All CAREC countries should consider establishing a visa-free policy as this would drive more demand for travel within CAREC, enabling airlines to launch more intra-CAREC flights.

Improving connectivity within CAREC is critical for boosting economic ties and tourism between CAREC countries. Improved connectivity would facilitate intra-CAREC tourism as well as facilitate visitors from outside the region to visit multiple CAREC countries and follow multi-stop Silk Road itineraries.

The COVID-19 impact study recommended that CAREC member countries and airlines focus on travel within CAREC in the initial recovery phase. It included a list of several potential new intra-CAREC routes that could be launched during the pandemic or in the initial post-pandemic phase. This recommendation was achieved to a great extent as 19 new routes were launched within CAREC in 2021 and 2022 (Table 17). Several new intra-CAREC routes are being launched in 2023, starting with a weekly service connecting Baku and Urgench that was launched by AZAL in late January 2023.

Table 17: New Intra-CAREC Routes, 2021 and 2022

Airline	Route	Launch Date	Weekly Frequencies
Aero Nomad	Bishkek–Islamabad	August 2022	1, year-round
Aero Nomad	Bishkek–Lahore	August 2022	1, year-round
Air Astana	Almaty–Batumi	May 2021	Up to 5, summer only
AZAL Azerbaijan Airlines	Baku–Samarkand	October 2022	2, winter only
AZAL Azerbaijan Airlines	Baku–Fergana	December 2022	1 weekly
FlyArystan	Aktau–Kutaisi	May 2021	Up to 3, year-round
FlyArystan	Astana–Kutaisi	May 2021	Up to 5, year-round
FlyArystan	Atyrau–Kutaisi	May 2021	Up to 4, year-round
FlyArystan	Shymkent–Kutaisi	July 2021	Up to 2, summer only
Hunnu Air	Ulaanbaatar–Almaty	March 2022	2, year-round
Pakistan International Airlines	Islamabad–Baku	June 2022	1, summer only
Pakistan International Airlines	Karachi–Baku	March 2022	1, summer only
Pakistan International Airlines	Lahore–Baku	March 2022	2, year-round
Qazaq Air	Aktobe–Baku	August 2022	2, year-round
SCAT Airlines	Aktau–Nukus	May 2021	Up to 3, year-round
SCAT Airlines	Aktau–Urgench	March 2021	Up to 4, year-round
SCAT Airlines	Aktobe–Tbilisi	August 2021	2, year-round
Uzbekistan Airways	Samarkand–Almaty	June 2021	2, year-round
Uzbekistan Airways	Tashkent–Batumi	May 2022	2, summer only

CAREC = Central Asia Regional Economic Cooperation.
Notes: Uzbekistan Airlines also launched Aktau–Urgench in May 2021 and Aktau–Nukus in July 2021; these routes were transferred to Uzbekistan Express later in 2021, but were suspended in August 2022. Aktobe–Tbilisi was operated year-round from August 2021 to October 2022, but did not operate in winter 2022/2023. Uzbekistan Airways launched Samarkand–Almaty in June 2021, but suspended the route in October 2022. Air Astana also launched Samarkand–Almaty in June 2021, but suspended the route in October 2021. FlyArystan launched Samarkand–Almaty in March 2022 and suspended it in September 2022, but resumed the route in March 2023. New routes that were only briefly operated or routes that were served with only a few ad hoc flights are excluded.
Source: Author, based on data from OAG and other sources.

Air Astana is the largest airline in the intra-CAREC market and serves six destinations in other CAREC countries excluding the People's Republic of China, while its low-cost subsidiary FlyArystan is the third largest and serves five destinations in other CAREC countries (photo by Air Astana).

Five of the routes listed in Table 17 did not operate in the winter 2022/2023 season, but resumed for the summer of 2023. There are several other new intra-CAREC routes that were launched in 2021 or 2022, but are not currently operating and are not likely to be resumed. These are generally very short routes that were operated during an unusual period that land borders were closed but air borders had reopened. Once land borders reopened, these routes were no longer viable and were suspended. Examples include Bishkek–Turkistan and Tashkent–Turkistan (they are excluded from Table 17 as they were temporary routes with limited flights).

There were 35 regularly scheduled international routes connecting CAREC countries (excluding Afghanistan and the PRC) in 2022, compared to 27 routes in 2019. While 18 routes were launched, 10 of the 27 routes from 2019 did not operate in 2022. These 10 routes are Almaty–Ashgabat, Almaty–Osh, Almaty–Issyk-Kul, Ashgabat–Baku, Astana–Batumi, Astana–Baku, Astana–Dushanbe, Astana–Ulaanbaatar, Bishkek–Dushanbe, and Lahore–Tashkent. (Three of these routes were resumed in the first half of 2023: Almaty–Ashgabat, Astana–Baku, and Astana–Batumi. Turkmenistan Airlines operates Almaty–Ashgabat and Air Astana operates a summer-only Astana–Batumi service. Astana–Baku, which was served prior to the pandemic by Air Astana, is now served by FlyArystan and AZAL.)

Table 18 shows the 17 scheduled routes that were operated prior to the pandemic and were again operated in 2022. They are ranked based on the number of weekly flights that were operated in 2022.

The frequency on many intra-CAREC routes varies significantly depending on the time of year. Of the 35 routes that were operated in 2022, only three were served daily on a year-round basis—Baku–Tbilisi, Almaty–Tashkent, and Almaty–Bishkek.

Baku–Tbilisi had about 1,000 frequencies each way in 2022 or an average of almost three flights per day. Almaty–Tashkent had about 700 frequencies in 2022 or an average of two flights per day, while Almaty–Bishkek was third largest with about 400 frequencies or slightly more than one flight per day on average.

The next largest intra-CAREC routes, Astana–Tashkent and Baku–Tashkent, each had about 300 frequencies or an average of almost six flights per week. There were no other routes that had an average of five or more flights per week.

While overall connectivity has improved, the lack of frequency on intra-CAREC routes continues to be a major impediment to economic development and tourism. The typical intra-CAREC schedule of a few frequencies per week makes it difficult for quick

Table 18: Intra-CAREC Routes That Operated Pre-pandemic and Resumed by end of 2022

Route	Airline/Airlines	Weekly Frequencies
Baku–Tbilisi	AZAL, Buta Airways, Gulf Air	Up to 28, year-round
Almaty–Tashkent	Air Astana, Uzbekistan Airways	Up to 14, year-round
Almaty–Bishkek	Air Astana	Up to 12, year-round
Baku–Tashkent	AZAL, Uzbekistan Airways	Up to 8, year-round
Astana–Tashkent	Air Astana, Uzbekistan Airways	Up to 6, year-round
Aktau–Tbilisi	SCAT Airlines	Up to 6, year-round
Aktau–Baku	Buta Airways, FlyArystan	Up to 6, year-round
Almaty–Dushanbe	Air Astana, Somon Air	Up to 6, year-round
Almaty–Tbilisi	Air Astana	Up to 5, year-round
Dushanbe–Tashkent	Somon Air, Uzbekistan Airways	Up to 4, year-round
Bishkek–Tashkent	Uzbekistan Airways	Up to 4, year-round
Almaty–Baku	Air Astana	Up to 4, year-round
Baku–Batumi	Buta Airways	Up to 4, summer only
Astana–Bishkek	Air Astana/FlyArystan	Up to 3, year-round
Astana–Tbilisi	Air Astana	Up to 3, summer only
Tashkent–Tbilisi	Uzbekistan Airways	Up to 2, year-round
Bishkek–Ulaanbaatar	Hunnu Air	Up to 2, year-round

CAREC = Central Asia Regional Economic Cooperation.
Notes: Weekly frequencies are for all airlines operating the route combined. Astana–Bishkek was served by Air Astana until May 2022; FlyArystan took over the route in June 2022, suspended it in September 2022, but resumed it in June 2023. Bishkek–Ulaanbaatar was served pre-pandemic by Turkish Airlines, which operated Istanbul–Bishkek–Ulaanbaatar until January 2020, when it launched nonstop Istanbul–Ulaanbaatar. Bishek –Ulaanbaatar was launched in March 2022 by Hunnu Air; it was served year-round by Hunnu in 2022, but in 2023, is only being served in the winter season. Gulf Air operates from Baku to Tbilisi (one-way only) using fifth freedom rights as part of a Bahrain–Baku–Tbilisi–Bahrain service.
Source: Author, based on data from OAG and other sources.

business trips, which are common in the rest of the world when traveling regionally. It is also a barrier to developing cross-CAREC tourism as the schedule is not sufficient to enable a weekend or long weekend holiday to a nearby country. Higher frequencies would also facilitate Silk Road multi-stop itineraries for visitors from outside CAREC.

Passengers traveling between CAREC cities that do not have a daily nonstop service can use one-stop connections on days without a nonstop option, but one-stop connections add considerable time and expense. A nonstop intra-CAREC flight typically takes 1 to 3 hours, while a one-stop connection takes several hours and sometimes even a full day.

Facilitating LCC development on intra-CAREC routes is a principal recommendation of this study. Attracting more LCCs on intra-CAREC routes would lead to higher frequencies on existing routes and the launch of new routes.

There are currently only two LCCs operating intra-CAREC routes—Buta Airways and FlyArystan. A third LCC, Uzbekistan Express, operated a small number of intra-CAREC flights in its first year of operations (about 100 return flights over 1 year), but has not operated any intra-CAREC flights since August 2022.

In addition to Buta and FlyArystan, in 2022 there were 10 FSCs that operated scheduled services between CAREC countries (excluding Afghanistan and the PRC). These FSCs are based in seven CAREC countries. Air Astana is the largest airline in the intra-CAREC market, based on the number of destinations and number of flights. While Air Astana's share of the intra-CAREC

Table 19: Intra-CAREC Capacity Share by Airline, 2022 and 2019 (% of total seats)

Rank	Airline	2022 Share	2019 Share	Number of routes (2022)
1	Air Astana	30%	37%	9
2	Uzbekistan Airways	21%	24%	8
3	FlyArystan	15%	0%	7
4	Buta Airways	12%	9%	3
5	SCAT Airlines	6%	9%	4
6	AZAL Azerbaijan Airlines	5%	4%	2
7	Somon Air	3%	3%	2
8	Pakistan International Airlines	2%	0%	3
9	Uzbekistan Express	1%	0%	3
10	Hunnu Air	1%	0%	1
11	Qazaq Air	1%	1%	1
12	Aero Nomad	1%	0%	2
	Turkmenistan Airlines	0%	2%	0
	Avia Traffic	0%	1%	0
	Foreign airlines[a]	2%	9%	

CAREC = Central Asia Regional Economic Cooperation.
[a] Foreign airlines (airlines from outside CAREC) operating intra-CAREC routes with fifth freedom traffic rights include Gulf Air (in 2019 and 2022), Turkish Airlines (2019 only), and Lufthansa (2019 only).
Notes: Rank based on capacity share (% of total intra-CAREC schedule seat capacity) for 2022. Turkmenistan Airlines resumed services to other CAREC countries in 2023.
Source: Author, based on data from OAG and other sources.

market has dropped, the share of Air Astana Group has increased when including FlyArystan, which is now the third-largest competitor in the intra-CAREC market after Air Astana and Uzbekistan Airways.

As of summer 2023, LCCs were operating onlly 13 intra-CAREC routes. Buta Airways operates four routes within CAREC—Baku to Aktau, Batumi, Dushanbe, and Tbilisi, with Batumi only operating in the summer. FlyArystan also operates Aktau–Baku and has five routes to Kutaisi— from Aktau, Almaty, Astana, Atyrau, and Shymkent, with Shymkent only operating in the summer. FlyArystan also operates Astana–Baku, Astana–Bishkek, Astana–Tashkent, and Almaty–Samarkand, all of which, along with Kutaisi–Almaty, were launched or resumed in the first half of 2023. FlyArystan has briefly operated several other intra-CAREC routes that are not currently operating, including Almaty–Namangan, Almaty–Nukus, Almaty–Osh, Turkistan–Bishkek, and Turkistan–Tashkent (FlyArystan is also launching Astana-Urumqi in September 2023 and Astana-Dushanbe in October 2023).

FlyArystan has been very successful in the Georgia–Kazakhstan market, driving rapid growth and becoming in 2022 one of the 10 largest airlines in Georgia as well as the second-largest airline at Kutaisi. Buta Airways has been successful in the Azerbaijan–Georgia market. Both LCCs have had some success in the Azerbaijan–Kazakhstan market, albeit primarily on the short route connecting Baku with Aktau. Kazakhstan–Kyrgyz Republic and Kazakhstan–Uzbekistan were the only other country pairs in CAREC with LCC service in 2022.

In other regions, LCC options are much more common. Regional connectivity is also much higher in other regions.

For example, in Southeast Asia, intra-region flights accounted for 28% of total international seat capacity in 2022, with LCCs accounting for 48% of capacity. In comparison, in CAREC, intra-CAREC accounted for only 3.5% of total international seat capacity in 2022, with LCCs accounting for less than 30%. In Europe, intra-region flights accounted for 68% of total international seat capacity, with LCCs accounting for 52%. Europe is a bigger region, while Southeast Asia, although much more populated, is similar in size to CAREC with 11 countries.

While 18 new routes were launched, total intra-CAREC capacity only increased slightly (less than 5%) from 2019 to 2022. In 2019, intra-CAREC accounted for slightly over 3% of total international seat capacity, with the LCC portion less than 10% (Table 20).

In Central Asia, international seat capacity between the five countries accounted for only 4% of total international seat capacity in both 2019 and 2022.

Table 20: Intra-Regional Portion of Total International Seat Capacity by Region, 2022 and 2019

Region	2022 Portion	2019 Portion
Europe	68%	66%
Southeast Asia	29%	25%
Northeast Asia	24%	36%
Southwest Pacific	24%	22%
Latin America	23%	27%
Africa	23%	25%
Middle East	18%	17%
North America	10%	11%
South Asia	7%	7%
Central Asia	**4%**	**4%**
CAREC	**4%**	**3%**

CAREC = Central Asia Regional Economic Cooperation.
Notes: Kazakhstan, the Kyrgyz Republic, Tajikistan, Turkmenistan, and Uzbekistan are included in Central Asia and CAREC. Mongolia is included in Northeast Asia and CAREC. Azerbaijan and Georgia are included in Europe and CAREC. Pakistan is included in South Asia and CAREC. Latin America includes South America, Central America, and the Caribbean.
Source: OAG.

Table 21: Intra-CAREC Portion of Total International Seat Capacity by Country, 2022 and 2019

Country	2022 Portion	2019 Portion	2022 Number of Routes	2019 Number of Routes
Kazakhstan	20%	15%	19	14
Georgia	11%	5%	10	7
Uzbekistan	11%	10%	13	7
Azerbaijan	9%	9%	13	7
Kyrgyz Republic	6%	11%	4	5
Tajikistan	4%	7%	2	4
Mongolia	3%	5%	2	2
Pakistan	<1%	<1%	5	1
Turkmenistan	0%	10%	0	2

CAREC = Central Asia Regional Economic Cooperation.
Notes: Intra-CAREC excludes Afghanistan and the People's Republic of China. Number of routes exclude ad hoc routes or routes that had a very small number of frequencies for the year.
Source: Author, based on data from OAG and other sources.

This is the lowest figure among all regions, highlighting how underserved the intra-Central Asia market is. Central Asia is a small region, but other small regions (geographically) such as South Asia and North America had a higher level of intra-regional capacity.

It is also clear that the broader intra-CAREC market is underserved. Of the nine CAREC countries (excluding Afghanistan and the PRC), only Kazakhstan has a significant intra-CAREC portion of total international seat capacity (Table 21).

The relatively small size of the intra-CAREC market and the lack of intra-CAREC connectivity are major impediments to CAREC economically. The LCC penetration rate in the intra-CAREC market is also about 15 percentage points below the global average for intra-regional markets.

Policy changes and LCC growth could help drive improved connectivity within CAREC. Both are critical as LCCs cannot expand without a more favorable regulatory environment. LCCs need to be able to launch routes without any constraints and require a reasonable cost environment. Unfortunately, there are still regulatory constraints impeding development of more flights between CAREC countries and the costs are too high at most CAREC airports to make many potential new intra-CAREC routes viable.

Airport charges and taxes for all international flights are generally high in CAREC. These costs particularly become an issue for regional flights as the charges are typically the same regardless of the destination. Therefore, the cost of airport taxes, charges, and fees are proportionally much higher for a regional flight within CAREC than a flight to a destination outside the region.

For example, FlyArystan has incurred over $50 per passenger in charges and fees for flights from all CAREC destinations it has served except Kutaisi. It has not been able to sustain several intra-CAREC routes and most of its intra-CAREC flights are now from Kutaisi, which is an exception in CAREC as it has very low taxes and fees. Kutaisi is also exceptional in that it is an airport catering almost entirely to LCCs.

CAREC countries should consider policies to ensure taxes and charges for regional flights are reasonable. Otherwise, it will be very difficult to significantly improve regional connectivity. This applies to both LCCs and FSCs, although it is particularly an issue for LCCs as they cannot offer the low fares needed to stimulate the market if airports costs and taxes are high.

The intra-CAREC market is ideal for LCCs given the relatively short length of flights and the fact that the market generally consists of price-sensitive leisure passengers. However, it is difficult to attract LCCs without reasonable airport costs and supportive policies. Otherwise, LCCs in CAREC will continue to focus mainly on other markets, including domestic and international services to non-CAREC countries. Domestic flights generally benefit from lower airport costs and taxes, while international flights outside the region benefit from lower airport costs and taxes in non-CAREC countries.

Airports and tourism authorities in non-CAREC countries are also typically aggressive at incentivizing LCCs. CAREC airports are generally not competitive when it comes to attracting LCCs from other CAREC countries and focus more on attracting LCCs from outside CAREC than within.

Another challenge is the limited number of local LCCs in CAREC. The international market is dominated by foreign LCCs. As highlighted in the earlier section, foreign LCCs accounted for 80% of total international LCC capacity in CAREC in 2022. While local LCCs can narrow this gap, particularly if CAREC countries adopt policies that are more supportive of local LCC development, foreign LCCs will always be larger as they benefit from being based in larger home markets, resulting in economies of scale.

Foreign LCCs are unable to operate intra-CAREC routes unless there are policy changes that provide them with fifth and seventh freedom traffic rights. Seventh freedoms could be particularly useful at facilitating intra-CAREC growth as it would allow foreign LCCs that have bases in CAREC countries to serve intra-CAREC routes. For example, seventh freedom rights would enable Wizz Air to link Kutaisi with other CAREC countries, although

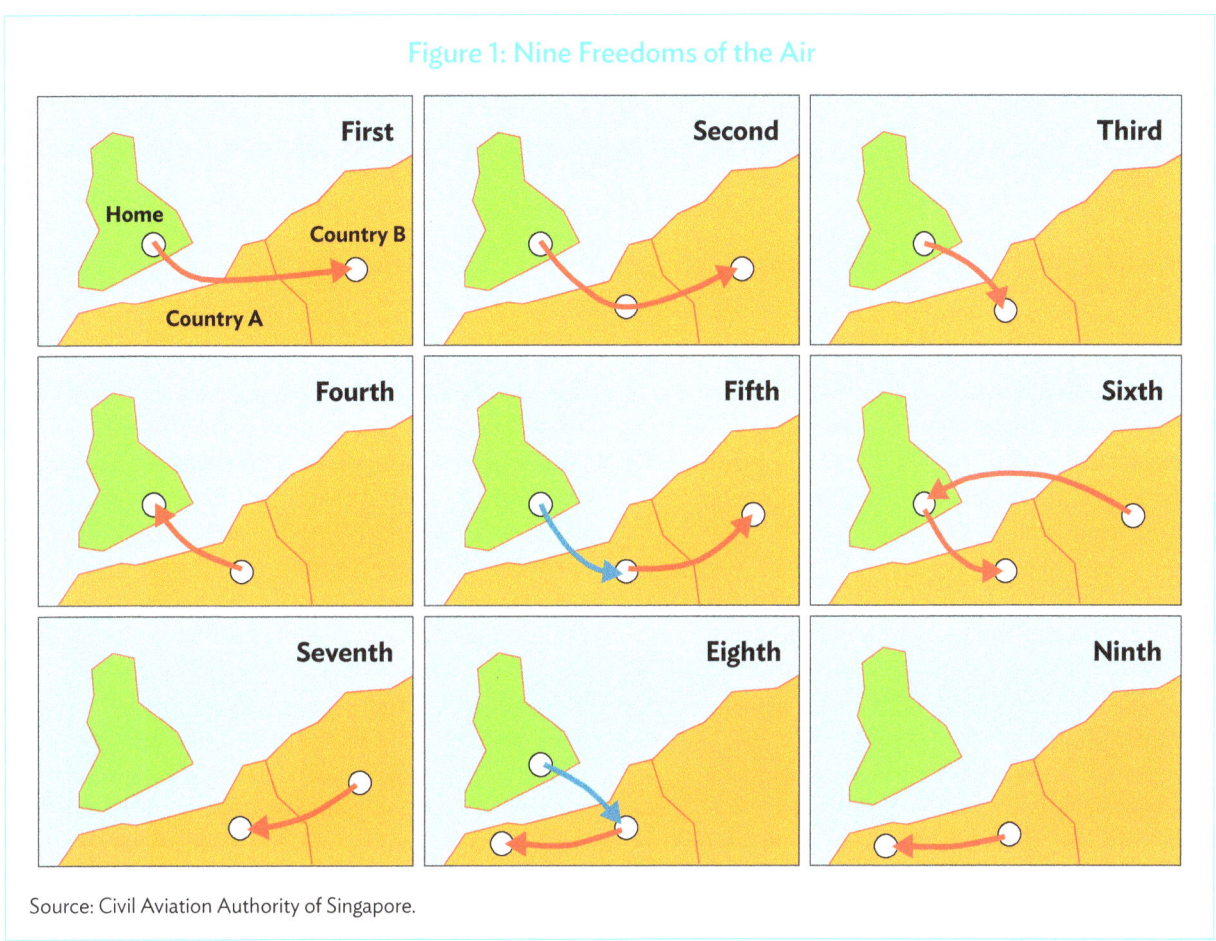

Figure 1: Nine Freedoms of the Air

Source: Civil Aviation Authority of Singapore.

it is a registered airline in Hungary (and European Union). Seventh freedoms can be controversial but can help develop markets that are unserved or underserved.

Fifth and seventh freedoms for CAREC LCCs would also enable more intra-CAREC routes. For example, FlyArystan would be able to set up bases in other CAREC countries with seventh freedom rights. With fifth freedoms, FlyArystan would be able to operate routes such as Tashkent–Baku as long as the flight originates in Kazakhstan, while Buta Airways could operate routes such as Tashkent–Almaty as long as the flight originates in Azerbaijan. The nine freedoms of the air are outlined in Figure 1.

Recommendations

CAREC countries should consider providing fifth and seventh freedom rights for intra-CAREC routes, enabling local as well as foreign airlines to launch more intra-CAREC routes and facilitate development of the intra-CAREC market, including LCC development.

CAREC countries should consider adopting a universal visa-free policy, which would facilitate cross-CAREC tourism and drive improved connectivity within CAREC, as well as boost the CAREC aviation and tourism sectors.

CAREC countries should consider reducing taxes, fees, and charges for intra-CAREC flights to help facilitate the development of more flights within CAREC and improve intra-CAREC connectivity.

CAREC countries should consider establishing programs to incentivize and support new intra-CAREC routes.

Opportunities: Domestic Market

There are also opportunities for CAREC LCCs to drive growth in the domestic market. However, these opportunities vary significantly depending on the country as several CAREC countries have limited domestic markets.

Kazakhstan is the largest domestic market in CAREC and has already benefited significantly from LCC stimulation since the launch of FlyArystan in May 2019. FlyArystan operates nearly 30 domestic routes (as of summer 2023), including several point-to-point routes that are not served by any other airline. It is already the largest domestic airline in Kazakhstan with market share of about 40% and is also now the largest domestic airline in CAREC (excluding the PRC).

Kazakhstan's domestic market has nearly doubled in size since FlyArystan's launch with low fares stimulating demand and persuading millions of travelers who previously relied on trains or buses. Kazakhstan has had one of the world's fastest-growing domestic air transport markets during this period. This would not have been possible without the launch of an LCC and policy adjustments that were implemented by the Kazakhstan government to facilitate LCCs.

For example, Kazakhstan previously required that all airlines provide free baggage, a regulation that needed to be removed given that charging for checked luggage and other items such as food is a fundamental component of the LCC model. Kazakhstan sensibly agreed to change this regulation, enabling LCCs to enter the local market. The policy and legislative changes that were done by Kazakhstan to facilitate FlyArystan's launch has been extremely successful, with the domestic market growing twice as fast as expected by aviation authorities, with low fares enabling Kazakhs that were previously traveling by train to fly for the first time.

Other CAREC countries can potentially learn from the Kazakhstan example and encourage LCCs to stimulate rapid growth in domestic air travel. However, realistically, only Pakistan is able develop its domestic market to the extent Kazakhstan has, given the other CAREC countries are much smaller.

Pakistan's domestic market has been served by LCCs since 2004, when airblue commenced operations. However, airblue has focused primarily on the international market since starting international flights in 2005. Prior to the pandemic, airblue accounted for less than 10% of domestic seat capacity in Pakistan. While airblue grew its domestic operation during the pandemic, when international flights were very limited, it still has less than a 15% share of domestic seat capacity and is now once again primarily focused on the Pakistan–Middle East market.

The launch in late 2022 of a second LCC in Pakistan, Fly Jinnah, has had an impact on the domestic market. Fly Jinnah already accounted for about a 20% share of domestic seat capacity in January 2023, which was only its third month of operations, and already had overtaken airblue, Air Sial, and SereneAir to become the second-largest domestic airline in Pakistan after Pakistan International Airlines.

However, Fly Jinnah will also likely focus on the international market once it is permitted to operate international flights, which it expects by the end of 2023. Its domestic capacity and market share has been flat since January 2023. Fly Jinnah currently operates only three A320s on five domestic trunk routes, with about a 23% share of domestic seat capacity in Pakistan (as of Q3 2023).

New airlines in Pakistan typically shift focus to the international market once they have five aircraft, which is the minimum number of aircraft required to commence scheduled international flights. For example, Air Sial initially focused on the domestic market after commencing operations in December 2020, but shifted focus to the international market after launching scheduled international flights in October 2022 following delivery of its fifth aircraft. SereneAir commenced operations in January 2017 and began international flights in March 2022, also after expanding beyond five aircraft. SereneAir now has a larger international than domestic operation.

Pakistan's domestic market is hugely underserved but has been challenging for new airlines—both LCCs and FSCs. There is no competition outside the main trunk routes and there are virtually no point-to-point routes connecting secondary cities like there is now in Kazakhstan. Most domestic capacity, including most of the LCC capacity, is on just two routes, connecting Karachi with Islamabad and Lahore.

Policy changes are required to drive growth in Pakistan's domestic market and to tap the huge potential of LCCs. Pakistan's domestic market has not grown in over 15 years. In the decade prior to the pandemic, domestic passenger traffic in Pakistan was stagnant, while in the same period international traffic doubled. In 2022, Pakistan's domestic market was almost back at 2019 levels, but 2019 levels (about 3 million annual passengers) were virtually the same as 2007 levels. In 2023, domestic seat capacity has been roughly the same as 2019 levels, despite the launch of Fly Jinnah.

Pakistan should have a much larger domestic market by now. The lack of growth is hurting Pakistan's economy and its ability to develop tourism. ADB and CAREC should consider a separate study analyzing the opportunities for LCC development in Pakistan, as the scale of the opportunities and the market characteristic are very different than other CAREC countries. The potential for LCC growth in Pakistan is massive as it is such a populated and drastically underserved country.

The domestic market potential of other CAREC countries is not as big. However, there are opportunities for LCCs to drive some domestic growth in Azerbaijan, the Kyrgyz Republic, and Uzbekistan. These three domestic markets now each have nearly 1 million passengers per annum and could double or triple in size with the right policies and support. However, these three markets are still much smaller than Kazakhstan or Pakistan, which have the potential to reach 10 million and 20 million passengers per annum, respectively.

Azerbaijan, the Kyrgyz Republic, and Uzbekistan all have LCCs, but in 2022 their domestic markets had no LCC service. This has changed in Uzbekistan as a new LCC, Silk Avia, launched operations in April 2023, focusing entirely on the domestic market. Silk Avia is following a regional low-cost model using turboprop aircraft, a smaller aircraft type used by only a few LCCs globally. This model could be followed in other CAREC countries to develop domestic markets, but it will be very difficult to achieve profitability.

Policy and regulatory changes are needed to encourage LCC growth—and growth, overall—in CAREC's smaller domestic markets. Unlike the international market, policy changes would not be about trying to facilitate a reduction in airfares, as domestic airfares in most CAREC countries are already low. Domestic airfares are regulated in many CAREC countries, which essentially makes it impossible for airlines to be profitable in the domestic market without subsidies.

While subsidizing domestic air services can be justified given the social and economic benefits of ensuring smaller or isolated communities are connected, CAREC countries should consider liberalization and other options that could potentially enable domestic operations to become commercially viable. Encouraging and facilitating privately owned LCCs would be sensible, resulting in better domestic connectivity across CAREC. Improved domestic connectivity would facilitate economic development as well as both domestic and international tourism.

Kazakhstan's FlyArystan commenced operations in May 2019 and has already become the largest low-cost carrier in CAREC (photo by FlyArystan).

Recommendations

CAREC countries should consider policies and programs to facilitate development of domestic air transport, particularly LCC development.

CAREC countries subsidizing domestic air travel and/or regulating domestic airfares should examine new options or funding mechanisms for both airports and airlines.

CAREC should consider a separate study on the opportunities for domestic LCC development in Pakistan, as the scale of the opportunities and the market characteristic are very different than in other CAREC countries.

Opportunities: International Market (Excluding Intra-CAREC)

The CAREC international market relies heavily on the Russian Federation, the Gulf Cooperation Council (GCC), and Türkiye. These markets currently account for around 80% of total international seat capacity in CAREC.

In 2022, the Russian Federation accounted for 24% of scheduled international seat capacity from CAREC (excluding Afghanistan and the PRC) (Table 22). The GCC accounted for 43%, including 23% for the UAE and 12% for Saudi Arabia, while Türkiye accounted for 15%.

All these markets have been growing, resulting in an even smaller share for the rest of the world. There are further growth opportunities in all these main markets—for both LCCs and FSCs, and for both foreign and local carriers.

Economic ties with the GCC are strong and there is a large population of CAREC citizens working in the GCC. The GCC also has become a large and growing source market for tourism in some CAREC countries.

The CAREC–Saudi Arabia market, in particular, has a lot of potential. Saudi Arabia is expected to emerge as one of the world's fastest-growing aviation markets over the next decade. CAREC countries are well placed to benefit from Saudi Arabia's ambitious hub aspirations, with commitments to triple airport capacity by 2030, given the geographic proximity and cultural ties.

Türkiye, meanwhile, has become the most popular holiday destination for residents of many CAREC countries. There are also close economic and cultural ties with Türkiye.

Airlines from all six GCC countries (Bahrain, Kuwait, Oman, Qatar, Saudi Arabia, and the UAE) and Türkiye have been expanding rapidly in CAREC, including LCCs. Airlines from CAREC have also been expanding in these markets, particularly Türkiye.

While facilitating further growth in these key markets is important, it is critical for CAREC to diversify. There is

Table 22: Top Five International Markets for CAREC Based on Share of Seat Capacity, 2022 and 2019

Rank	Country	Share in 2022	Share in 2019
1	Russian Federation	24%	24%
2	United Arab Emirates	23%	19%
3	Türkiye	15%	11%
4	Saudi Arabia	12%	11%
5	Qatar	5%	4%
	Top 5	**78%**	**70%**
	GCC	43%	38%

CAREC = Central Asia Regional Economic Cooperation, GCC = Gulf Cooperation Council.
Note: GCC also includes Bahrain, Kuwait, and Oman; each of these markets accounted for 1% to 2% of total international seat capacity in 2022.
Source: OAG.

growing interest in CAREC countries from airlines based in Southeast Asia, South Asia, Northeast Asia, and the European Union (EU), particularly LCCs. However, attracting LCCs from these regions will be challenging.

LCCs from these regions are attracted by the surging demand for air travel to/from Central Asia, but are dissuaded by high airport costs and taxes. In some cases, there are also regulatory constraints and they have struggled to secure approvals to launch the routes they would like to serve.

There are also visa issues, particularly with India. Several CAREC countries are keen to develop India as a source market for tourism, but have struggled to attract Indian LCCs. The recent launch of services to India by FlyArystan and to four CAREC countries by Indian LCC IndiGo is a major breakthrough, but is just a start. There is potential for significantly more Indian LCC routes to CAREC.

Outbound travel from India is growing rapidly, driven by economic growth and rapid expansion of India's middle-class population. CAREC countries are well placed to benefit from this growth as they are close to India geographically and have products which appeal to Indian travelers (such as ecotourism and Silk Road tourism). However, attracting Indian travelers is very competitive and requiring visas makes it much harder to develop any source market.

CAREC countries should consider lifting visa requirements for India. CAREC countries should also consider programs and incentives to attract Indian LCCs. Indian LCCs are typically more focused on other growth markets that are bigger, easier to access, and cheaper to operate from, but can potentially be enticed to launch services to more CAREC destinations.

Several CAREC airports are reluctant to reduce charges and put in place incentive programs to attract LCCs from new markets because, so far, these have not been needed to attract LCCs from Türkiye and the GCC. Several LCCs from the GCC and Türkiye have been able to justify expanding in CAREC countries despite high airport charges and other costs, as demand has been sufficient to pass on these costs to passengers. However, this has resulted in relatively high airfares in these markets despite significant LCC expansion and there is a limit to the growth that can be achieved at the current high level of airfares.

Eventually, lower airfares will be needed to stimulate further growth in these markets. Much lower average fares are common on similar-length flights in other markets such as Europe, South Asia, and Southeast Asia. High airfares have been identified by several tourism authorities in CAREC countries as the biggest impediment in achieving international visitor growth targets. It will be difficult to reduce international airfares in CAREC without reducing airport costs and taxes.

While LCCs from the Middle East and Türkiye have so far accepted the relatively high airport costs of CAREC, the same cannot be assumed of LCCs from other regions. Some LCCs from other regions may still launch flights to CAREC countries and there are some recent examples. However, these flights are often charters or seasonal, for example, charter services that were operated to Georgia by Thai AirAsia X in 2022 and the services that are currently being operated to Kazakhstan and Uzbekistan by VietJet Air. It is difficult attracting LCCs to launch year-round regularly scheduled services from Southeast Asia or Western Europe, but the benefits of such flights to tourism and the overall economy are massive.

Lower airport costs and taxes would help attract scheduled services by foreign LCCs from outside the GCC or Türkiye. It will be difficult to develop new markets without significant discounts on airport fees and charges, as well as marketing incentives.

CAREC countries are keen to diversify and attract more flights from these markets given the potential economic benefit. CAREC airports are also keen to diversify and attract a more diverse portfolio of airlines, particularly LCCs. With the right policies and strategies, CAREC can succeed at attracting more air services and LCCs from outside the traditional markets.

flydubai is the largest foreign low-cost carrier in CAREC with 18 destinations across eight CAREC countries in the summer of 2023 (photo by flydubai).

Recommendations

CAREC airports should re-examine their structure of prices and charges to ensure they are not dissuading airlines from new markets from launching services, particularly LCCs.

CAREC countries should consider programs, policies, and strategies to tackle high international airfares, which have become the largest impediment to tourism growth.

CAREC countries should introduce new policies and strategies that facilitate a diversification of their international air transport markets by reducing reliance on the Russian Federation, the GCC, and Türkiye.

Opportunities: Airport Infrastructure Focused on Low-Cost Carriers

There are opportunities in CAREC to focus on LCCs as airports are expanded and new airports are developed. LCC terminals or LCC-focused terminals could facilitate a reduction in airport fees and charges and help resolve infrastructure constraints.

Several CAREC countries are now planning major airport expansion or development projects. Some CAREC countries have multiple airport projects in their pipeline, and some are looking at public–private partnership (PPP) options for funding these projects.

Airport infrastructure upgrades are needed urgently to keep up with growth, improve service levels, and raise efficiency levels to international standards. PPPs have become increasingly popular as they provide the capital to accelerate infrastructure development while bringing in the expertise needed to improve efficiency levels and grow non-aeronautical revenues. CAREC airports generally are much less efficient and have a much smaller non-aeronautical portion of revenues than similarly sized airports in other regions.

Improvements in the airport sector are particularly important to facilitate LCC growth, as LCCs find it difficult to make their model work at inefficient and expensive airports. With the right strategies and policies, CAREC airports can attract more LCCs. For some airports, this could include dedicated LCC terminals, which are quick and relatively inexpensive to develop as they are typically simple and do not have amenities such as aerobridges.

The first LCC terminal in CAREC is planned in Astana, with FlyArystan the only tenant and investor. FlyArystan also intends to open an LCC terminal in Shymkent. These projects are discussed in the Kazakhstan case study and could become a model for other CAREC airports.

Kutaisi Airport in Georgia can also be used as a potential model for other CAREC airports. While it does not have an LCC terminal, Kutaisi is a simple and efficient airport with no aerobridges designed for LCCs. Kutaisi has grown rapidly and could become the largest LCC airport (based on LCC passenger traffic) in CAREC in 2023. Kutaisi's role in driving aviation growth in Georgia, and the policies and low tariffs that have made this possible, are discussed in the Georgia case study.

Investment is needed not only at major airports in CAREC but at smaller airports that primarily or entirely handle domestic traffic. Most of these airports are too small to attract major airport investors, but there are other options for funding these airports, both to cover ongoing operations and modernization or upgrades, as often, the facilities at these airports are old and in poor condition. Attracting LCCs to smaller airports is critical, as smaller markets often consist of primarily price-sensitive leisure or worker traffic.

For example, in Kazakhstan, there is an opportunity to take over, modernize, and improve several smaller domestic airports that are now owned by local governments. This is discussed in the Kazakhstan case study. Domestic airport challenges as well as overall airport policy issues are also discussed in the other five other case studies that follow this section.

Recommendations

1. CAREC countries should consider PPPs and other options for facilitating development of airport infrastructure and for improving airport efficiency levels.
2. CAREC airports should consider developing LCC terminals and focusing more on LCCs as they expand.

CASE STUDY 1
Azerbaijan and Buta Airways

AZAL Azerbaijan Airlines became the first FSC in CAREC to establish an LCC or low-cost brand in March 2016 when it launched AZALJET.

AZALJET was initially used to take over flights to 15 of 27 AZAL's international destinations. However, AZALJET ceased operations in August 2017 and was replaced by Buta Airways, which began operations in September 2017.

The launch of Buta was essentially a rebranding of AZALJET, as Buta took over AZALJET aircraft and routes. The two brands had essentially the same product, with both charging passengers extra for some items that were free when traveling under the AZAL brand. Neither had or have a business class product, which is available on virtually all AZAL-branded international flights.

Charging for bags, seats, meals, and only offering an economy class seat are typical components of the LCC model. However, Buta is not a typical LCC in this respect as it provides free snacks (sandwiches), coffee, and drinking water, and does not charge for the first 10 kilograms (kg) of check-in luggage. Buta also uses unusually small aircraft for an LCC, with economy seats in a two-by-two configuration without any middle seats. It charges extra for extra-legroom seats (the first row and emergency row) and for seats at the front of the cabin, but otherwise seat assignments are free of charge, which is also unusual for LCCs.

Buta's ancillary revenues are therefore low for an LCC. While Buta's product does not quite match AZAL's economy class product—which includes meals, a full selection of beverages, and 20 kg of check-in luggage—offering some frills limits the ability to upsell and generate non-ancillary revenues.

Buta's costs are also significantly higher than most LCCs. This has made it difficult for Buta to compete with foreign LCCs. Buta was operating about 20 routes prior to the pandemic and currently operates around 20 routes, competing with foreign LCCs on several of these routes (as of summer 2023).

The higher costs compared to other LCCs are mainly due to using much smaller aircraft. Buta's fleet has always consisted entirely of Embraer E190s, a regional jet that has 106 seats in Buta's all-economy configuration. Competing LCCs generally use Airbus A320s or Boeing 737s with at least 174 seats, resulting in much lower unit costs.

Buta also has higher costs than competitors because it is a division of AZAL rather than a separate airline with its own AOC. Some legacy- or full-service-related costs that are incurred by AZAL are passed on to Buta due to this structure.

Buta competes against LCCs that are also much larger, and therefore its competitors benefit from economies of scale. Buta has only eight aircraft and has not expanded since 2018, when it took the seventh and eighth E190.

AZAL should consider changing Buta's fleet to larger aircraft and separating Buta from AZAL or launching a new LCC subsidiary with larger aircraft. Larger aircraft, such as A320s, which have up to 186 seats in all economy-configuration, would result in lower and more competitive unit costs. A separate company with its own AOC would allow Buta or a new LCC to negotiate separate contracts with vendors, leveraging its position as an LCC.

AZAL already has two all-economy 174-seat A320ceos, which operate predominantly in the domestic market.

AZAL could use Buta—or a new LCC that replaces Buta—to take over these aircraft and domestic services. Some of AZAL's three existing two-class A320ceos can also be converted into a single-class configuration and transferred to Buta. This is how FlyArystan and Uzbekistan Express were started, using Air Astana and Uzbekistan Express A320ceos that were reconfigured. FlyArystan also now operates new A320neos, which would be another option for Buta.

AZAL is modernizing and expanding its narrow-body fleet with 12 new generation A320neos and A321neos by the end of 2024 (three of which were delivered in late 2022 and early 2023). While these aircraft are intended for AZAL, some of the older generation A320ceos that AZAL now operates could be transferred to Buta or a new LCC. It is also possible to allocate some of the A320neos to Buta or a new LCC, particularly given that at least three of these aircraft are slated to be delivered in a single-class 186-seat configuration. Most of the A320neos/A321neos are slated to be delivered in dual-class configuration and used to streamline the fleet as older types such as 757s are phased out.

AZAL also has placed orders for eight more 787s, including five aircraft which will be delivered by 2030, and allow it to phase out 767s and A340s. It currently has two 787-8s that were delivered in 2014.

Without A320s, Buta will not be able to grow, as AZAL is not intending to acquire any additional E190s and has been looking to phase out the type over the next few years. Without A320s, Buta also cannot compete effectively with other LCCs.

In late July 2023, AZAL announced plans to merge the AZAL and Buta brands under a single brand, AZAL, and have an LCC fare called "Buta Budget" on all AZAL flights. AZAL should instead consider turning Buta into a pure LCC with A320s—or establishing a new LCC with a strong and pure LCC strategy. Merging Buta into AZAL and offering "Buta Budget" as an airfare option will not resolve most of the challenges Buta has faced or significantly improve AZAL's ability to compete with LCCs.

AZAL was a pioneer in CAREC by establishing an LCC 6 years ago. This was a sensible strategy as AZAL recognized the potential of LCCs, before any other FSC or flag carrier in CAREC. However, AZAL did not and has still not fully embraced the LCC model. A purer and totally independent LCC is needed to tap the full potential of LCCs in Azerbaijan.

The decision to establish an LCC to take over AZAL's E190s, which were already in single-class configuration when they operated under the AZAL brand, was in many respects driven by a desire to reduce losses with the E190 operation, rather than to create an LCC with growth potential. Buta cannot grow under the current model and Buta (and AZAL) will continue to lose market share if AZAL's LCC strategy is not adjusted. The E190 fleet is now slated to move back to the AZAL brand as part of the recently announced AZAL-Buta merger and is expected to be phased out entirely over the next few years. While this is sensible AZAL has not yet addressed the fact that Azerbaijan needs a strong local LCC with a cost structure, product, and fleet that is competitive with foreign LCCs, which continue to expand rapidly in its home market.

Foreign LCCs expand rapidly

Foreign LCC capacity in Azerbaijan increased by over 80% from 2019 to 2022, as the number of foreign LCCs in the market more than doubled from five to 13. Buta shrunk during this period and its share of LCC capacity in its home market dropped from 50% in 2019 to 31% in 2022 (Table 23).

The biggest increases in foreign LCC capacity have occurred in the Saudi Arabia and Türkiye markets. Both are key markets for both Buta and AZAL.

Türkiye's AnadoluJet launched services during the pandemic to Baku from both Ankara and Istanbul's Sabiha Gokcen, which are Buta routes. AnadoluJet has quickly become the second-largest foreign LCC in Azerbaijan after flydubai. In 2023, AnadoluJet further expanded in Baku with a third route to Izmir, which was launched in June 2023 and is also a Buta route.

Another Turkish LCC, Pegasus, also started competing on the Baku–Sabiha Gokcen route during the pandemic. Prior to the pandemic, Pegasus was only serving Baku

Table 23: Low-Cost Carriers in Azerbaijan Ranked by Seat Capacity Share, 2022 versus 2019
(% of total capacity)

Rank	Airline	2022 Share	2019 Share
1	Buta Airways (Azerbaijan)	31	50
2	flydubai (UAE)	16	22
3	AnadoluJet (Türkiye)	11	0
4	flynas (Saudi Arabia)	10	5
5	Wizz Air Abu Dhabi (UAE)	7	0
6	Pegasus (Türkiye)	7	2
7	Air Arabia (UAE)	7	15
8	Jazeera (Kuwait)	3	3
9	FlyArystan (Kazakhstan)	2	0
10	Wizz Air (Hungary)	2	2
11	flyadeal (Saudi Arabia)	2	0
12	SalamAir (Oman)	1	0
13	Bees Airline (Ukraine)	1	0

CAREC = Central Asia Regional Economic Cooperation, UAE = United Arab Emirates.
Notes: Bees Airline launched services to Baku in 2021 and 2022 until Russia's war in Ukraine started. Air Arabia Abu Dhabi is included under Air Arabia.
Source: Author, based on data from OAG and other sources.

from Izmir with limited frequencies. Pegasus added a third route in June 2023, when it launched Baku–Dalaman, which was not previously served by any airline.

From Saudi Arabia, flynas has expanded rapidly and a second Saudi Arabian LCC, flyadeal, has entered the market. Flynas only began serving Azerbaijan in 2018 and expanded rapidly just before as well as during the pandemic. In 2022, flynas served Baku with up to 18 weekly flights, and in 2023 with up to 17 weekly flights. In its summer schedule, flynas often has three A320s at Baku at once with flights from Dammam, Jeddah, and Riyadh. Buta competes on the Dammam and Riyadh routes, while the AZAL brand is mainly used for Jeddah. Flyadeal launched a summer-only service on the Baku–Riyadh route in 2022 and on the Baku–Jeddah route in 2023.

There also has been a significant increase in Azerbaijan–UAE capacity due to the launch of services to Baku in late 2021 from Abu Dhabi by both Air Arabia Abu Dhabi and Wizz Air Abu Dhabi. These new services are in addition to flights from Dubai by flydubai and from Sharjah by Air Arabia. Dubai and Sharjah capacity has not grown, but overall capacity to the UAE has grown due to the new Abu Dhabi services. The number of Baku–Abu Dhabi flights is reaching a record 16 frequencies per week in September 2023 compared to only three per week prior to the pandemic. Flydubai remains the largest foreign LCC in the Azerbaijan market with four flights per day during the summer season, although its market share has declined due to the increase in the overall market.

The overall surge in LCC capacity from the GCC has been beneficial for Azerbaijan, particularly its tourism sector. Saudi Arabia has quickly emerged as one of Azerbaijan's largest source markets from a very small base a few years ago. There were no regularly scheduled services between Azerbaijan and Saudi Arabia until 2018 and at the time, there was very few visitors from Saudi Arabia. Saudi Arabia is now the fifth-largest source market for Azerbaijan, accounting for about 5% of total visitors. This would not have been possible without the new LCC services and the lifting of visa restrictions for Saudi citizens.

Buta Airways launched in 2017 and in the summer of 2023 served 20 destinations from Baku with a fleet of eight Embraer E-190s (photo by Buta Airways).

Further rapid growth from Saudi Arabia is expected, once again driven by LCCs. Azerbaijan tourism authorities are also eager to use LCCs to drive similar growth in other new or undeveloped source markets. However, this is not feasible without policy changes and a reduction in airport charges. LCCs from Saudi Arabia and other GCC countries have been able to expand in Baku despite very high airport costs and charges. However, similar growth in other markets cannot be achieved if the status quo is maintained. GCC growth may also hit a ceiling without a reduction in airport costs and charges.

Lower airport costs would facilitate lower fares and help Azerbaijan achieve its goals for developing tourism. High airfares have been identified by tourism authorities as the biggest impediment in attracting more tourists. High airfares also have impeded growth of the outbound segment as Azerbaijan residents are not able to afford as many trips overseas.

High fares were particularly an issue in 2022 as Azerbaijan did not reopen its land borders, resulting in very high demand and airfares, as flying was the only option both for outbound travelers and inbound tourists. (Azerbaijan land borders were still closed as of summer of 2023, benefiting airlines as airfares remained very high, particularly to Georgia and Türkiye, as most travelers in these markets typically drive.)

Azerbaijan's aviation and tourism sectors could benefit from reform and liberalization

Market liberalization is controversial as it would impact AZAL, but is needed for Azerbaijan to meet tourism aspirations, including a doubling of visitor arrivals over the next few years, and to compete effectively. Azerbaijan's aviation sector still has a vertical Soviet-style structure, with the airport and flag carrier controlled by a single company. There are no privately owned passenger airlines and airport costs are very high. Uzbekistan had a similar structure until a few years ago, when it pursued rapid liberalization, resulting in Uzbekistan Airways and Uzbekistan Airports becoming separate companies and in the launch of new privately owned airlines. Private sector participation in the airport sector has also started in Uzbekistan.

It would be sensible for Azerbaijan to follow Uzbekistan with similar reforms. If Azerbaijan does not change, it will fall behind and it will be difficult to compete, particularly for international tourists. Azerbaijan tourism authorities believe it is now losing potential tourists to Uzbekistan, as well as Armenia and Georgia, as these countries all have more liberal aviation policies.

Azerbaijan should also consider further visa reform as the current e-visa system makes it difficult to compete with countries that have no visa requirements. For example, it is easier for some of Azerbaijan's neighbors to attract tourists as they offer free visa, free entry while Azerbaijan charges for e-visas. The e-visa charge is relatively low, but it is still an extra step that dissuades some travelers.

Market liberalization and lower airport charges will make it harder for AZAL to compete. However, AZAL can also restructure and become more competitive. Both AZAL and Buta would benefit from restructuring and a new strategy.

As highlighted earlier in this case study, Buta could separate from AZAL, switch to larger and more efficient aircraft, and fully embrace the LCC model. It could focus on short-haul routes that already have foreign LCC competition or that have high growth potential with LCC stimulation. AZAL could diversify its network by focusing more on destinations to the east. AZAL's network has traditionally been imbalanced with very few flights to the east, which makes it hard to develop Baku as a hub.

Azerbaijan could benefit from network diversification

Transit passengers currently only account for about 20% of total traffic at AZAL and about 10% of total traffic for Baku. AZAL has an opportunity to attract more transit passengers, for example, from Malaysia or Pakistan to Saudi Arabia, and India or Uzbekistan to the UAE. While transit would drive faster traffic growth and support several new potential routes that would help grow inbound tourism, AZAL should be cautious and focus on niche opportunities rather than rely heavily on transit as it is a very competitive segment. Focusing on regional connections to underserved destinations in CAREC and other nearby countries could be a viable strategy as it would avoid significant overlap with major network airlines from the Gulf.

In CAREC, new services to Pakistan and Uzbekistan particularly have a lot of potential. Pakistan International Airlines launched limited flights to Baku in 2022 and AZAL is planning to launch services to Pakistan in late September 2023. Azerbaijan and Pakistan have been working on completing their first air services agreement, which would help facilitate more regular flights. Until now, flights between the two countries, which enjoy close ties, have been operated using temporary traffic rights.

AZAL is also keen to further expand in Uzbekistan, where it began serving Samarkand in late 2022 and both Fergana and Urgench in early 2023. However, Samarkand and Fergana services were suspended in May, with Urgench continuing only as a seasonal route with one weekly frequency. Samarkand and Fergana services could resume in the future, and more frequencies are possible for Urgench as well as Tashkent.

AZAL aims to operate services to seven CAREC countries by 2030 as part of its network development strategy. AZAL currently serves five CAREC countries—Georgia, Kazakhstan, the Kyrgyz Republic, Tajikistan, and Uzbekistan—with Pakistan slated to launch in September 2023 and the PRC potentially launching in the near term.

AZAL added Tajikistan in May 2023, when it used the Buta brand to launch flights to Dushanbe. The Kyrgyz Republic followed in July 2023 when AZAL launched flights to Bishkek. However, both services operate only once per week, although Dushanbe was initially announced as a thrice-a-week route. Block bookings from travel agents typically underwrite low-frequency routes—such as Baku to Bishkek, Dushanbe, Fergana, Samarkand, and Urgench—making them hard to sustain once the commitments from the agents expire.

In Georgia, Buta serves Tbilisi and Batumi, with the Batumi service only operating in the summer. In Kazakhstan, Buta serves Aktau, while AZAL serves

Almaty and added Astana in March 2023. FlyArystan competes against Buta on the Aktau route and launched Baku–Astana service in June 2023. Azerbaijan and Kazakhstan expanded their air services agreement in June and 42 weekly flights are now permitted from each side compared to 32 previously. This provides ample space for growth; in the summer of 2023, there were only 20 weekly passenger flights between the two countries, up from 17 in summer of 2019. The market also has been served by Qazaq Air since August 2022, when it launched its Baku–Aktobe service, but another Kazakhstan carrier, SCAT, has not served Baku since just prior to the pandemic.

Meanwhile, AZAL's new fleet of A321neos and additional 787s should facilitate network expansion on longer routes to the east. Malaysia, India, Japan, the PRC, and the Republic of Korea all have potential and are high-priority new source markets for Azerbaijan's tourism sector. Azerbaijan tourism authorities began marketing efforts in many of these countries prior to the pandemic and are eager to step up these efforts.

A service to India was finally secured in summer of 2023 with IndiGo, which launched four weekly flights on the Baku–Delhi route in August 2023. The addition of IndiGo results in 13 foreign LCCs serving the Baku market, compared to 11 in summer 2022 and, significantly, is the first from Asia. In addition to the IndiGo launch, airBaltic relaunched service on the Baku–Riga route in May 2023 after a 4-year hiatus.

Expansion in Western Europe is also a priority as it helps Azerbaijan attract more tourists. AZAL expanded its Western European network in the summer of 2023 by adding or resuming services to Barcelona, Paris, and Vienna. This gives AZAL six destinations in Western Europe, including Berlin, London, and Milan. AZAL plans to add Geneva in late September 2023 and more expansion in Europe from AZAL is possible including Rome. Wizz Air launched its Baku–Rome service in July 2023, giving Wizz two European destinations from Baku along with Budapest, which it has served since 2013.

AZAL has suspended New York, which prior to the pandemic was its only long-haul route, and does not intend to resume services to North America. AZAL needs new markets not only to support future growth but also to fill the void from markets that have been impacted by Russia's war in Ukraine. Ukraine was the group's fourth-largest market, accounting for 6% to 7% of total traffic. The Russian Federation was its largest market, accounting for about 30% of traffic before the crisis.

Buta and AZAL were unable to serve the Russian Federation for about 3 months after the invasion started, which impacted their first half 2022 performance, leading to lower-than-normal market share for the full year. AZAL and Buta resumed Russian Federation flights in June 2022, but their Russian Federation capacity is still lower than pre-crisis levels while Russian carriers are well above 2019 levels.

The group also has been unable to restore capacity to Iran, another key market for Buta before the pandemic. It was only able to operate one weekly flight to Iran in 2022 and this limitation is still in place (as of summer of 2023).

Route development programs and initiatives would help facilitate new routes—from both AZAL and foreign airlines. Some programs, including a scheme for discounted airport fees, were in place prior to the pandemic, but were limited and only offered to a small number of airlines (both LCCs and FSCs). The scheme was suspended during the pandemic but should be resumed and expanded. Ganja could also soon have flights to Tbilisi as Georgian Wings, which began serving Baku from Tbilisi in September 2023, is also planning to serve Ganja.

It is never easy to balance the needs of a government-owned flag carrier and the economic benefits that come from competition. However, there are policies and programs that can benefit all airlines and AZAL can step up to become a more effective competitor.

Azerbaijan liberalized significantly in the several years prior to the pandemic, removing traffic right restrictions and establishing an e-visa system. Foreign airlines generally do not have any access issues and even fifth freedom rights are usually granted when requested. However, access is only one factor as foreign airlines can be dissuaded by high airport costs, particularly from an airport that is part of a company that also includes a competing airline and the only ground-handling supplier.

In more recent years, neighboring countries have liberalized further while Azerbaijan has essentially maintained the status quo. Now is the time for Azerbaijan to accelerate liberalization and consider a new aviation strategy. Alignment with a tourism strategy is also critical.

Azerbaijan has massive aviation and tourism potential. Traffic should well exceed 2019 levels in 2023. In the first 6 months of 2023, passenger traffic at Baku was 25% above 2019 levels. In summer of 2023, international seat capacity in Azerbaijan was about 20% higher than in 2019.

Rapid growth would benefit both local and foreign airlines, the tourism sector, and the overall economy. Baku Airport would also benefit with higher traffic volumes and new practices resulting in higher efficiency, as well as potentially enabling lower airport fees and charges.

With the right policies and programs, Azerbaijan could also potentially attract more traffic at secondary airports.

There are seven airports in Azerbaijan, all of which are under the same airport company, with two more slated to open in 2023 and 2024. However, only four airports have commercial services and only Baku and Ganja have regular year-round international services. Lankaran and Nakhchivan currently have limited seasonal international services. Ganja is very small and currently (as of summer 2023) only has flights to Istanbul and Moscow.

The only regular domestic route is Nakhchivan–Baku, which is served several times per day with low subsidized airfares. The domestic market had a temporary spike in traffic in 2022, with Nakhchivan–Baku flights increasing to 15 per day at one point due to a lack of road access. In summer of 2023, there were about 10 flights per day. However, the current domestic structure makes it challenging for airlines due to the very low fares AZAL is required to offer on all domestic flights. Prior to the pandemic, there were about 600,000 domestic passengers per annum in Azerbaijan.

AZAL Azerbaijan Airlines is renewing its narrow-body fleet with new A320neos and A321neos, replacing A320ceos which could potentially be transferred to Buta Airways or a new low-cost carrier subsidiary (photo by Airbus).

Azerbaijan should reconsider its domestic air transport policy as it reviews its overall aviation strategy. There is an opportunity to improve domestic connectivity, which would boost tourism in the more isolated areas, under a new domestic strategy for both airports and AZAL. The commercial viability of domestic flights is challenging but LCCs could improve the potential viability, and LCCs could also be used to develop new international routes from some of the secondary airports with incentives and discounts. For example, Gabala has a lot of tourism potential if air services can be developed.

However, most of the opportunities are at Baku. Rapid growth is feasible for Baku, necessitating airport expansion. Baku Airport has capacity to handle 9 million passengers, but has already been experiencing congestion during peak periods. Baku handled 4.7 million passengers in 2019. It was slightly short of a full recovery in 2022, but Baku is on pace to easily surpass 5 million passengers for the first time in 2023.

The airport would benefit from an airside link connecting terminal 1 with terminal 2 to improve connectivity. Terminal 2, which reopened for international flights in June 2023 after being closed during the pandemic, caters to LCCs with slightly lower charges and could be developed as a pure LCC terminal. Private sector investment has not been considered previously but should be looked at in future.

Recommendations for Azerbaijan

1. Consider following Uzbekistan in restructuring and liberalizing its aviation sector.
2. Adopt a new aviation strategy and make sure there is alignment with its tourism strategy.
3. Consider further visa liberalization by replacing its e-visa system with an expanded visa-free list.
4. Work with other CAREC countries in facilitating Silk Road tourism and developing more new air services between CAREC countries.
5. Consider a new strategy for AZAL Group, with Buta Airways separated from AZAL Azerbaijan Airlines and operating independently under a pure LCC model.
6. Consider changing Buta's fleet to high-density narrow-body aircraft, which would enable it to compete more effectively against foreign LCCs.
7. Look at new options for developing domestic air transport.
8. Consider policies and programs to facilitate LCC growth.
9. Review airport taxes charges and fees, including ground handling fees, to ensure they are competitive.
10. Consider private sector participation in the airport sector and look at opening an LCC terminal at Baku.

CASE STUDY 2
Georgia and Kutaisi Airport (Wizz Air Base)

Georgia has benefited from a high LCC penetration rate since Hungary-based LCC group Wizz opened a base at Kutaisi Airport in September 2016. While Wizz is not a Georgian carrier—and therefore is considered a foreign LCC rather than a CAREC LCC in this study—its Kutaisi base has had a significant impact on Georgia's aviation market. There are potential meaningful lessons for other CAREC countries from Wizz's Kutaisi base, which is the only example of a foreign airline base in CAREC, as well as Georgia's overall success at attracting LCCs since adopting a liberal aviation policy in 2005.

Wizz carried over 800,000 passengers to and from Georgia in 2019, making it the largest airline in the country with a 16% share of the total market. In 2022, Wizz was again the market leader with about 600,000 passengers carried and a 13% share. The largest Georgia-based airline, Georgian Airways, carried 500,000 passengers in 2019 and only 149,000 passengers in 2022, which made it the third- and ninth-largest airline in Georgia, respectively, in said periods.

In 2019, LCCs accounted for six of the 10 largest airlines in the Georgia market and a 37% share of total scheduled airline seat capacity. In 2022, LCCs also accounted for six of the 10 largest airlines in the Georgia market, with their overall capacity share growing to 55%. In 2022, 16 LCCs operated scheduled services to Georgia with the top six (Wizz, Pegasus, flydubai, flynas,

Kutaisi Airport has a modern and spacious terminal that was designed for low-cost carriers (photo by Brendan Sobie).

FlyArystan, and Buta) accounting for 42% of total seat capacity. Based on passenger traffic, Georgia reported that LCCs grew from a 33% share in 2019 to a 55% share in 2022, with the top six LCCs accounting for a 40% share of total passenger traffic in 2022.

LCCs dominate at Kutaisi, which has been positioned as an LCC airport since it reopened in 2012. While Wizz started to operate flights to Kutaisi in 2012, the airport was handling only about 200,000 passengers per annum before the Wizz base was established. Kutaisi's traffic grew rapidly from 2016 to 2019, driven primarily by Wizz. In 2019, Kutaisi handled 874,000 passengers, with Wizz accounting for over 95% of total traffic.

Kutaisi handled 822,000 passengers in 2022, representing a 94% recovery. While Kutaisi passenger traffic was above 2019 levels from May 2022, traffic was still down the first 4 months of the year when there were still COVID-19 testing and vaccination requirements in Georgia. Annual traffic for 2022 was also impacted by a 3-week closure in October, when all Kutaisi flights were moved to Tbilisi as Kutaisi's only runway was repaired. If it were not for this closure, Kutaisi traffic in 2022 would have nearly reached 2019 levels.

Wizz Air's passenger traffic in Georgia dropped by 27% in 2022 compared to 2019 as it initially only brought back two of the three aircraft that had been based at Kutaisi prior to the pandemic. The 27% decline includes the passengers Wizz Air carried at Tbilisi during the 3-week closure of Kutaisi in October 2022, but excludes passengers carried by the group's new affiliate in the UAE, Wizz Air Abu Dhabi, which launched flights to Kutaisi in late 2021. When including the Abu Dhabi route, which operated two to five flights per week in 2022, the decline for the Wizz group was still over 20% and Wizz's overall share of traffic at Kutaisi dropped to less than 80%.

In 2022, Kutaisi was served by only two other international airlines, FlyArystan and Belarusian flag carrier Belavia. Georgia's AK Air (also known as Vanilla Sky) had the only domestic service, a once weekly flight to Mestia using 19-seat aircraft.

FlyArystan has expanded rapidly at Kutaisi since commencing services to Kutaisi in May 2021. FlyArystan carried about 140,000 passengers to and from Georgia in 2022, which made it the 10th largest airline in Georgia overall, quite an accomplishment given this was its first full year serving Georgia. As is the case with Wizz, FlyArystan does not usually serve Tbilisi or Batumi, but temporarily moved its Kutaisi flights to Tbilisi in October 2022 during the Kutaisi Airport closure.

Kutaisi Airport aimed to exceed 1.5 million annual passengers in 2023. This should be achievable given current airline schedules. Wizz brought back a third aircraft to Kutaisi in June 2023 and has up-gauged all its aircraft based at Kutaisi from A320s to larger A321s, resulting in significantly higher seat capacity. There also has been growth from FlyArystan and Wizz Air Abu Dhabi as well as the launch of flights by Russian carrier Red Wings.

Scheduled seat capacity for Kutaisi in summer of 2023 was slightly more than double compared to the summer 2019 levels (based on OAG data). Wizz planned to add a fourth aircraft to its Kutaisi base in October 2023, which should drive further capacity growth in the last 2 months of the year. For the full year in 2023, scheduled seat capacity was roughly double 2019 levels, indicating Kutaisi could end the year with about 1.7 million passengers. In the first half of 2023, Kutaisi passenger traffic was already up 83% compared to 2019 levels to 667,000.

The Wizz group operated 27 routes from Kutaisi in summer of 2023 compared to 22 in summer of 2022, based on OAG data. Kutaisi overall had 28 routes in 2022, with FlyArystan operating 4, and 1 route each for Belavia and AK Air/Vanilla Sky. This increased to 35 routes in summer of 2023, with FlyArystan adding a fifth Kutaisi route (Almaty) and Red Wings launching service at Kutaisi (Moscow), as well as the five additional routes from Wizz (Brussels Charleroi, Frankfurt Hahn, Hamburg, Madrid, and Poznan).

Kutaisi's rapid growth prior to the pandemic contributed to the overall rapid growth of Georgia's aviation market. Total passenger traffic in Georgia increased more than fivefold in the decade prior to the pandemic, from less than 800,000 in 2009 to 5.2 million in 2019. Kutaisi accounted for 900,000 of the additional 4.4 million passengers, while Tbilisi accounted for 3 million and Batumi 500,000.

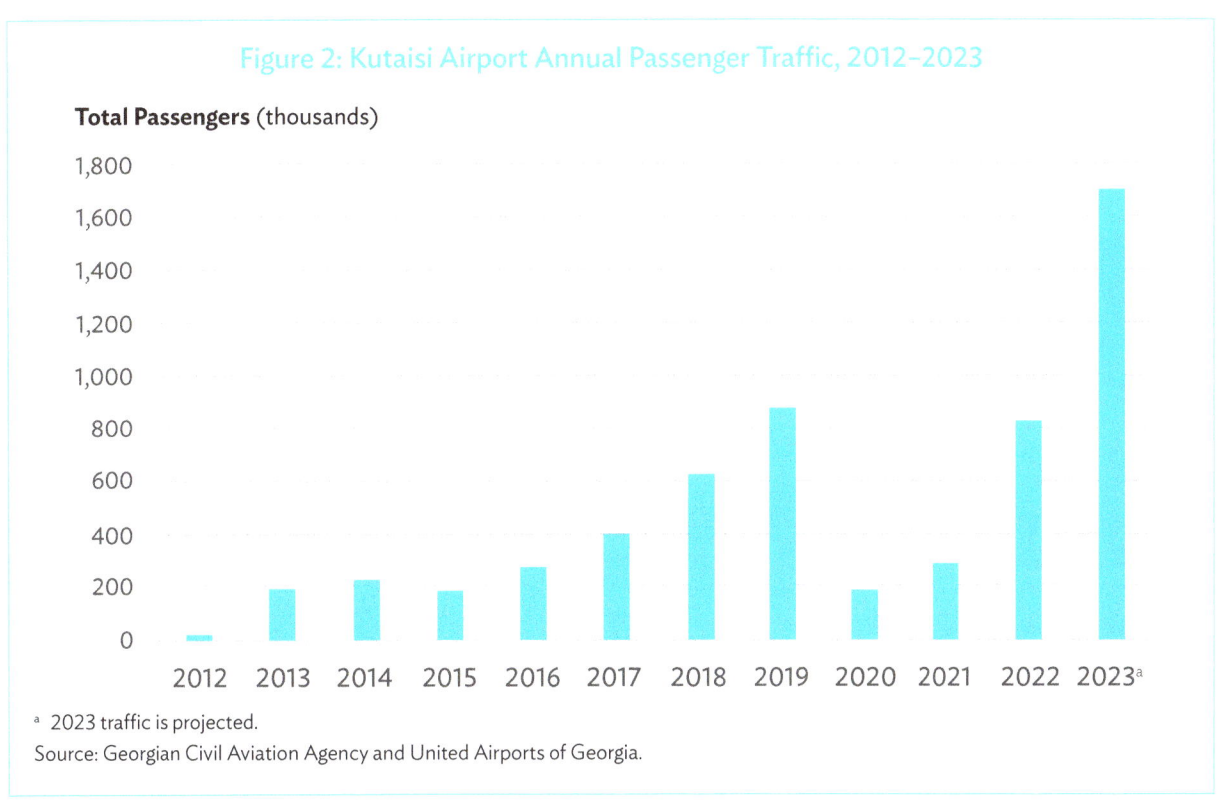

Figure 2: Kutaisi Airport Annual Passenger Traffic, 2012–2023

a 2023 traffic is projected.
Source: Georgian Civil Aviation Agency and United Airports of Georgia.

Georgia was the fastest growing aviation market in CAREC during this period, demonstrating how market liberalization and LCCs can drive rapid growth. While Kutaisi became the first LCC airport in CAREC and is a focus of this case study given its success at attracting LCCs, Tbilisi and Batumi have also achieved rapid LCC growth.

In 2022, LCCs accounted for 50% of scheduled seat capacity at Tbilisi and 43% at Batumi. While this is not quite the level of Kutaisi, where LCCs accounted for 94% of seat capacity, all three of Georgia's international airports are standouts in CAREC. Tbilisi was the second-largest international LCC airport in CAREC in 2022 with about 1.8 million LCC seats, behind only Baku in neighboring Azerbaijan, which had about 1.9 million international LCC seats. Kutaisi and Karachi were the next largest international LCC airports in CAREC, with each having about 1 million international LCC seats in 2022.

Kutaisi is now close to overtaking both Tbilisi and Baku as the largest LCC airport in CAREC. Kutaisi had about 1.9 million scheduled LCC seats in 2023. In 2023, Kutaisi was one of the fastest-growing airports in CAREC and globally, an impressive achievement that is made possible by a policy and pricing structure that is geared toward attracting LCC growth.

Georgia's liberal aviation policy has been very successful

Georgia initially adopted a liberal aviation policy in 2005 and has since negotiated over 20 open skies agreements. Georgia joined the European Common Aviation Area (ECAA) in 2010, essentially resulting in open skies with another 30 European countries as the ECAA is considered a single market for aviation services.

Overall, Georgia has about 40 air service agreements and while nearly half are not considered open skies, due to a lack of interest from the other country, there is generally no limitation on third and fourth freedoms. Foreign airlines, including foreign LCCs, have therefore enjoyed unfettered access from their home markets (all of Europe for ECAA carriers such as Wizz). This has enabled foreign LCCs to tap into Georgia's growing popularity as a tourist destination (Table 24).

In the decade prior to the pandemic, Georgia was remarkably successful at attracting LCCs and—in parallel—tourism. Georgia also was successful at achieving a quick recovery from COVID-19 with passenger traffic above 2019 levels in Q4 2022, with LCCs driving this recovery. As outlined in an earlier section and table in this study, Georgia's LCC penetration rate increased from 37% in 2019 to 55% in 2022, compared to the global average of 30% in 2019 and 33% in 2022.

In the decade prior to the pandemic, Georgia was among the fastest-growing aviation markets globally. After a slight contraction in 2009, passenger traffic in Georgia grew by at least 10% every year from 2010 to 2018, with a compound annual growth rate of over 20%. However, it will be challenging to match in the post-pandemic era the high double-digit annual growth that Georgia was able to achieve from 2009 to 2018 (Figure 3).

Passenger traffic in Georgia grew by a more modest 4% in 2019, with a slight reduction at Tbilisi due to the suspension of all Russian carrier flights in mid-2019.

The Russian Federation was a major market for Georgia, accounting for more than 30% of total international seat capacity (and 28% of international passenger traffic) in Georgia prior to late June 2019, when the Russian Federation government banned Russian carriers from serving Georgia. Ukraine was another major market, accounting for 7% of total seat capacity prior to the pandemic (and 9% of passenger traffic).

Two Ukrainian carriers, full-service flag carrier Ukraine International Airlines and LCC SkyUp, were among the 10 largest airlines in Georgia in 2019. Two Russian carriers, Ural Airlines and Aeroflot LCC subsidiary Pobeda, were also among the top 10 airlines in Georgia in 2019, despite not being able to operate any services to Georgia in the second half of the year (it was among the top five in the first half of the year).

There were seven Russian airlines serving Georgia prior to the suspension, which was lifted in May 2023. The lack of flights from Russian carriers for nearly 4 years is in stark contrast to other CAREC countries, some of which have experienced a major surge in flights from Russian

Table 24: Top 10 Airlines in Georgia Based on Passenger Traffic, 2019 and 2022

Airline	Country	2019	2022
Wizz Air	Hungary/EU	825,000 (#1)	588,000 (#1)
Turkish Airlines	Türkiye	572,000 (#2)	547,000 (#2)
Georgian Airways	Georgia	500,000 (#3)	149,000 (#9)
Ukraine International Airlines	Ukraine	208,000 (#4)	Not in Top 10
flydubai	UAE	204,000 (#5)	228,000 (#5)
Ural Airlines	Russian Federation	190,000 (#6)	No Services
Pegasus Airlines	Türkiye	181,000 (#7)	409,000 (#3)
Pobeda	Russian Federation	181,000 (#8)	No Services
SkyUp	Ukraine	156,000 (#9)	Not in Top 10
Air Arabia	UAE	144,000 (#10)	Not in Top 10
Belavia	Belarus	Not in Top 10	244,000 (#4)
AZAL	Azerbaijan	Not in Top 10	209,000 (#6)
Israir	Israel	Not in Top 10	197,000 (#7)
flynas	Saudi Arabia	Not in Top 10	162,000 (#8)
FlyArystan	Kazakhstan	No Services	139,000 (#10)

EU = European Union, UAE = United Arab Emirates.
Notes: AZAL traffic includes AZAL Azerbaijan Airlines and Buta Airways. Wizz Air traffic excludes Wizz Air Abu Dhabi (2022) and Wizz Air UK (2019). Traffic is rounded to the nearest thousand.
Source: Georgian Civil Aviation Agency.

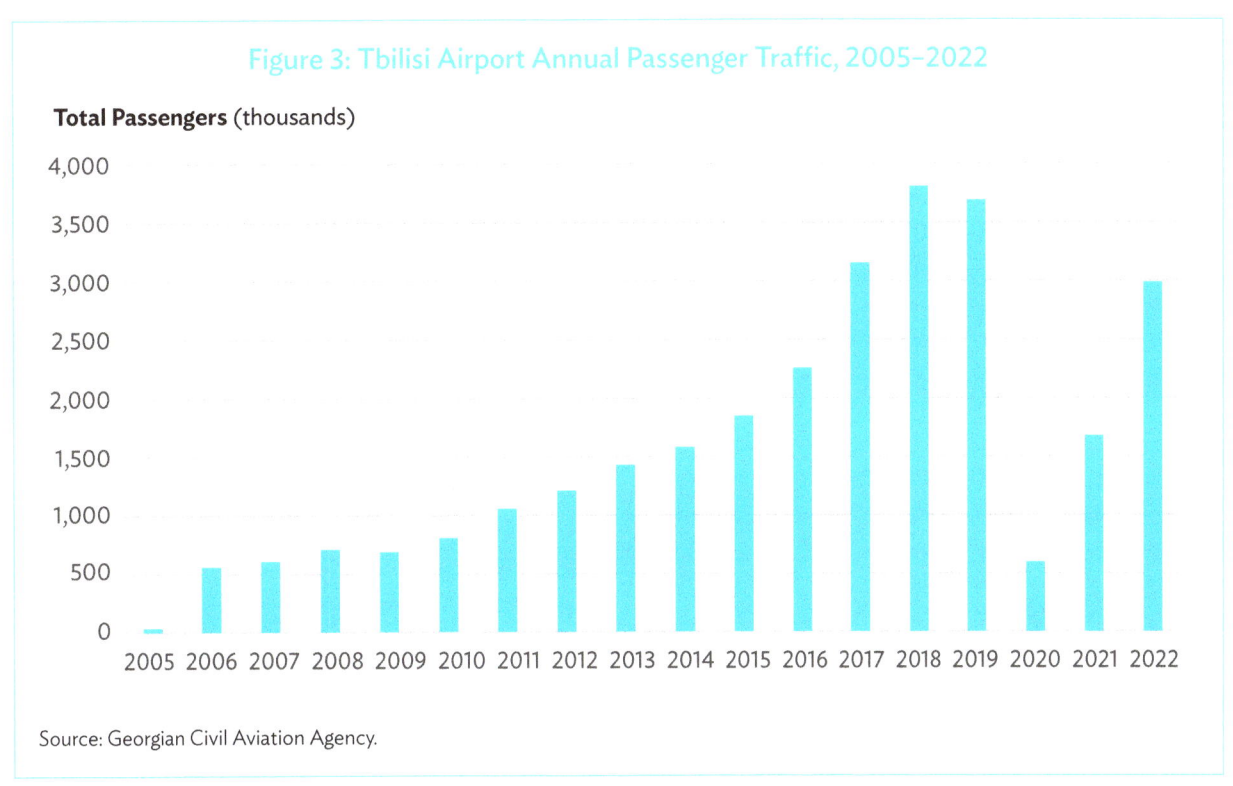

Figure 3: Tbilisi Airport Annual Passenger Traffic, 2005–2022

Source: Georgian Civil Aviation Agency.

carriers following the start of Russia's war in Ukraine (as outlined in other sections of this study). While Georgia–Russian Federation flights resumed in May 2023, there is a very limited number from only three airlines (Azimuth Airlines, Georgian Airways, and Red Wings). In July 2023, there were an average of four daily flights between Georgia and the Russian Federation, compared to nearly 20 prior to the suspension.

There have not been any flights between Georgia and Ukraine since the start of the Russian invasion in early 2022. A return of Ukrainian carriers is not possible without an end to the invasion and the recovery of the Ukrainian aviation sector. Passenger traffic in Georgia should still exceed 2019 levels (over 5 million passengers) in 2023 despite very few Russian Federation flights and no Ukraine flights, as other markets have expanded to fill the void. However, it will be difficult to achieve significant growth in overall passenger traffic without a more significant recovery of the Russian Federation market and a return of the Ukraine market.

Significant growth at Tbilisi beyond 2018 levels, when the airport handled a record 3.8 million passengers, could be particularly challenging without the resumption of more Russian Federation services and Ukraine services. In the first 6 months of 2023, Tbilisi passenger traffic was at 84% of 2019 levels.

In Q3 2023, scheduled seat capacity at Tbilisi was again slightly above 2019 levels, although still below 2018 levels (capacity at Tbilisi declined in the second half of 2019 due to the suspension of services by Russian carriers). Tbilisi Airport handled 3 million passengers in 2022 and could again reach 3.8 million passengers in 2024.

Batumi also relied heavily on the Russian Federation and Ukraine, but it is a much smaller and highly seasonal market. Batumi was the first airport in Georgia to achieve a full recovery (in terms of monthly traffic) and annual traffic for 2022 was at 99% of 2019 levels with about 620,000 passengers handled.

In the first 6 months of 2023, Batumi passenger traffic was at 96% of 2019 levels. Passenger traffic at Batumi was 37% higher than 2019 levels in the first four months but this was on a very small base as most of Batumi's traffic is in the summer months. Scheduled airline capacity at Batumi for summer of 2023 was significantly below 2019 levels. Batumi traffic for the full year in 2023 is therefore likely to be below 2019 levels. (While the winter market has grown as Batumi now has more year-round residents and visitors, the much larger summer market was smaller in 2023.)

Batumi Airport grew rapidly in the decade prior to the pandemic, from less than 100,000 passengers in 2009 to 599,000 in 2018, and a record 624,000 in 2019 (Figure 4). The summer season dominates, with monthly traffic that is up to six times higher than winter. Turkish airport operator TAV took over Batumi and Tbilisi Airport in 2007 as part of a concession that ends in 2027.

Kutaisi is accounting for all the growth in Georgia in 2023 as its annual scheduled seat capacity is doubling compared to 2019, driving overall growth in the Georgia market, while there are reductions at Batumi and Tbilisi. Kutaisi's share of international seat capacity in Georgia grew from 16% in 2019 to 28% in 2023. In the first 6 months of 2023, Kutaisi passenger traffic was 83% above 2019 levels. Total passenger traffic in Georgia was flat (at 2.5 million for both the first six months of 2023 and the first six months of 2019) with the increase at Kutaisi offsetting the declines at Batumi and Tbilisi.

Future Batumi growth is uncertain

Batumi has emerged as a popular summer holiday destination and has been particularly successful at attracting high-end international visitors. Batumi's appeal as a high-end destination bodes well for a resumption of growth in the post-pandemic era despite relatively high airport costs. However, operational constraints with the existing airport, which is located close to the center of the city with a unidirectional runway, limit Batumi's growth potential.

A new airport just across the border in Türkiye also impacts Batumi Airport's outlook. The Rize-Artvin Airport opened in May 2022 less than 100 kilometers (km) from Batumi. Previously, Batumi Airport attracted traffic from Türkiye, as it was the closest airport for the Turkish province of Artvin. Batumi Airport also previously attracted some traffic from Rize province, located about halfway between Batumi and Trabzon, which previously had the closest airport on the Türkiye side of the border about 200 km from Batumi.

Rize-Artvin Airport changes the dynamic of the Batumi market as it overlaps with Batumi Airport's catchment

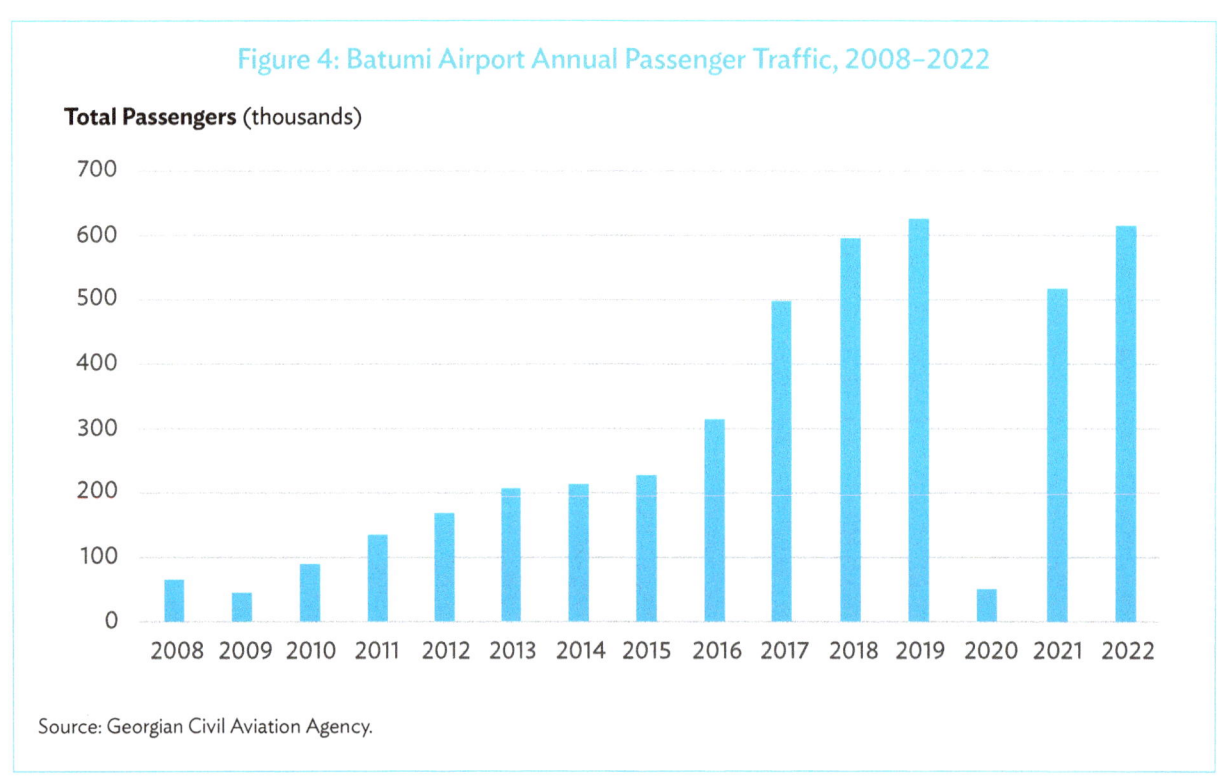

Figure 4: Batumi Airport Annual Passenger Traffic, 2008–2022

Source: Georgian Civil Aviation Agency.

Batumi Airport has a small terminal with no aerobridges but is conveniently located near the center of the city (photo by Brendan Sobie).

area, resulting in Rize-Artvin attracting passengers from Türkiye that were previously driving to Batumi, as well as attracting some of Batumi's passengers. While a new airport for Batumi was under consideration that would not have any operational constraints, the proposed new airport is about 50 km from Batumi, making it only slightly closer to Batumi than Rize-Artvin. Georgia is currently not considering a new airport for Batumi and (as of July 2023) is focusing on developing a new airport outside Tbilisi, which will replace the existing Tbilisi Airport.

The proposed new Batumi Airport was also only about 80 km from Kutaisi, which is already able to attract some Batumi traffic as well as some Tbilisi traffic, given its location in the middle of Georgia. It does not make sense to invest in a new airport that is so close to Kutaisi, and Georgia should consider looking at options for expanding and improving the usability of Batumi Airport, leveraging the investments that have been made at the existing airport in recent years. A new terminal opened at Batumi Airport in 2021, increasing capacity to 1.2 million passengers.

Kutaisi can also be positioned to serve some of the Batumi market, particularly the LCC segment, as highway upgrades are expected to reduce travel time between Kutaisi Airport and Batumi to only about 1 hour. Closing Batumi Airport to commercial traffic and reducing the number of international airports to just two (Kutaisi and the new Tbilisi Airport) is a possibility. However, Georgia should consider keeping Batumi Airport open for up to 1.2 million passengers per annum as the airport's convenient location near the city helps Batumi attract visitors from key source markets such as Israel.

More rapid growth for Kutaisi is possible

Over the next few years, Kutaisi is best positioned for rapid growth as it does not have the constraints of Batumi or Tbilisi and relies less on the Russian Federation or Ukraine (only a few flights per week in each market). Very low fees and charges also make Kutaisi attractive, particularly to LCCs. Kutaisi aims to attract several new airlines while also continuing to work with Wizz and FlyArystan on further expansion.

Kutaisi is mainly served from Europe and, prior to the pandemic, all of Kutaisi's routes were to Europe. However, Kazakhstan emerged as a major new market during the pandemic and there is potential to develop routes to other CAREC countries. There is also potential to develop several new routes to the Middle East to supplement the service from the UAE that was launched by Wizz Air Abu Dhabi in late 2021 and was expanded in summer of 2023.

Georgia should seek fifth and seventh traffic rights from several countries, particularly in Asia and the Middle East, as this could facilitate growth at Kutaisi with more routes to the east. Wizz can now generally only operate European routes from its Kutaisi base as operating non-European routes requires seventh freedoms. Georgia's liberal air transport policy does not preclude seventh freedoms or fifth freedoms, which are available in a few markets such as Georgia–Azerbaijan, but it needs to convince more countries to provide these rights. This would be particularly beneficial in facilitating the development of air travel between Kutaisi and other CAREC countries.

Kutaisi is one of the lowest-cost airports in CAREC and is the only airport in CAREC focusing specifically on LCCs. Kutaisi's standard charges and fees total about $24 per passenger. For new routes, there are discounts that reduce the total to only about $10 per passenger. Until 2023, there was also a discount to $8.50 for those airlines generating over 55,000 annual passengers on a specific route.

Georgia has been able to keep the costs at Kutaisi very low as the airport and ground handling provider is operated by a government company, United Airports of Georgia (UAG). Kutaisi has not been a profitable airport due to the minimum tariff policy, which results in very low aeronautical revenue, and has traditionally not generated significant non-aeronautical revenues. However, Kutaisi is strategically important for Georgia and profitability has not been the objective as it is designed to facilitate growth in passenger traffic, resulting in broad economic benefits, by providing LCCs an alternative to the high tariffs at Batumi and Tbilisi.

At Tbilisi and Batumi, UAG only provides security services, while the airport is operated by a private company, TAV. UAG offers discounts on security fees for new airlines and new routes, but this does not have a significant impact as security fees account for a very small portion of the total charges, costs, and fees incurred by airlines at an airport. UAG and the Georgian National Tourism Administration (GNTA), both of which are under Georgia's Ministry of Economy and Sustainable Development, work together in trying to attract airlines to Tbilisi and Batumi. However, UAG has very little leverage in determining the costs and charges at Tbilisi and Batumi, which are often an impediment to airlines launching services or expanding existing services at these airports.

Georgia understandably has been focusing on Kutaisi for growth as it has the capacity, is significantly less expensive, and is under government ownership. While Tbilisi is by far the largest city in Georgia and is by far the biggest destination for international tourists, the current airport is congested (with traffic levels that are above its designed capacity during peak periods) and outdated. Kutaisi is a more modern facility and, in some respects, has a better product despite its much cheaper cost.

Kutaisi's LCC-focused strategy has been successful and could be emulated by other CAREC countries. However, there is a limit to how many airlines and routes Kutaisi can realistically attract given its location, which is 250 km from Tbilisi. Buses from Kutaisi Airport to Tbilisi take 4 hours. Passengers with early morning departures need to take an overnight bus from Tbilisi to catch flights. Batumi is closer, at about 130 km from Kutaisi Airport, with buses taking 2 hours. However, Batumi is a much smaller market and for many passengers, a 2-hour bus ride is still considered inconvenient.

The journey to Kutaisi is too long for many travelers, particularly business travelers and international tourists. Kutaisi has had more success attracting Georgian citizens heading to Europe for holidays or to visit friends and family living in Europe. This is a very price-sensitive segment of the market and generally outbound travelers in Georgia are more price sensitive than inbound travelers.

In 2019, international visitors accounted for over 80% of total passenger traffic at Batumi and over 70% at Tbilisi, but only about 50% at Kutaisi. Nearly 1.4 million visitors entered Georgia at Tbilisi Airport in 2019, compared to 258,000 at Batumi Airport and 216,000 at Kutaisi Airport.

There is an opportunity for Kutaisi to attract more inbound tourists. Improving the train connection from Kutaisi Airport to Batumi and Tbilisi would help. A train option was established in 2022, but passengers need to take a bus from the airport to a nearby train station. Tickets on the train are often not available as demand for passengers heading between Tbilisi to Batumi is high, leaving few to no seats available at Kutaisi. The train schedule is also not aligned well with flight schedules. Georgia needs to boost the number of trains and allocate seats to Kutaisi Airport passengers. Establishing a stop at the airport, which was planned several years ago, should also be reconsidered.

Georgia should also consider stepping up the promotion of Kutaisi Airport as the gateway to mountainous regions. Several remote regions of Georgia have potential to attract more international tourists and Kutaisi is the closest international airport for most of these regions.

However, Kutaisi Airport will never be able to attract nearly as many international tourists as Tbilisi Airport. Highway improvements will reduce the travel time between Kutaisi and Tbilisi, but the journey will still be at least 2 hours. Tbilisi will always be by far the most popular destination for international tourists followed by Batumi. While Tbilisi and Batumi have much higher charges and fees than Kutaisi, most airlines including LCCs are not interested in Kutaisi as they are predominantly flying tourists that are keen on only visiting Tbilisi or Batumi.

Tourism growth is dependent on Tbilisi growth

Attracting more airlines and routes to Tbilisi is therefore more feasible from a market perspective. Several routes are currently underserved or entirely unserved. Potential new scheduled routes from Tbilisi include Bangkok, Beijing, Berlin, Budapest, Bucharest, Brussels, Delhi, Mumbai, Prague, Shanghai, and Seoul (IndiGo launched Tbilisi-Delhi in August 2023 and Eurowings is planning to launch Tbilisi-Berlin in December 2023 as well as Tbilisi-Prague in April 2024).

India, the Republic of Korea, and the PRC are priority new source markets for tourism authorities. Tbilisi is currently not well linked with Asia. India is finally being linked for the first time with the highly anticipated launch of services from IndiGo (although another Indian LCC, SpiceJet, was already been using Tbilisi as a fuel stop for some flights to Europe). In the PRC, there is only a service to Urumqi from China Southern. Georgia should consider extending its visa-free regime to India and the PRC to help attract more services from these countries. It also needs to further increase marketing activities in India, the PRC, and the overall Asia region.

The Republic of Korea, Japan, and Thailand are also target markets. Georgia has been trying to attract Thai AirAsia X to launch a scheduled service between Tbilisi and Bangkok. Thai AirAsia X launched a Tbilisi–Bangkok charter service in 2019 and resumed the service in 2022, but this service has not been operated in 2023. There was also a charter service from Seoul that was operated by Korean Air prior to the pandemic, which could be reinstated and eventually upgraded to scheduled.

There are also opportunities for Tbilisi to attract more flights to the Middle East and Central Asia. These were the growth markets in 2022, helping partially fill the void left by the Russian Federation and Ukraine. There were up to 170 weekly flights (during peak summer months) between Georgia and the Middle East in 2022, compared to up to 130 weekly flights in 2019. Georgia–Central Asia frequencies increased to up to 38 in 2022,

compared to up to 22 in 2019. In addition, there have been an increase in the number of flights from Georgia to Belarus and Türkiye. There are opportunities in all these markets to continue attracting more flights.

Several new airlines started serving Tbilisi during the pandemic, including AnadoluJet, Air Arabia Abu Dhabi, Condor, Eurowings and flyadeal. All of these are LCCs, except Condor, which is generally considered a leisure rather than low-cost airline, although often has LCC-like pricing.

Of the 16 LCCs that operated scheduled services to Georgia in 2022, 13 of these served Tbilisi. The other three served Kutaisi, although temporarily operated to Tbilisi during Kutaisi's closure in October. Eight of the 16 LCCs also served Batumi in 2022, although generally only in the summer season.

IndiGo and Türkiye's SunExpress entered the Georgia market in summer of 2023 with both also serving only Tbilisi. SunExpress launched three twice weekly Tbilisi routes (to Ankara, Antalya, and Izmir) in June 2023.

In addition to all the new LCCs, several of the existing LCCs have expanded rapidly. For example, Pegasus more than doubled its passenger traffic in Georgia from 2019 to 2022. In 2022, Pegasus was the third-largest airline overall in Georgia, but in 2019 it was only the seventh largest.

While visitor numbers have not yet fully recovered (as of the first half of 2023), visitor spending has fully recovered due to an increase in the average length of stay and an increase in the number of high-end tourists (considered bigger spenders). Tourism authorities continue to work on attracting more upmarket tourists and aim to increase the portion of visitors that arrive by air. Georgia would like to permanently increase the portion of visitors arriving by air from only 20% prior to the pandemic to 40%. (There was already a significant increase in this metric in 2022 and the first half of 2023 as the land border with Azerbaijan remained closed, but this is considered temporary as eventually the land border with Azerbaijan will reopen.)

Attracting more new air services to Tbilisi is critical to meet Georgia's tourism goals. While the GNTA and UAG have very limited leverage in bringing down high airport costs and fees, they have marketing programs to help support the launch of new routes. There are also schemes to provide ground handling discounts to new airlines, but these are not that significant. Other programs, schemes, and incentives should be considered. The GNTA and UAG should beef up efforts to attract more international air services to Tbilisi as the airport has not been very active in developing routes.

Prior to the pandemic, Georgian authorities tried to mitigate the impact of high costs at Tbilisi with a special program that secured services from leading European LCC Ryanair, which was persuaded to launch services to Georgia in late 2019. This program or arrangement included two routes from Tbilisi and two routes from Kutaisi that were intended to generate a combined 170,000 passengers per annum. However, the arrangement was suspended in March 2020 due to the pandemic. Ryanair only served Georgia for 5 months prior to the suspension and at this point has no plans to resume services to Tbilisi or Kutaisi.

It would be difficult for authorities to again provide the scheme that was offered to Ryanair. However, other programs or initiatives are possible. Without any support or policy changes, it could be difficult for Tbilisi to resume passenger growth, which is critical for Georgia's tourism sector and the overall economy.

While Tbilisi Airport overall is now operating close to capacity, traffic is not evenly distributed and there are periods of the day where there is ample capacity. Authorities should work to incentivize more flights during the off-peak periods, which would help improve airport efficiency and make better use of the existing infrastructure until it is replaced or expanded.

In addition to trying to attract new services, particularly from potential source markets, it is important to work with existing airlines and incentivize them to add capacity. Additional capacity from Georgia's main source markets is crucial for the resumption of tourism growth and the overall economy. Additional capacity, particularly from LCCs, could also bring lower fares, which would help make Georgia more attractive as a destination.

Tourism authorities are concerned with high airfares at Tbilisi, which have dissuaded potential tourists from visiting Georgia and impeded a full recovery from the pandemic. While high airport costs are a factor, the high airfare is primarily driven by a lack of airline capacity and a supply–demand imbalance. There has been an influx of Russian residents crossing the Georgia border by land and using Georgian airports to hop on flights to other destinations. This has led to higher demand for air services from Georgia, thus increasing average airfares.

More airline capacity would help alleviate this issue, but attracting airlines is not easy. Georgia relies almost entirely on foreign airlines, which accounted for 97% of total passenger traffic in 2022. However, many foreign airlines are currently limited in their ability to add capacity due to human resources and aircraft constraints. Foreign airlines that are expanding have many destinations to select between and Tbilisi is not always the most attractive due to high airport costs.

Georgia should relook at its aviation strategy to make sure the right policies and strategies are in place to support the resumption of growth. Alignment with its tourism strategy is also important, although tourism should not be the only driver.

Tourism accounted for 8.4% of Georgia's GDP in 2019, according to the National Statistics Office of Georgia. The broader tourism and travel sector accounted for 26.3% of Georgia's GDP in 2019, according to World Tourism and Travel Council data. Georgia relies on tourism more than any other CAREC country and has among the highest tourism contribution to GDP rates globally.

Georgia would benefit from a new domestic air transport strategy

While the biggest opportunities are in attracting more foreign airlines, particularly LCCs and the inbound segment, Georgia should focus on more than just the international market. A new domestic aviation strategy is also urgently needed. Domestic airports and local airlines have an important albeit relatively small role, and could also benefit from policy changes.

Georgia has two very small government-owned domestic airports, Mestia and Ambrolauri, located in mountainous areas. Mestia reopened in 2011 and Ambrolauri, which has a new modern terminal, reopened in 2017. Ambrolauri has handled only about

2,000 passengers per annum since the reopening. Mestia is bigger as it attracts more international tourists but still very small with traffic now at about 10,000 passengers per annum. Operating these airports require significant subsidies and their only routes are also heavily subsidized.

In the first six months of 2023 there were about 10,000 domestic passengers in Georgia. Mestia accounted for about half this traffic while Ambrolauri accounted for only about 10%.

In recent years, AK Air/Vanilla Sky has been the only airline operating domestic services in Georgia. Mestia has been served with an average of one flight per day from Natakhtari, a small airport outside Tbilisi that is owned by Vanilla Sky's partner company, and one to two flights per week from Kutaisi. These flights carry mainly international tourists but only have 19 seats as the short runway at Mestia (as well as at Natakhtari) cannot accommodate larger aircraft.

Ambrolauri also cannot accommodate larger aircraft and has been served with two to three weekly flights from Natakhtari. Ambrolauri flights generally carry domestic tourists as international tourism has not yet been developed in the Ambrolauri region due in part to a lack of high-end hotels and other tourism infrastructure.

AK Air/Vanilla Sky also has been operating flights from Natakhtari to Batumi and, until 2022, from Tbilisi to Batumi. Natakhtari–Batumi is operated with the 19-seat aircraft, while Tbilisi–Batumi was operated until 2022 with a larger 30-seat aircraft that is too big for Natakhtari. Both Batumi routes have typically only operated with one daily fight, but the Tbilisi–Batumi route did not operate for the last several months of 2022 and has not operated at all in 2023 as AK Air's only 30-seat aircraft has been grounded for maintenance.

AK Air has only one 30-seat aircraft, an Embraer EMB-120 Brasilia that has not operated since early 2022. It has two 19-seat Let L-410s but has been primarily relying on a wet-leased L-410 that is operated by an airline from the Czech Republic. AK Air's L-410 fleet was grounded entirely in June 2023, forcing it to rely entirely on wet-leased aircraft. Its contract with the government to provide domestic services had been temporarily extended several times over the last year due to delays in preparing a new tender and was due to expire at the end of 2023.

AK Air/Vanilla Sky carried about 22,000 passengers in 2019. There was a slight decline in passenger traffic in 2022 to about 18,000 passengers. However, Mestia/Ambrolauri traffic was higher than 2019 levels as Batumi traffic dropped, as the Brasilia was out of service for several months.

AK Air has been keen to add more services on the Natakhtari–Mestia route as most flights are now fully booked well ahead of time. AK Air also has been keen to add flights on the Kutaisi–Mestia route, which is popular with European tourists that use Kutaisi to transfer from cheap Wizz flights, and to start a new route from Batumi to Mestia. AK Air has also been interested in serving Batumi from Telavi, a city outside Tbilisi that has an airport that was part of the Georgian Aviation University and is now in the process of being taken over by UAG. Telavi Airport is now used for flight training but there is a proposal to upgrade the airport with security infrastructure, which would be needed to support commercial flights. There is also a proposal to upgrade Natakhtari Airport to accommodate larger aircraft.

All of AK Air's routes have been subsidized by the government, which needs to approve any new route or additional frequencies. The entire operation is funded by the government with a budget of about $8 million per annum although typically not all of this has been used. As part of the program, airfares are regulated and are well below cost with the government essentially covering the difference. Seats on the Natakhtari–Ambrolauri and Kutaisi–Mestia routes are sold for only about $19 one-way. Natakhtari–Mestia is sold for about $34, while Natakhtari–Batumi and Tbilisi–Batumi are sold for about $48. All seats are sold at the same airfare, assuming they are available (often there are no more seats available).

It is not unusual for governments to subsidize rural domestic air services to maintain connectivity to smaller communities and ensure affordable access to residents. However, it is rather unusual to subsidize routes catering to tourists. Georgia could look at other options for promoting development of Ambrolauri and Mestia while potentially increasing the airfare for tourists, particularly international tourists.

Ambrolauri and particularly Mestia, given its more isolated location and better tourism infrastructure, would benefit from more capacity. More flights would generate much-needed revenues for local tourism and local economies. It could be feasible to support more flights by adjusting the subsidy scheme, increasing the airfare, and launching tourist marketing programs to raise awareness.

Ambrolauri and Mestia will still require support as these routes and airports are not commercially viable. Ambrolauri and particularly Mestia are remote and need air services.

However, the need to continue subsidizing domestic flights to Batumi is more questionable as Batumi is easily accessible from the Tbilisi area by highway and rail. Similar domestic routes in Europe (in terms of length and availability of rail services) are being phased out for sustainability reasons. Georgia should be investing in further improving rail services and capacity (there is an insufficient number of trains, particularly in the summer season), and considering sustainability as it relooks at its domestic aviation market.

Georgian carriers are small

Georgian Airways previously operated some domestic flights between Tbilisi and Batumi, but these flights were not subsidized and struggled commercially. Georgian Airways does not intend to resume domestic services unless they are subsidized. It currently (as of summer of 2023) operates regularly scheduled international flights from Tbilisi to only six destinations—Amsterdam, Larnaca, Moscow, Paris, Tel Aviv, and Vienna—using a fleet of three Boeing 737s (two 737-700s and one 737-800). A Boeing CRJ200 regional jet and Bombardier Challenger 850 business jet are also under Georgian Airways' AOC, but these aircraft are now only used for charters. It also has several charter routes or infrequent scheduled routes (less than 50 return flights per year) using the 737 fleet.

An Armenian partner airline, Armenia Aircompany (also known as Armenia Airlines), operates 737s from Yerevan to Tbilisi and Russian destinations. Connections are offered between Armenia Aircompany's Yerevan-Tbilisi flights and Georgian Airways-operated Europe and Israel flights. Armenia Aircompany also provided a connection option via Yerevan for passengers traveling between Georgia and the Russian Federation during the suspension of Russian carrier flights to Georgia.

Georgian Airways established in early 2022 a separate cargo carrier, Georgian Airlines. There are currently three 737-800 freighters under the new Georgian Airlines AOC. While Georgian Airways does not have big plans for expanding its passenger operation, it has ambitious plans for the cargo side, including more 737-800 freighters and 767 wide-body freighters, the first of which was delivered in August 2023. Georgian Airlines plans to place some of the additional freighters under the Armenian AOC.

Georgia's largest cargo carrier, Geo Sky, established a passenger operation in 2023 initially with a 737-800 that was wet leased to an airline in Africa. In late July 2023 it launched a scheduled domestic passenger operation using an ATR 72 turboprop that is wet leased from a European carrier. Geo Sky has established a new brand, Georgian Wings, for the domestic passenger operation, which consists of 12 weekly Tbilisi-Batumi flights that at least for now are not being subsidized.

Georgian Wings also launched three weekly flights from Tbilisi to Baku in September 2023 and is planning to launch international flights to Ganja, Samsun and Trabzon. Georgian Airways until September 2023 was the only Georgian airline operating scheduled international passenger flights. Myway Airlines operated scheduled passenger flights prior to the pandemic but its passenger aircraft over the last few years have been wet leased to airlines in other countries, primarily in Africa. A new passenger airline in Georgia launched in 2022, Tbilisi Airways, but has only been operating charter flights as well as wet leasing its only aircraft to airlines in other countries.

Cargo has generally become the focus for Georgian carriers as cargo is a more attractive and less competitive market. There are currently five airlines in Georgia operating freighters— CAMEX Airlines, Easy Charter, Georgian Airlines, Geo Sky, and Myway Airlines. Geo Sky is the most established and the largest of these airlines, operating a fleet of several 747 freighters and adding a 757 freighter in late 2022, while the others are all relatively new. CAMEX Airlines is the latest start-up, having commenced operations in September 2022 using 737 freighters. The Georgia-based freighter fleet has grown significantly over the last few years while the number of passenger aircraft has been reduced.

Wizz Air has three aircraft based at Kutaisi Airport, with a fourth aircraft expected by the end of 2023 (photo by Wizz Air).

While almost all the freighters operated by Georgian carriers are used outside of Georgia, carrying cargo between other countries, there is an opportunity to establish Georgia as a transit hub for cargo. For example, Georgian Airlines plans to use its new fleet of 767s to serve the Europe–Asia cargo market using Tbilisi as a hub. CAMEX has a similar plan to add a medium-size wide-body freighter, which would be used to carry cargo between Europe and Asia via Tbilisi.

While establishing a cargo hub in Georgia will not be easy, it is more commercially feasible than establishing a passenger hub. A passenger hub requires more scale, which Georgian carriers lack, making it nearly impossible to compete with major flag carriers in larger countries. Georgian passenger carriers are generally not able to compete effectively against foreign airlines, which now dominate the Georgian market.

Georgia's long-standing policy of not owning or protecting a flag carrier has been successful. Having a completely open or liberal market has enabled rapid growth in passenger traffic, facilitating development of tourism and the broader economy. This growth has been driven almost entirely by foreign airlines and any future growth will likely continue to be driven by foreign airlines. Georgian Airways is the only remaining Georgian carrier with scheduled international jet services following the failure of several other passenger airlines. Georgian Airways also has struggled to some extent and restructured in 2022 as part of a court-supervised rehabilitation process.

The outlook for Georgian passenger carriers will remain challenging. Establishing a large Georgian passenger carrier, following either a full-service network model or an LCC model, is not realistic. However, there are still possible niche roles for local passenger carriers.

Georgian Airways plans to stick with its niche full-service model, focusing mainly on routes that do not have significant competition. It will continue to operate aircraft with two classes of service: Georgian Airways' 737-700s have 12 business class seats along with 121 economy seats, while its 737-800 has 12 business class and 156 economy seats. Only modest expansion on the passenger side is planned with one additional 737-800 potentially joining the fleet.

While small and not ambitious, Georgian Airways is an important player in the overall Georgian aviation market. In addition to operating both scheduled and charter flights, the company has catering, ground handling, and aircraft refueling businesses.

AK Air is also an important player in the overall aviation market with businesses under the parent company, including an aircraft maintenance operation and an airport that could potentially be expanded to accommodate jets, including wide-body freighters. The parent company has two AOCs (although as of July 2023, both were inactive) with AK Air used for the commercial aircraft and Serviceair for general aviation. It also has a tour operator business and has a small hotel with restaurant at Natakhtari Airport.

AK Air has an opportunity to expand by acquiring larger regional aircraft and could potentially adopt a regional LCC model while still focusing on niche routes (both domestic and international) that have limited or no competition. There is also an opportunity to acquire electric aircraft that could be used to serve remote mountainous regions and facilitate sustainable development of regional tourism. However, any expansion will pose challenges and AK Air would be impacted by any changes in Georgia's domestic air transport strategy. Georgia has been planning to hold a new competition to select an airline to operate the subsidized domestic services.

Georgia should factor the needs and the importance of local airlines while assessing options for developing the local aviation sector, particularly domestic services, in a sustainable and viable manner. Any new domestic air transport strategy should challenge the status quo and at the same time facilitate growth, particularly in mountainous regions with tourism potential. Any new international air transport strategy should maintain the liberal policies that have facilitated Georgia's remarkable growth story but with adjustments aimed at driving a new growth chapter in the post-pandemic era.

Recommendations for Georgia

1. Adopt a new aviation strategy covering both the domestic and international markets.

2. Push for fifth and seventh traffic rights from several countries to facilitate further passenger growth, including more routes to other CAREC countries.

3. Beef up efforts to attract more international air services to Tbilisi, and consider policies and programs to facilitate a resumption of growth at Tbilisi.

4. Work to incentive more flights during the off-peak period at Tbilisi Airport, which would help improve efficiency and make better use of the existing infrastructure until it replaced or expanded.

5. Look at options for expanding and improving the usability of Batumi Airport rather than investing in a potential new airport that would overlap with Kutaisi Airport's catchment area.

6. Consider improving the train connection from Kutaisi Airport to Batumi and Tbilisi and reconsider establishing a railway station at the airport.

7. Step up promotion of Kutaisi Airport as a gateway for international tourists and promote tourism in the nearby mountainous regions.

8. Look at new options for subsidizing and developing domestic air transport as well as new options for promoting growth at Ambrolauri and Mestia airports.

9. Consider sustainability as it revisits its domestic air transport market.

CASE STUDY 3
Kazakhstan and FlyArystan

The evolution and rapid growth of Kazakhstan's air transport market since the launch of FlyArystan is the best example in CAREC of how a local LCC can transform a market.

While FlyArystan is a division rather than independent subsidiary of Air Astana, it follows several more components of the LCC model than Buta Airways or Uzbekistan Express, the two other low-cost brands in CAREC. For example, FlyArystan charges for checked baggage, food and drinks, and seat assignments. It relies heavily on ancillary revenues and sells several non-aviation items such as insurance.

FlyArystan also has its own sales and marketing teams, which gives it a lot more independence than Buta or Uzbekistan Express. FlyArystan sells and distributes its tickets like most LCCs with a direct distribution model that relies heavily on its website. It does not sell tickets via global distribution systems, which are used by travel agents around the world but come with a cost. While FlyArystan sells connecting itineraries between two FlyArystan flights, it does not offer connections or interline with Air Astana. It plans to consider interlines in the future as its international network expands, but if it does offer connections with Air Astana (or any other airlines), it will be via a low-cost platform and not offered on global distribution systems.

FlyArystan has its own head office, which has an LCC feel with open seating. Unlike Buta and Uzbekistan Airways, FlyArystan has its own management team and staff. The only exception are pilots, which are supplied by Air Astana as all FlyArystan flights are

FlyArystan introduced self-service kiosks at Almaty Airport in October 2022 and has since rolled them out across its domestic network (photo by Brendan Sobie).

under Air Astana's AOC and IATA designation code. This is not ideal as if FlyArystan was a separate airline, it would be able to have a separate contract with pilots and would have more control of its operation. However, FlyArystan has a more efficient flight operation than Air Astana as it has higher utilization of aircraft and pilots. It also does not overnight any crew, which results in lower costs although its pilots fly for both brands.

Overall, FlyArystan has been able to achieve very low unit costs, or cost per available seat kilometer of about $0.04 excluding fuel. This is low by global standards and extremely low for CAREC. Unit costs should decline further as FlyArystan expands, which is typical for any LCC as economies of scale improve with larger fleets. Unit costs should also decline further if it separates from Air Astana and secures its own AOC.

Transitioning from a brand to a subsidiary of the Air Astana Group and applying for its own AOC has always been part of the FlyArystan long-term plan since its inception. It is likely this transition will occur within the next year as FlyArystan is now aiming to secure its own AOC in early 2024. This will make FlyArystan a full or proper LCC. It would be sensible for Buta and Uzbekistan Express to also make this transition, but both have a lot more work to do in adopting a pure LCC model.

FlyAyrstan has followed a pure LCC model since its launch on 1 May 2019 despite not having its own AOC. Securing its own AOC will further cement FlyArystan's position as a pure LCC, resulting in even lower unit costs. However, the transition to its own AOC will have some challenges, including the need to secure its own traffic rights and airport slots for international services, which could result in FlyArystan not being able to maintain some of the international services it has successfully developed while using Air Astana's AOC.

As highlighted earlier in this study, FlyArystan has quickly become the largest LCC in CAREC. In 2022, FlyArystan carried 3.3 million passengers and was the only LCC in CAREC (local or foreign) that carried over 3 million passengers. It was nearly twice the size of airblue, which was the second-largest CAREC LCC, and more than five times larger than Uzbekistan Express or Buta Airways.

FlyArystan was initially targeting 4.8 million passengers for 2023, which would make it the largest CAREC airline overall (including both LCCs and FSCs), surpassing full-service sister airline, Air Astana. Air Astana was the largest CAREC airline in 2022 with 4.1 million passengers and was initially targeting 4.6 million passengers in 2023, which would put it above Air Astana's previous high mark of 4.4 million in 2019.

However, it is now likely that FlyArystan will not overtake Air Astana until 2024 due to a slower than initially expected Q1 2023, as pilot resource issues forced it to temporary reduce capacity by up to 75% in flights on some days. Aircraft delivery delays were among the issues that impacted its ability to achieve 4.8 million passengers in 2023. In May 2023, the Air Astana Group revised its 2023 target to 8.5 million passengers, which still represents growth of 16% compared to the 7.35 million carried in 2022, but falls short of the 28% growth initially expected due to engine and other supply chain issues. FlyArystan will likely end up with between 3.5 million and 4 million passengers in 2023, which is still quite an achievement for an airline that is only 4 years old although growth has slowed considerably since 2021.

FlyArystan already surpassed the 3-million-passenger milestone in 2021 after carrying 1.5 million in 2020 and 700,000 in 2019. In 2021, FlyArystan became the largest domestic airline in Kazakhstan, surpassing both Air Astana and SCAT Airlines.

The domestic market has grown rapidly

Kazakhstan was the world's fastest-growing domestic air transport market in 2021 with passenger traffic over 30% above 2019 levels. In 2022, domestic traffic was only about 35% above 2019 levels, but growth would have been more significant if it were not for a very slow start to the year due to the unrest in January 2022. Almaty Airport was shut for 1 week in January 2022 and domestic traffic declined by almost 50% compared to the prior month (December 2021). The domestic market quickly recovered and was back to 2021 levels by March and was above 2021 levels for the rest of the year.

The impact of FlyArystan on the domestic market has been staggering and the rapid recovery Kazakhstan's air transport market has enjoyed would not have been possible without FlyArystan. Domestic traffic at Almaty Airport, Kazakhstan's largest airport, will likely exceed 5 million passengers in 2023. In 2018, the year before FlyArystan's launch, there were only 2.8 million domestic passengers in Almaty.

Domestic traffic at Almaty was up 19% in 2019 with growth accelerating rapidly in the second half as FlyArystan only launched in May (Figure 5). There was a decline in domestic passenger traffic by 18% in 2020 due to the lockdowns and domestic travel restrictions imposed at the beginning of the pandemic. However, there was an increase of 63% in 2021, or an increase of 34% compared to 2019. There was only a 1% increase in 2022, impacted by the big drop in January, as monthly traffic was up by at least 3% for 7 of the 12 months. In the first 6 months of 2023, domestic traffic at Almaty was up 16% compared to the same period of 2022 and by about 70% compared to the same period of 2019. Almaty is now the largest domestic airport in CAREC.

Domestic traffic in Almaty has increased by about 70% since the launch of FlyArystan. Domestic passenger growth at Astana, which has a slightly smaller (about 5%) domestic market than Almaty, and the overall Kazakhstan domestic market has also grown by about 70% since FlyArystan's launch.

Most of the domestic growth since 2018 has been driven by FlyArystan, which accounted for about 40% of domestic traffic in Kazakhstan in 2022. FlyArystan's domestic market share reached 43% in summer of 2022 and its domestic market share remained above 40% in Q4 2022. However, FlyArystan's market share dropped significantly in early 2023 as it temporarily slashed capacity due to a pilot resource issue. FlyArystan's capacity was back at second half of 2022 levels from June 2023, pushing its domestic market share back to about 40%

Prior to the reduction in capacity, FlyArystan was operating an average of about 58 domestic flights per day. The cuts were mainly implemented in late January 2023, resulting in a February 2023 schedule of about 27 domestic flights per day on average. This temporarily put FlyArystan below Air Astana and SCAT, but for the full year FlyArystan should again be the domestic market leader. In the peak summer

Figure 5: Almaty Airport Annual Domestic Passenger Traffic, 2018–2022

Source: Author, based on data from TAV.

months of 2023, FlyArystan was operating an average of slightly more than 60 domestic flights per day.

In 2022, SCAT accounted for about 25% of domestic seat capacity, compared to about 36% for FlyArystan and 32% for Air Astana. Qazaq Air, a small regional airline, accounted for most of the remaining 7%. There are other regional operators in Kazakhstan, but they are very small and, combined, account for less than 1% of scheduled domestic passenger traffic.

FlyArystan's share of traffic was slightly higher than its capacity share as it has higher average load factors than its competitors, which is typical for an LCC. The Air Astana Group's share of domestic traffic reached as high as 80% during some months of 2022 and for the year was around 70%. Prior to the launch of FlyArystan, Air Astana's domestic market share had slipped to less than 50%. The launch of an LCC was clearly the right decision, enabling Air Astana to win back domestic market share and drive rapid growth.

At the beginning of 2023, FlyArystan was operating 26 domestic routes and eight scheduled international routes, with domestic flights accounting for about 90% of its total capacity. In July 2023, FlyArystan was also operating 26 domestic routes while its scheduled international network grew to include 13 routes.

FlyArystan has stimulated demand in Kazakhstan's domestic market by offering low fares and opening point-to point-routes (routes bypassing the main hubs of Almaty and Astana) that were previously underserved. This stimulation effect began in the 10 months prior to the pandemic, with FlyArystan flying 1 million passengers from May 2019 until the start of the pandemic in March 2020. However, the biggest impact was in 2021 as domestic travel surged, stimulated by low fares and also driven by limited options for international holidays due to border closures. FlyArystan flew 3.1 passengers in 2021, including nearly 3 million domestic passengers.

FlyArystan again flew nearly 3 million domestic passengers in 2022 as it was impacted by the unrest in January and new aircraft delivery delays. However, its international traffic increased to nearly 400,000 passengers in 2022 as more borders reopened.

FlyArystan currently serves 14 of the 20 airports in Kazakhstan that have commercial services, up from 13 in 2022 as it resumed services to Oskemen (also known as Ust-Kamenogorsk) in May 2023. The Air Astana brand currently only serves 10 airports in Kazakhstan, while SCAT serves 15 and Qazaq 14 (based on OAG schedules for summer of 2023). SCAT and Qazaq have regional aircraft, which enables them to serve small airports or very thin routes, some of which are subsidized by the government with low fixed fares to ensure affordability for residents of isolated communities. Qazaq is entirely a regional operator, while SCAT also operates larger aircraft.

FlyArystan is the only domestic airline at two airports—Semey and Karaganda—and is the market leader at another eight airports (based on schedules from December 2022 or prior to the temporary capacity cuts that impacted its schedule in first half 2023). FlyArystan has bases at five airports—Almaty, Aktau, Atyrau, Astana, and Shymkent—which are also the five largest airports in Kazakhstan. Almaty and Astana are large hub airports, while Aktau, Atyrau, and Shymkent are considered regional hub airports, each handling at least 1 million passengers per annum. The other 15 airports are smaller although seven also have some international services (Table 25).

FlyArystan is the market leader in all nine of the smaller airports it serves (based on 2022 data). It is also the market leader in Aktau, while Air Astana is the market leader in Almaty and Astana. SCAT is the market leader in Shymkent, where it is based, and in five smaller airports.

FlyArystan operates alongside Air Astana on most of the major domestic trunk routes, which are also generally served by SCAT and in some cases by Qazaq. Air Astana is still the largest competitor on the main domestic routes including Almaty to Aktau, Atyrau, Astana, and Shymkent. Air Astana no longer operates many of the smaller domestic routes from Almaty and Astana, having essentially transferred some of these routes to FlyArystan, which is now often the largest (and sometimes is the only airline) on these routes.

FlyArystan also has several exclusive point-to-point routes (bypassing Almaty and Astana). Some of these

Table 25: Kazakhstan Airports Ranked by Domestic Seat Capacity

Rank	Airport	IATA Code	Airlines Listed Based on Size (2022)
1	Almaty Airport	ALA	Air Astana, FlyArystan, SCAT, Qazaq
2	Astana Airport	NQZ	Air Astana, FlyArystan, SCAT, Qazaq
3	Aktau Airport	SCO	FlyArystan, SCAT, Air Astana
4	Shymkent Airport	CIT	SCAT, FlyArystan, Air Astana, Qazaq
5	Atyrau Airport	GUW	FlyArystan, SCAT, Air Astana, Qazaq
6	Aktobe Airport	AKX	FlyArystan, Air Astana, SCAT, Qazaq
7	Turkistan International Airport	HSA	FlyArystan, Qazaq, SCAT
8	Ust-Kamenogorsk Airport[a] (Oskemen)	UKK	SCAT, Air Astana, Qazaq
9	Oral Ak Zhol Airport (Uralsk)	URA	FlyArystan, Air Astana, Qazaq, SCAT
10	Karaganda Airport	KGF	FlyArystan
11	Kyzylorda Airport	KZO	FlyArystan, Air Astana, Qazaq
12	Kostanay Airport	KSN	FlyArystan, Air Astana
13	Semey Airport	PLX	FlyArystan
14	Zhezkazgan Airport	DZN	SCAT
15	Pavlodar Airport	PWQ	FlyArystan, SCAT
16	Taraz Airport	DMB	SCAT
17	Taldykorgan Airport	TDK	Qazaq
18	Petropavl Airport	PPK	SCAT
19	Kokshetau Airport	KOV	SCAT
20	Usharal Airport	USJ	N/A

[a] FlyArystan resumed Ust-Kamenogorsk in May 2023.

Notes: Ranking is based on scheduled seat capacity in 2022. Usharal was not served by any of the four main airlines in 2022, but was served by Qazaq and SCAT in summer of 2023.

Source: Author, based on OAG schedules data.

were not served previously and on some of the larger point-to-point routes such as Aktau–Atyrau, FlyArystan is now the only airline. FlyArystan has two daily flights on Aktau–Atyrau (based on summer of 2023 schedules), which historically was served with one daily flight from Air Astana and one to two daily flights from SCAT.

Air Astana and FlyArystan focus on different segments of the market and therefore do not overlap that much on trunk routes, with FlyArystan catering more to price-sensitive leisure traffic. FlyArystan mainly competes on the main domestic routes against SCAT, which is a low-fare competitor although not considered an LCC. Qazaq is also a low-fare competitor but is not considered an LCC. Qazaq competes on some domestic trunk routes, including Almaty–Astana, although it has much smaller aircraft. Qazaq also has two CAREC routes, Aktobe-Baku and Almaty-Bishkek (launched in September 2023), and four Russian Federation routes.

SCAT started 2023 with a fleet of 32 aircraft that consists of several aircraft types ranging from 50-seat Bombardier CRJ200 regional jets to a 290-seat Boeing 767-300ER, which is used for international charters such as Almaty–Phuket and is operated under SCAT's charter subsidiary Sunday Airlines. SCAT generally uses Boeing 737s on trunk routes, including high-density all-economy 213-seat Boeing 737-9s and 189-seat 737-8s. Qazaq has only one aircraft type, 78-seat all-economy Dash 8 Q400 turboprops, with five currently in its fleet.

The Air Astana Group started 2023 with a fleet of 43 aircraft, including 29 at the full-service brand and 14 aircraft at FlyArystan. The full-service fleet ranges from 108-seat Embraer E190-E2s to 223-seat 767-300ERs. All the aircraft under the Air Astana brand have both business and economy cabins.

FlyArystan's fleet was still at 14 aircraft at the end of the first half of 2023. However, it added a 15th aircraft in July 2023 and another in August 2023, resulting in a fleet of 11 180-seat A320ceos and 5 188-seat A320neos. Most of its A320ceos were taken over from Air Astana and retrofitted into all-economy configuration while the 5 A320neos were all delivered new since September 2022.

SCAT and Air Astana adjust their strategies

While Qazaq and SCAT are primarily domestic operators, they reduced their focus on the domestic market in 2022 to pursue expansion on Kazakhstan–Russian Federation routes, where there was a void left by the Air Astana Group. Air Astana and FlyArystan both served the Russian Federation prior to Russia's war in Ukraine, but have not resumed services to the Russian Federation since the start of the crisis due to insurance reasons.

SCAT has been particularly aggressive in expanding to the Russian Federation, with its Russian Federation capacity more than quadrupling compared to pre-COVID levels. In addition to carrying local passengers between the Russian Federation and Kazakhstan, SCAT has been using Russian Federation flights to feed the rest of its international network, which includes Armenia, Georgia, Pakistan, Türkiye, Saudi Arabia, and Uzbekistan. Pakistan was added in July 2023 with twice weekly service from Almaty to Lahore. SCAT also has a larger charter operation with destinations that include Bahrain, Maldives, Thailand, and Türkiye (Istanbul has scheduled services while Antalya and others are served with charters).

SCAT has been expanding and modernizing its fleet by acquiring new Boeing 737 MAX family aircraft. SCAT could reach 3 million annual passengers in 2023, which would make it one of the largest airlines in CAREC.

SCAT's international seat capacity in summer of 2023 was more than double pre-pandemic levels, although it is still about half the size of Air Astana in the international market and less than half the size of the Air Astana Group. Air Astana Group international seat capacity was still slightly short of 2019 levels in summer of 2023 but expansion by SCAT and foreign airlines drove a more than 10% increase in total international seat capacity (based on OAG data for the summer season of 2023 versus 2019). The Kazakhstan government stated in May 2023 that international flights had increased to 488 per week compared to 442 prior to the pandemic.

Air Astana has shifted focus to other international markets, enabling it to restore most of its international seat capacity despite not having any services to the Russian Federation and Ukraine, which accounted for nearly 30% of its international capacity before the pandemic. The Russian Federation also accounted for 6% to 7% of FlyArystan's capacity prior to the start of the Russian invasion.

Air Astana launched several new international destinations during the pandemic, including Batumi in Georgia, Bodrum in Türkiye, Heraklion in Greece, Malé in Maldives, Padgorica in Montenegro, and Phuket in Thailand as it shifted its focus to point-to-point leisure traffic and reduced its reliance on connecting traffic. Jeddah in Saudi Arabia and Tel Aviv in Israel are planned new destinations for 2023, growing Air Astana's network from only one destination in the Middle East (Dubai) to three. Almaty–Tel Aviv service launched in September 2023 followed by Almaty–Jeddah in October 2023.

Air Astana has more than doubled its capacity to Türkiye, which is now its largest market, accounting for 24% of the group's international seat capacity in 2022 (based on OAG schedules data). The group had 13 Türkiye routes in 2022. Six were under the full-service brand, including the new Almaty–Bodrum service, while FlyArystan had seven. The four main Kazakhstan–Türkiye routes—Almaty and Astana to Antalya and Istanbul—are all under the Air Astana brand and accounted for about 75% of the capacity.

In Q1 2023, the group operated seven Türkiye routes, the main four routes and Atyrau–Istanbul from Air Astana as well as Aktau–Istanbul and Turkistan–Sabiha

Gokcen (a secondary airport outside Istanbul) from FlyArystan. Several of Air Astana Group's other Türkiye routes are seasonal and resumed in summer of 2023.

FlyArystan has been relatively conservative in expanding in the international market and has so far focused mainly on the domestic market. However, FlyArystan will likely focus more on the international market over the next several years as domestic growth could start slowing down as the market becomes more mature.

Kazakhstan aviation authorities expect domestic growth of 5% to 10% per annum over the next several years. This represents a dramatic slowdown from the growth that was achieved from 2018 to 2022. There are now about 8 million passengers per year flying domestically in Kazakhstan and given the size of the population and income levels, there is a limit to how much more the market can be stimulated. Kazakh carriers therefore need to shift focus to the international market, particularly FlyArystan given its expansion plans.

FlyArystan has ambitious fleet expansion plans and expects to have a fleet of at least 26 aircraft by the end of 2025. It now plans to take delivery of two additional aircraft over the last few months of 2023 for a total of 18 aircraft by the end of 2023, which is two short of its initial target of operating 20 aircraft by the end of 2023.

Low-cost carriers start to penetrate the international market

While most of FlyArystan's capacity so far has been in the domestic market, it has not been shy in experimenting with international routes, including to other CAREC countries. Some international destinations have been successful, particularly Kutaisi in Georgia, but others such as Bishkek in the Kyrgyz Republic and Samarkand in Uzbekistan have not been consistent.

In Q1 2023, FlyArystan's scheduled international network consisted of only five destinations—Baku in Azerbaijan, Dubai in the UAE, Istanbul in Türkiye, Kutaisi in Georgia, and Samarkand in Uzbekistan. In summer of 2023, its scheduled international network did not include Dubai, but grew to also include Ankara in Türkiye, Bishkek in the Kyrgyz Republic, Delhi in India, Tashkent in Uzbekistan and Urumqi in the PRC for a total of nine destinations.

Kutaisi is FlyArystan's largest international destination and is now served from five cities in Kazakhstan—Aktau, Almaty, Astana, Atyrau, and Shymkent. The Shymkent route is only operated in the summer season, while Almaty is the most recent addition, launching in June 2023.

Baku was initially served from Aktau, with Astana added in June 2023. The Almaty–Samarkand service was suspended in September 2022 but resumed in March 2023. It did not operate again in July and August 2023 but was slated to resume again in September 2023.

The Astana–Bishkek service was also suspended in September 2022 but resumed in June 2023. Astana–Tashkent was launched for the first time in July 2023 (although FlyArystan briefly served Tashkent from Turkistan in 2021) and Astana-Urumqi was slated to launch in September 2023, resulting in 13 scheduled routes within CAREC (as of September 2023). FlyArystan planned to launch Astana-Dushanbe in October 2023, resulting in 14 scheduled routes within CAREC. FlyArystan is now exploring several other potential CAREC destinations including Mongolia and Pakistan. It is also looking at several potential new destinations outside CAREC including to Oman, Saudi Arabia and non-CAREC parts of China such as Xian.

Outside of CAREC, Türkiye and now India are the only countries with scheduled services. Istanbul is served from Aktau and Turkistan, with the Aktau flights operating to Istanbul Airport and the Turkistan flights to Sabiha Gokcen Airport. Astana-Ankara and Shymkent-Delhi were launched in May and Almaty-Delhi is slated to launch in late September, resulting in six non-CAREC scheduled international routes for FlyArystan. Dubai was served earlier in 2023 from Aktau and Shymkent but only for the winter season.

FlyArystan continues to experiment with new international destinations. In May 2023, it resumed services from Aktau to Yerevan in Armenia but dropped the route for a second time at the end of June. FlyArystan initially suspended services to Yerevan in September 2022, having initially launched

Almaty–Yerevan in May 2022 and Aktau–Yerevan in June 2022. Aktau–Yerevan is still served by SCAT.

FlyArystan also has several international charter routes, including to Sharm El Sheikh in Egypt, Doha in Qatar, and Antalya in Türkiye. Even when including the charters, about 84% of FlyArystan's capacity was in the domestic market in the summer of 2023.

Türkiye is a key market and will continue to be served with a mix of scheduled flights and charters, with the latter typically only operating on a seasonal basis. Without an LCC subsidiary, it would be difficult for Air Astana to compete with Turkish LCCs. While Air Astana is keen to continue building its full-service operation in Türkiye, there are several routes which are more suitable for an LCC, including Almaty–Ankara.

Ankara had not previously been served by FlyArystan or Air Astana, but two Turkish LCCs; AnadoluJet and Pegasus both launched services to Kazakhstan from Ankara in 2022. AnadoluJet currently serves Ankara from both Almaty and Astana, while Pegasus only serves Ankara from Almaty.

Pegasus expanded its Kazakhstan operation in 2022 from two to 13 weekly flights. Prior to the pandemic, it had just three weekly flights to Kazakhstan and only served the Almaty–Sabiha Gokcen route. It now has seven routes to Kazakhstan, serving Almaty, Astana, and Shymkent from both Sabiha Gokcen and Antalya as well as Almaty–Ankara, although some of these services are seasonal.

AnadoluJet has a smaller Kazakhstan operation with three routes, including Ankara to Almaty and Astana and Antalya to Almaty. However, its full-service parent Turkish Airlines is the largest foreign airline in Kazakhstan and operated nine Kazakhstan routes in 2022.

Pegasus is now the second-largest foreign LCC in Kazakhstan after flydubai, which also serves Almaty, Astana, and Shymkent. flydubai's relaunched services in February 2023 to Shymkent, which it last served in early 2019.

Flydubai became the second LCC after Air Arabia to serve Kazakhstan when it launched Dubai–Almaty in 2014. In 2022, flydubai carried about 300,000 passengers on its Dubai to Almaty and Astana services. Flydubai was the third-largest foreign airline in Kazakhstan in 2022 (and the largest foreign LCC) after Turkish Airlines and Aeroflot.

Around 30 foreign airlines operated scheduled flights to Kazakhstan in 2022, including nine LCCs. The number of foreign LCCs was up from only five in 2019.

Five LCCs launched scheduled services to Kazakhstan in 2021 or 2022, including AnadoluJet, Buta Airways, Jazeera Airways, Uzbekistan Express, and Wizz Air

Pegasus is the second-largest foreign low-cost carrier in Kazakhstan and is the third largest in CAREC with 10 destinations in five CAREC countries in the summer of 2023 (photo by Pegasus).

Table 26: International Low-Cost Carrier Seat Capacity in Kazakhstan Ranked by Airline, 2022 versus 2019

Rank	Airline	2022 Seats	2019 Seats	Airports Served (2022)
1	FlyArystan	480,000	<10,000[a]	Almaty, Aktau, Aktobe, Astana, Atyrau, Shymkent, Turkistan, Uralsk
2	flydubai	340,000	230,000	Almaty, Astana
3	Pegasus Airlines	140,000	60,000	Almaty, Astana, Shymkent
4	Wizz Air Abu Dhabi	110,000	0	Almaty, Astana
5	Air Arabia	80,000	70,000	Almaty
6	Jazeera Airways	60,000	0	Almaty, Turkistan
7	AnadoluJet	30,000	0	Almaty, Astana
8	Uzbekistan Express	30,000	0	Aktau, Aktobe
9	Buta Airways	20,000	0	Aktau
10	Wizz Air	10,000	30,000	Astana
N/A	airBaltic	0	20,000	Almaty

LCC = low-cost carrier, N/A = not applicable.

[a] FlyArystan had less than 10,000 international seats in 2019 as it only launched international services in December 2019 with a service from Almaty to Moscow; 480,000 international seats in 2022 include charters. Seats are rounded to the nearest 10,000 and are approximate. Charter services by foreign LCCs are excluded.

Source: Author, based on OAG schedules data and other sources.

Abu Dhabi. Uzbekistan Express is not currently serving Kazakhstan.

Latvia-based airBaltic and Hungary-based Wizz Air, which served Kazakhstan in 2019, also do not currently serve Kazakhstan. Wizz resumed Budapest–Astana in summer of 2021 but suspended the route, which was initially launched in 2017, in March 2022. AirBaltic launched seasonal only services between Riga and Almaty in 2018 and operated the route for two summers but has not operated the service since the pandemic.

While airBaltic and Wizz Air still did not operate any services to Kazakhstan in 2023, two other LCCs entered the market with the launch of services from IndiGo and SalamAir. SalamAir started Muscat–Almaty in July 2023 and IndiGo is launching Almaty–Delhi in September 2023.

Total international LCC capacity in Kazakhstan has more than tripled since prior to the pandemic, increasing from about 400,000 seats in 2019 to about 1.3 million seats in 2022. This resulted in Kazakhstan's international LCC penetration rate increasing from only 6% in 2019 to 21% in 2022, as outlined in an earlier section of this study.

Foreign LCC capacity doubled from 400,000 seats in 2019 to about 800,000 seats in 2022, with FlyArystan accounting for the rest. FlyArystan had virtually no international capacity in 2019 as it only launched its first international service in December 2019.

In 2022, FlyArystan was only about one-third bigger than flydubai in its own international market, carrying slightly less than 500,000 international passengers in 2022 compared to about 300,000 for flydubai (Table 26). This highlights how small FlyArystan's international operation is although in 2022, it operated international flights (including charters) from eight cities in Kazakhstan. In summer of 2023, FlyArystan had a bigger international network but was still only about 50% bigger than flydubai in Kazakhstan's international market.

Kazakhstan should support even more international LCC capacity—from FlyArystan as well as foreign LCCs. More LCC flights would stimulate demand, driving faster growth in Kazakhstan's international market. While Kazakhstan has had remarkable LCC-driven domestic growth over the last few years, the international market is still relatively underserved.

There are opportunities to attract more LCCs from the Middle East, particularly Saudi Arabia. Kazakhstan has been working on attracting Saudi Arabian LCC flynas, which in August 2022 announced plans to launch service to Almaty from Jeddah starting November 2022. The route did not launch in 2022 as initially planned, but flynas planned to begin serving Almaty in early October 2023 with three weekly flights from Jeddah. Omani LCC SalamAir also began serving Almaty in July 2023 with two weekly seasonal flights from Muscat.

There are also opportunities to start attracting LCCs from Western Europe and Asia. There are currently no LCCs serving Kazakhstan from the EU. There are also no scheduled services from an Asian LCC although Viet Nam's VietJet launched charter services to Kazakhstan in late 2022 with services from Nha Trang in Viet Nam to both Almaty and Astana.

VietJet could operate scheduled flights to Kazakhstan in future. The charters that were operated to Nha Trang for Kazakh travel agents in winter 2022–2023 were popular with both Kazakh citizens and Russian citizens, with the latter crossing the border to take the flights due to a lack of direct flights from the Russian Federation during Russia's war in Ukraine. VietJet continued to operate flights from Nha Trang to both Almaty and Astana in summer of 2023.

Malaysia-based LCC group AirAsia also has been looking at launching services to Kazakhstan, sending a delegation of executives to Almaty and Astana in October 2022. AirAsia could begin serving Kazakhstan as early as Q4 2023, initially with service to Almaty from Kuala Lumpur. Air Astana served Kuala Lumpur prior to the pandemic and was initially not planning to resume this service, leaving a potential void in the market. However, Air Astana in now planning to resume Almaty–Kuala Lumpur by the end of 2023, which could impact AirAsia's plans. AirAsia is also considering flights to Almaty from Bangkok, a route that is also served by Air Astana.

Kazakhstan–India is also a big potential growth market that could be stimulated by Indian LCCs. Prior to FlyArystan's launch of Shymkent–Delhi services in May 2023, Air Astana had the only service in the Kazakhstan–India market, linking Almaty with Delhi. This has changed dramatically with the launch of flights from FlyArystan and IndiGo, which will both serve Almaty-Delhi starting in late September 2023.

While for now there are only two India-Kazakhstan routes, both FlyArystan and IndiGo are likely to expand. FlyArystan is aiming to add services from Almaty to Mumbai. It also aims to serve secondary cities in India such as Jaipur. Attracting more LCC capacity in the Kazakhstan–India market will help Kazakhstan attract Indian tourists and result in several new nonstop routes between Kazakhstan and India.

Within CAREC, Pakistan and Mongolia are potential LCC markets. Pakistan is now served from Kazakhstan with a new flight from SCAT but with LCC services, there is potential to attract more Pakistani tourists and further improve economic ties. The Kazakhstan-Mongolia market is currently served by Hunnu Air, which operates two weekly Almaty–Ulaanbaatar flights, and prior to the pandemic was also served by SCAT with Astana–Ulaanbaatar flights. FlyArystan has looked at both Pakistan and Mongolia as potential new markets.

Korean LCCs are another potential target. Kazakhstan–Republic of Korea is a big market due to close cultural ties and a large Korean community in Kazakhstan. This market is currently only served by Air Astana and Asiana, which are partners, and securing an independent Korean LCC could stimulate growth.

Visa reform drives growth but tourism is still undeveloped

Most Kazakhstan–Asia expansion, including potential LCC flights to the Republic of Korea, would require foreign LCCs as FlyArystan plans to focus only on the short-haul segment with routes of 4 hours or less. It has no intention of adding wide-body aircraft, which are now operated by LCCs in several Asian countries, including Indonesia, Japan, Malaysia, the Philippines, the Republic of Korea, Singapore, Thailand, and Viet Nam. Citizens from all these countries as well as India and the PRC no longer require visas or e-visas to enter Kazakhstan, which is critical in developing a new source market.

A new international terminal is under construction at Almaty Airport, which is expected to open in 2024 and increase the airport's capacity to 14 million passengers per year (photo by Brendan Sobie).

India and the PRC were added to Kazakhstan's visa-free list in 2022, which should help drive growth from these markets in the post-pandemic era. Without this development it is unlikely FlyArystan would have launched flights to India or the PRC. Kazakhstan had 90 countries on its visa-free list as of mid-2023 and tourism authorities expect the list to exceed 100 countries by the end of 2023. E-visas are now offered for another 100 countries.

Kazakhstan began its visa-free program in 2014 with only 19 countries, but the list has since been gradually extended. Kazakhstan should consider further liberalizing its visa policy. The initial visa liberalization phase drove an almost 50% increase in visitor numbers from 2014 to 2018. There were about 9 million visitors per annum to Kazakhstan prior to the pandemic, but most of these visitors crossed over by land and outbound travel dominates Kazakhstan's international air transport market. The Russian Federation is Kazakhstan's largest source market and has become an even a bigger source market since Russia's war in Ukraine. Russian visitor numbers are now well above pre-COVID levels, while visitor numbers from other key source markets have not yet fully recovered.

Kazakhstan is still a relatively unknown destination and has massive inbound tourism potential, which can only be unleashed with improved international connectivity. There is particularly a lot of potential for ecotourism and digital nomads, two emerging trends globally that Kazakhstan is well positioned to benefit from with the right products. There is also growing interest in Silk Road itineraries combining Kazakhstan with other CAREC countries, particularly the Kyrgyz Republic and Uzbekistan.

Kazakhstan tourism authorities have been working on developing source markets in several Asian countries as well as in the GCC. There is also a push in Europe, including in France, Germany, and Italy. Kazakhstan was able to attract its first service from Italy in 2022, a twice weekly year-round route from Milan to Almaty operated by Italian leisure airline Neos. Securing a flight from Paris has been another priority. However, route development initiatives are often disjointed.

Kazakhstan has multiple tourism agencies—from the federal, regional, and city levels. This makes it difficult to work with airlines and develop source markets. There are some programs in place to support new routes and tourism authorities have been working with airlines, particularly Air Astana and FlyArystan. However, more programs are needed and cooperation between aviation and tourism stakeholders, including between government ministries, should be improved. Kazakhstan should revisit its aviation and tourism strategies to make sure they are aligned, and introduce more joint programs to facilitate development of international services, particularly LCCs.

Open skies policy is not actually open

There are several barriers impeding international air transport growth, particularly foreign LCC growth, including market access issues and high airport costs. Kazakhstan should consider adopting more liberal policies to facilitate international LCC growth as this would be beneficial to Kazakhstan's economy, particularly the tourism sector.

Kazakhstan's open skies policy, which was initially adopted in 2019 and has been extended until 2027, only has had impact on routes that Kazakh carriers do not serve. This policy has made it easier to develop new routes as any foreign airline applying for a route that is not already served by a Kazakh carrier has been able to secure unlimited rights, including fifth freedom rights if required. However, this policy inhibits competition as it does not provide fifth freedom rights to any route served by a Kazakh carrier. Foreign carriers are also still subject to limitations in Kazakhstan's bilateral air service agreements, which restrict the number of frequencies and routes that airlines are permitted to operate. Kazakhstan's open skies policy is unusual in this respect and should not really be considered "open skies" given these major limitations. It also excludes two of Kazakhstan's airports, Atyrau and Uralsk, although the two main airports and 11 of the secondary airports are included.

Air service agreements can still be expanded to enable more flights from foreign airlines, including LCCs. Kazakhstan currently has about 40 air service agreements. Kazakhstan expanded its air services agreement with the UAE in 2021 and with Türkiye in 2022. These are Kazakhstan's two largest markets after the Russian Federation and have experienced rapid LCC-led growth in recent years.

The most recent agreement with Türkiye expanded the total number of weekly frequencies permitted for each side from 40 to 93, increased the number of destinations, and added second-carrier designations from each side on the core Almaty–Istanbul and Astana–Istanbul routes. The expanded air services agreement resulted in an almost immediate increase in the number of flights from both Kazakh and Turkish carriers, including LCCs.

While the expanded agreement with Türkiye is encouraging, there are still limitations in this key market and there is a need to expand the number of flights permitted yet again. Some Turkish carriers are keen to add more capacity but are restricted.

Kazakhstan was willing to negotiate increases in the number of flights from Türkiye and the UAE as Kazakh carriers were interested in expanding in these markets. However, in other cases, Kazakhstan is not willing to negotiate an increase as there is no or limited interest from Kazakh carriers.

Kazakhstan was also not willing to negotiate an open skies agreement with Türkiye or the UAE, which would remove the need for future extensions. Every new negotiation takes time along with resources, and expanded air service agreements often are way behind demand, leading to a market being undersupplied for sometimes long periods as airlines are unable to add flights.

In the first 7 months of 2023, Kazakhstan expanded its air service agreements with Azerbaijan, Qatar, the United Kingdom, and Uzbekistan. While these agreements have provided airlines with the ability to add flights in these key markets, there are still restrictions on frequencies and therefore there is no open skies.

Kazakhstan's aviation policy is to not consider open skies and instead maintain restrictions, using the caps that are negotiated as part of air service agreements, for countries that have subsidized airlines. This includes Türkiye, the UAE, and Qatar. While this policy is somewhat understandable as Kazakhstan does not want to open the gates to markets that have what it considers to be an unlevel playing field, it sacrifices growth. Kazakhstan authorities try to be accommodating when it comes to LCCs, including from the countries that subsidize airlines, but several foreign LCCs are still impacted by the current policy, which is detrimental to consumers and the overall economy, particularly the tourism sector.

Adopting a more liberal open skies policy would be controversial but beneficial to the overall market. Protecting Kazakh carriers becomes less necessary as they grow and mature. Air Astana is now a leading international airline and, with the launch of FlyArystan, Kazakhstan now has its own LCC that is mature enough to compete effectively with foreign LCCs.

The appetite to liberalize the air transport sector could also increase following the initial public offering of Air Astana, which has been planned for over a decade and could finally occur in 2024. Air Astana has been 51% owned by Kazakhstan sovereign wealth fund Samruk-Kazyna and 49% owned by United Kingdom-based BAE Systems since the airline launched in 2002. SCAT is 100% privately owned, while Qazaq is 100% owned by Samruk-Kazyna. Qazaq is a small player that Kazakhstan could divest as part of a possible new aviation strategy.

Kazakhstan has been generally supportive of LCCs, and the government made critical changes to its aviation policy in 2019 to enable the launch of FlyArystan. For example, airlines were previously required to provide free checked baggage, but the government sensibly changed this policy. Without a supportive regulatory environment, it would have been impossible for an LCC to succeed in Kazakhstan's domestic market. This is an important lesson for other CAREC countries that continue to have similar policies.

Airport charges are cheap for domestic but expensive for international

Kazakhstan's domestic air transport market is regulated, which has enabled the government to make sure airport costs are low enough to support LCCs. Aviation authorities have tried to maintain charges at the lowest possible level as they recognize that higher charges impact airfares and the ability of citizens to fly, particularly given that income levels are not high enough to support high domestic fares.

The standard domestic airport charges are therefore relatively low. FlyArystan would not have been able to achieve its rapid growth without this domestic regulation, which has not been revised for many years, resulting in low domestic airport charges without any increases.

FlyArystan also has been able to negotiate discounts with most of the airports it serves in Kazakhstan, enabling it to pay less per domestic passenger than Air Astana. At all airports in Kazakhstan, FlyArystan now pays less than $10 per domestic passenger for taxes, fees, and charges, and on average it pays about $6 per domestic passenger. This is a very reasonable amount and has facilitated low fares which has stimulated demand, driving higher volumes of passengers for airports.

Many airports were initially reluctant to provide discounts on fees (taxes and charges are regulated) when FlyArystan launched and did not understand the LCC model. Some continue to be reluctant, refusing to provide discounts as volumes increase. Some airports also still refuse to turn around an aircraft in the 30 minutes that is typical for an LCC. One airport is still not able to accept mobile or home-printed boarding passes, which are important for LCCs as self-service technology drives efficiencies and reduces the need for check-in counters.

However, most airports have become receptive as they started to become more familiar with the LCC model and realized lower costs would lead to higher traffic volumes. Airports also have started to recognize that LCCs generally use fewer services. For example, FlyArystan using buses and remote stands rather than gates and aerobridges whenever possible. In October 2022, FlyArystan introduced check-in kiosks across all the airports it serves in Kazakhstan, providing a self-service option to print bag tags and a boarding pass for those passengers not using mobile or home-printed passes. The 48 kiosks have resulted in further staff savings and have freed up space in congested departure halls. The kiosks are only used for FlyArystan domestic flights and are the only airport kiosks in all of Central Asia.

The international environment is more difficult as it is unregulated. While some airports provide discounts and are aggressive at trying to attract new international services, costs are generally high for international flights. Regulating one sector of the market (domestic) but not both has resulted in a distortion.

As is the case throughout Central Asia and CAREC, high airport costs along with access issues are the main impediments, impacting the ability to grow Kazakhstan's international market. Airport fees and charges for international flights are relatively high in Kazakhstan, although not the highest in the region, as they are well above international norms despite poor service standards. The cost of important items such as ground handling and fuel are also well above international norms.

There is limited to no competition for airport-related services. For fuel, Kazakh carriers have access to cheap local fuel, but foreign airlines pay a significantly higher rate for imported fuel. For ground handling, local airlines also have an advantage as they are able to provide their own ground handling services (Kazakhstan, unlike some other CAREC countries, permits local airlines to self-handle).

Foreign airlines have no choice but to pay whatever ground handling and fuel rates airports decide to charge. This puts foreign airlines at a competitive disadvantage as, unlike the local carriers, they cannot bypass the high prices for ground handling and fuel that is charged by Kazakhstan airports. This makes it much more difficult to attract foreign airlines, particularly LCCs, as the LCC model relies on low costs to provide low fares to passengers.

The fuel issue is particularly concerning as airports in Kazakhstan are unique in that they provide fuel while in other countries, fuel is typically provided by fuel companies with multiple suppliers often at a single airport. Fuel is the largest source of revenue at the main international airports in Kazakhstan, but only foreign airlines are buying this fuel as the local airlines can access their own, much cheaper fuel. The fuel sold to foreign airlines generates significant profits for airports and essentially cross-subsidizes other part of the operation that benefit local carriers.

While some airports offer ground handling discounts to new foreign airlines, these are not across the board and are generally not that significant. For example, at Almaty, ground handling discounts are a relatively modest 20% and only cover the first year of operations. Fuel discounts are not usually considered.

Kazakhstan should look at introducing programs and policies to facilitate a reduction in airport costs, fees, and charges. Foreign airlines that have additional capacity coming online have a choice of new destinations and these costs often make Kazakhstan uncompetitive. While Kazakhstan has done a lot to facilitate domestic LCCs, a lot more still can be done from a policy and regulatory perspective in the international market.

The high international fees and charges is partly due to the low domestic fees and charges, which essentially force airports to cross-subsidize as the domestic fees and charges they are required to offer are below cost. However, airports still could potentially reduce international fees and charges by switching to a more volume-focused model where airlines, particularly LCCs, are incentivized to expand. There are also opportunities for all airports in Kazakhstan to improve their efficiency and expand non-aeronautical areas, which could enable airports to reduce international charges without having to increase domestic charges or impacting their profitability.

Kazakhstan airports should work more closely with LCCs, both local and foreign, to facilitate international growth. Airports may be reluctant to introduce discounts and incentive programs for international services as international operations often subsidize domestic operations. It is also difficult to reduce international fees and charges as Kazakhstan's airports are relatively inefficient and have much lower portions of non-aeronautical revenue compared to global norms. However, it is important for airports to recognize the long-term benefits of higher international traffic levels, which also have implications for the broader economy.

Airports need to be modernized

Kazakhstan's airports have a wide mix of ownership models with several airports or terminals that are owned outright by private companies. Only two airports have so far come under a PPP structure with one terminal now under a 30-year concession agreement. Several airports are still government-owned but by different local and federal government entities.

Most of Kazakhstan's airports are inefficient and outdated. For many years there was no development, leading to quality and efficiency issues. Airport infrastructure is now improving; a new airport opened in Turkistan in late 2020 and a long-overdue terminal expansion project is now underway in Almaty. Passenger terminals are also being rehabilitated at several smaller airports, including Kostanay and Uralsk, while a new terminal is being constructed at Kyzylorda. However, more major airport infrastructure upgrades are needed, and it is critical that Kazakhstan makes the necessary investments without further increasing airport costs as this would further erode its competitiveness in attracting airlines.

Kazakhstan should consider adopting an airport strategy that provides a clearer direction for the sector and better positions all airports for growth. The main airports are generally pursuing their own strategies in isolation, which is not in the best interest of airlines or consumers, while smaller airports would benefit from a new program that would help fund long-overdue modernization and improve management standards. Without a coherent strategy, the airports will continue to be developed in a fragmented manner, which is detrimental to Kazakhstan's aviation sector and overall economy.

Several of Kazakhstan's smaller airports are technically bankrupt and have trouble paying bills. It is not unusual for some of these airports to be behind in paying basic items such as electricity and salaries. It is almost impossible for these airports to fund larger maintenance projects such as runway and apron resurfacing. Several repaving cycles have been missed and conditions have deteriorated at many airports to the point that work in many cases is now needed urgently. A new funding scheme for smaller airports would enable the required upgrades without having to increase fees and charges. A project being introduced in 2023, which provides subsidies to cover operating costs of government-owned airports handling less than 200,000 passengers per year, is an encouraging new development in this area. There is also a new initiative providing credit lines to privately owned airports to help fund infrastructure rehabilitation projects and procurement of new equipment. The government should continue considering other new projects or schemes to facilitate airport modernization.

Management of Kazakhstan's smaller airports is generally poor. Municipal governments generally lack the competence to manage airports and even those regional governments that, in theory, have the funds are electing not to invest in their airports. There are opportunities for these airports to significantly improve efficiency and productivity as well as generate more non-aeronautical revenues. These airports typically rely almost entirely on aeronautical revenues. Some lack even basic amenities such as coffee shops.

As these airports are refurbished and modernized, it is important not to suddenly increase taxes and fees as this would impact demand. Domestic air travel in Kazakhstan, particularly outside the main cities, is highly price sensitive. As Kazakhstan's airports consider new strategies, it is sensible to focus more on LCCs. Airports should try to stimulate traffic by keeping fees and charges low. Kazakhstan's airports should consider terminals that are designed specifically for LCCs. As LCCs can use simple facilities that require minimum investment, LCC terminals would facilitate faster growth in the near term.

FlyArystan aims to open Kazakhstan's first LCC terminal at Astana Airport, which would be used only for FlyArystan domestic flights. Astana Airport's domestic traffic is now over 4 million passengers per annum, but its current domestic terminal (terminal 2) has capacity for only 2.7 million passengers per annum. This terminal was already operating above capacity prior to the pandemic, when there were about 3.2 million annual passengers, and became particularly congested during the pandemic due to rapid growth in domestic traffic. The planned new LCC terminal is a sensible quick solution to the current terminal constraints as it can be quickly developed by repurposing a VIP terminal.

Astana Airport expects the new LCC terminal would be capable of handling up to four flights at a time but will be simple with basic amenities and no gates or aerobridges. It is expected to handle 600,000 to 1.9 million passengers per annum, freeing up space in terminal 2 for other domestic airlines.

Astana Airport expects the LCC terminal will be open for about 4 years, when the planned expansion of terminal 2 is expected to be completed, more than doubling capacity from 2.7 million to 5.5 million passengers per annum. However, it is possible the LCC terminal can become a permanent fixture as it is a more suitable space for FlyArystan.

FlyArystan's international flights (as well as international flights by foreign LCCs) at Astana will continue to operate from T1, which is a modern terminal with ample capacity. T1's capacity is 5.2 million passengers per year, while only about 1.8 million international passengers are expected at Astana in 2023, matching 2019 levels.

The LCC terminal is critical for Astana Airport's growth as it enables FlyArystan to continue expanding, which Astana would not be able to otherwise accommodate given the constraints of the current terminal. The terminal costs only about $4 million and, while bringing in a private investor was initially considered, Air Astana Group has decided to make the investment itself.

This project could become a model for other airports in Kazakhstan and throughout CAREC.

A simple facility with parking stands and buses rather than gates facilitates fast aircraft turnaround times, which is a critical component of the LCC model. It is also convenient for passengers, particularly domestic travelers.

FlyArystan is also planning to open an LCC terminal at Shymkent using the existing terminal once Shymkent Airport opens a new terminal, which will used by all other airlines. It is keen to have similar LCC terminals in other Kazakhstan airports, including other major airports such Almaty and some of the smaller airports.

Almaty Airport is now planning a common-use concept for its new terminal, which is now under construction and is slated to open in 2024. However, FlyArystan would prefer a dedicated LCC space.

The new owners of Almaty Airport, Türkiye's TAV, plan to use the new terminal for all international flights (both LCC and FSC), while the existing terminal will be used for all domestic flights. Almaty Airport is now very congested and operating well above capacity. Once the new terminal opens, the airport's overall capacity will increase to 14 million passengers. The airport's only current terminal has a designed capacity of up to 1,200 passengers per hour, but at peak periods, Almaty is now handling 3,000 passengers per hour.

The new terminal at Almaty represents a massive improvement in service levels as compared to the outdated and congested current terminal. The transit product is particularly poor at the current terminal and the new terminal will resolve this issue with a transit area. Transit traffic at both Almaty and Astana is now well below pre-COVID-19 levels as Air Astana has dropped its earlier more transit-focused strategy, which drove a more than a doubling of transit traffic in Kazakhstan from less than 500,000 passengers in 2016 to 1 million in 2019. Transit accounted for 24% of Air Astana's traffic in 2019 but is now in the low single digits as the airline prefers to carry point-to-point passengers.

Air Astana has no intention for now of building back transit traffic, which is almost always lower yielding than point-to-point traffic. However, over time, transit traffic will inevitably grow again in Kazakhstan as transit is often needed to help fill additional capacity. FlyArystan already sells connecting itineraries and may need to rely on transit more as it expands its international network. Air Astana could start connecting with FlyArystan and will likely start again selling more transit between Air Astana flights as it resumes expansion, although it is unlikely the 24% transit figure will again be reached.

There are also opportunities to grow transit at SCAT, which has started targeting transit traffic to feed its Russian Federation flights. There are also potential opportunities to work with foreign LCCs to develop transit or stopover traffic. For example, AirAsia has looked at using Almaty as a potential stopover point and/or hub for flights to Europe.

There are opportunities in the intra-CAREC market

Improved transit services at airports could also help facilitate growth in traffic between Kazakhstan and other CAREC countries. Kazakhstan has more intra-CAREC capacity than any other CAREC country. With the launch of services to Pakistan and the

FlyArystan currently operates 11 180-seat A320ceo and 5 188-seat A320neo aircraft. This particular A320neo, EI-KBH was initially delivered to Air Astana and is now back at Air Astana after being operated by FlyArystan in a 180-seat configuration from September 2021 to June 2023 (photo by FlyArystan).

resumption of services to Turkmenistan in summer of 2023, Kazakhstan is now connected to all CAREC member countries.

Kazakhstan aviation authorities are keen to further develop intra-CAREC flights but believe local demand is weak. New regional routes to other CAREC countries often fail as demand cannot be stimulated even with low fares.

Kazakhstan could look at initiatives to help support intra-CAREC flights, including improving transit products and promoting Silk Road multi-country itineraries. Kazakhstan can also focus on improving economic ties with other CAREC countries and promoting intra-CAREC tourism. There is generally a lack of economic ties and tourism between Kazakhstan and other CAREC countries, although Georgia has been an exception with Kazakh visitor numbers to Georgia increasing by 76% in 2019 and 16% in 2022 (compared to 2019 levels).

FlyArystan has been very successful in Georgia, which accounted for nearly 30% of its total international passenger traffic in 2022. However, its experience with other CAREC airports has been more mixed with high fees and other limitations such as long aircraft turnaround times making it difficult to achieve profitability. FlyArystan has been able to make Baku work despite high costs and has resumed services to Bishkek, Samarkand, and Tashkent after earlier suspending services to these CAREC destinations. However, it does not intend to resume Osh, Namangan, or Nukus, all of which were served briefly in 2021 or 2022 with a mix of scheduled and charter flights.

FlyArystan could drive intra-CAREC growth in several country pairs like it has in the Kazakhstan–Georgia market. However, it will continue to be challenging to grow these markets without changes in both the demand and regulatory environments. FlyArystan has encountered regulatory issues when securing approvals from some other CAREC countries.

Kazakhstan could take a lead in pushing for CAREC countries to adopt policies aimed at facilitating intra-CAREC LCC growth. There are now several LCCs based in CAREC that could benefit from more liberal policies and learn from the FlyArystan example.

FlyArystan can also potentially operate fifth freedom routes between other CAREC countries and establish bases in other CAREC countries, which would require seventh freedoms. Kazakhstan and other CAREC countries should consider providing fifth and seven freedoms within CAREC to facilitate intra-CAREC growth.

Without more liberal policies and programs incentivizing new routes, it will continue to be difficult to develop the intra-CAREC air transport market. As it has the largest intra-CAREC market and now the largest CAREC LCC, Kazakhstan should consider taking the lead at the CAREC level and advocate new CAREC-wide policies aimed at facilitating LCC growth within CAREC.

Recommendations for Kazakhstan

1. Shift its focus to the international market.
2. Consider more liberal policies in the international market to facilitate LCC growth.
3. Adjust its open skies policy to include more country pairs and fifth freedom rights.
4. Revisit its aviation and tourism strategies to make sure they are aligned, improve coordination between aviation and tourism stakeholders, and introduce more joint programs to facilitate development of international services.
5. Consider further liberalizing its visa policy and increase efforts to promote international tourism.
6. Implement programs and policies to reduce international airport charges, ground handling fees, and the high price of fuel for foreign airlines.
7. Consider programs to improve efficiency and expand non-aeronautical revenues.
8. Look at accelerating airport infrastructure upgrades while making sure any investments do not result in further increasing airport costs.
9. Adopt an airport strategy that provides a clearer direction and provides a new funding mechanism for small airports that facilitates long-overdue modernization and improve management standards.
10. Consider developing LCC terminals, following the example of FlyArystan's planned new LCC terminal at Astana Airport.
11. Implement as soon as possible plans to transition FlyArystan of Air Astana from a brand to an airline by securing a separate AOC.
12. Consider working with other CAREC countries to improve intra-CAREC connectivity and introduce policies that would facilitate LCC growth.

CASE STUDY 4
Kyrgyz Republic and Air Manas

The Kyrgyz Republic is a unique market in Central Asia in that it has had a liberal aviation policy and has been served by LCCs for several years. LCCs started to have a significant presence in the Kyrgyz market a decade ago due to the launch of services by Air Manas, Central Asia's first local LCC, and two foreign LCCs. In this respect, the Kyrgyz Republic was well ahead of other CAREC countries. But as one of the smaller markets, the early success of LCCs, which was made possible by liberal aviation policies, went largely unnoticed.

LCCs have continued to expand in the Kyrgyz Republic in the last few years, driven by foreign LCCs. However, the LCC penetration rate in the Kyrgyz Republic is now below the Central Asian and CAREC average as other markets have experienced a bigger surge in LCC services.

In 2022, LCCs accounted for only about 16% of total seat capacity in the Kyrgyz Republic, including a 19% share of international seat capacity. Seven foreign LCCs operated scheduled services to the Kyrgyz Republic in 2022 (Table 27) compared to only two in 2018.

Türkiye's Pegasus Airlines and flydubai are the largest and most-established LCCs in the Kyrgyz market, accounting for nearly 60% of LCC capacity in 2022. Flydubai became the first foreign LCC in the Kyrgyz Republic in 2012, followed by Pegasus in 2013. Also in 2012,

Manas Airport in Bishkek requires expansion following rapid growth in the Kyrgyz Republic's aviation market, driven by foreign low-cost carriers and new local airlines such as Aero Nomad (photo by Brendan Sobie).

Air Manas adopted the LCC model after securing investment from Pegasus, which acquired a 49% stake. Air Manas adopted the Pegasus Asia brand in 2013 and rebranded back to Air Manas in 2015, although Pegasus maintained its 49% stake until 2019.

Air Manas/Pegasus Asia was a pioneer in many respects as it introduced the concept of LCCs to local travelers. This was not easy as it was following a pure LCC model and passengers were not used to paying extra for items such as checked baggage and seat assignments. Air Manas was able to gain some traction, but it has always been a small player with its fleet never growing beyond three aircraft.

Air Manas was reduced to just one aircraft in 2018, an old Boeing 737-400, as the newer 737-800 it was leasing from Pegasus was returned. Air Manas suspended operations in late 2019 after Pegasus dropped its investment and resumed services in April 2021 with an Airbus A220 leased from a Russian leasing company. However, it suspended services again in May 2022 due to issues operating a Russian-owned aircraft after sanctions were imposed on the Russian Federation.

Over the years, Pegasus Airlines has generally been larger in the Kyrgyz Republic international market than Air Manas, which, prior to the pandemic, focused mainly on domestic services. Pegasus is now the fifth-largest foreign airline in the Kyrgyz Republic overall after three Russian carriers (Ural Airlines, Aeroflot Airlines, and S7 Airlines) and Turkish Airlines. flydubai is seventh largest, behind another Russian carrier (Nordwind Airlines).

Russian carriers dominate the Kyrgyz Republic market, accounting for 56% of total international seat capacity in 2022. The largest Kyrgyz Republic-based airline, Avia Traffic, which currently only serves the Russian Federation, accounted for another 10% share. However, LCCs have a strong presence on other routes, accounting for a 57% share of non-Russian Federation capacity in 2022, up from 35% in 2019.

LCCs accounted for 8 of the top 12 airlines in the non-Russian Federation market in 2022, led by Pegasus with a 23% share. Air Manas had only a 1% share as it was only operating one aircraft, mostly on non-Russian Federation routes, prior to suspending services in May 2022.

Manas International Airport OJSC, which operates all the airports in the Kyrgyz Republic, handled 3.6 million international passengers in 2022, an over 40% increase compared to the 2.5 million handled in 2019. The Russian Federation market has been a key driver of this growth with the Kyrgyz Republic–Russian Federation seat capacity up by 45% in 2022 compared to 2019 levels (based on OAG schedules data). However, the non-Russian Federation market also has grown significantly, driven primarily by LCCs.

Non-Russian Federation seat capacity was up 30% in 2022 compared to 2019 levels, and when excluding the PRC, seat capacity was up 44%, roughly matching the Russian Federation increase. China Southern was the eighth-largest foreign airline in the Kyrgyz Republic in 2019 but did not resume regular services to Bishkek until early 2023, when the PRC reopened borders.

While traffic from the Russian Federation has surged since the start of Russia's war in Ukraine, traffic was already at higher than 2019 levels in 2021. The Kyrgyz Republic–Russian Federation seat capacity increased by 14% in 2021 compared to 2019 levels, followed by a further 27% year-over-year increase in 2022 (based on OAG schedules data). The Kyrgyz Republic was a very unusual market in 2021 as it was one of only a few countries globally that had an increase in international passenger traffic compared to 2019 levels. Airports in the Kyrgyz Republic handled a combined 2.6 million international passengers in 2021, up slightly from the 2.5 million handled in 2019.

The domestic market is small and unprofitable

Domestic passenger traffic in the Kyrgyz Republic also has increased although it is a small domestic market. There were 800,000 passengers in the Kyrgyz domestic market in 2022, compared to 700,000 in 2021 and 600,000 in 2019. Air Manas had about a 20% share of the domestic market prior to suspending services, providing an LCC option on the Bishkek–Osh route.

Tez Jet Airlines has been the domestic market leader for several years and is entirely a domestic operator. The other Kyrgyz Republic-based carriers, Avia

Table 27: Kyrgyz Republic International Capacity Share by Airline, Excluding Russian Federation (%)

No.	Airline	Country	Model	2022 Share	2019 Share
1	Turkish Airlines	Türkiye	FSC	25%	28%
2	Pegasus Airlines	Türkiye	LCC	23%	17%
3	flydubai	UAE	LCC	11%	13%
4	Air Astana	Kazakhstan	FSC	11%	15%
5	Jazeera Airways	Kuwait	LCC	10%	1%
6	Air Arabia	UAE	LCC	8%	3%
7	Uzbekistan Airways	Uzbekistan	FSC	4%	6%
8	Aero Nomad Airlines	Kyrgyz Republic	FSC	2%	0%
9	SalamAir	Oman	LCC	2%	0%
10	AnadoluJet	Türkiye	LCC	1%	0%
11	Air Manas	Kyrygz Republic	LCC	1%	2%
12	FlyArystan	Kazakhstan	LCC	1%	0%
	China Southern	PRC	FSC	<1%	10%
	Others			1%	5%
	Total LCC			57%	35%
	Total FSC			43%	65%

FSC = full-service carrier, LCC = low-cost carrier, PRC = People's Republic of China, UAE = United Arab Emirates.
Note: Ranking based on 2022 share.
Source: Author, based on OAG schedules data and other sources.

Traffic and Aero Nomad, focus mainly on the international market although they also compete on the main domestic route connecting Bishkek and Osh. Tez Jet, Avia Traffic, Aero Nomad, and Air Manas are all 100% privately owned and are the only local scheduled passenger airlines currently operating in the Kyrgyz Republic.

Aero Nomad is a new airline that launched services in late 2021 and operates several routes to the Russian Federation as well as to India and Pakistan. Avia Traffic launched in 2003 and has since focused on the Russian Federation along with operating domestic services, although over the years experimented with other international routes. Tez Jet launched in 2014 and is essentially a domestic subsidiary of Avia Traffic as the two airlines have mainly the same owners.

The Kyrgyz Republic is the only Central Asian country (and the only CAREC country other than Georgia) without a government-owned flag carrier. Government-owned Air Kyrgyzstan ceased operations in 2017.

For several years, the Kyrgyz Republic has had an open local market without any restrictions on launching local airlines. Most of the local airlines are controlled by foreign investors, including three cargo airlines that launched services in 2021 (Aerostan, Moalem, and Sapsan).

Air Manas is the only local LCC although it initially operated as a full-service airline from 2009 to 2012. While Tez Jet, Avia Traffic, and Aero Nomad are considered full-service airlines, they operate all-economy aircraft and are low-fare competitors.

Domestic airfares are inexpensive and, on average, are less than $50 one-way, leaving little room for LCC stimulation. The government does not regulate domestic fares or provide any subsidies or financial support. However, domestic services are generally unprofitable as it is a price-sensitive market and there is political pressure to keep fares low. The average domestic airfare has not increased in the Kyrgyz Republic in several years and airlines feel compelled to continue operating domestic services as a social obligation despite no requirements.

There are currently six airports in the Kyrgyz Republic with scheduled services, all of which are operated by Manas International Airport OJSC. Three are very small airports that only have domestic services—Batken, Isfana, and Jalal-Abad. Each of these airports only handles about 20,000 passengers per year. Bishkek, Osh, and Issyk-Kul are international airports, but Issyk-Kul, located near the town of Tamchy on the northwest end of Lake Issyk-Kul, is small.

Issyk-Kul Airport handled only 80,000 international and 10,000 domestic passengers in 2022 and is mainly served from the Russian Federation. The airport was upgraded just prior to the pandemic, enabling year-round operations and regular international flights. Passenger traffic at Issyk-Kul grew from only 16,000 in 2019 to 111,000 in 2021, but dropped slightly in 2022.

Bishkek and Osh are the main airports and, combined, their throughput has doubled over the last decade. Bishkek handled 2.7 million passengers in 2022 (Figure 6), including almost 800,000 domestic and over 1.9 million international passengers. Osh handled 2.3 million passengers in 2022 (Figure 7), including almost 800,000 domestic and almost 1.6 million international passengers. In 2013, Bishkek had less than 1.4 million passengers, while Osh had less than 1 million.

International passenger traffic at both Bishkek and Osh has continued to grow rapidly in 2023, driven by further growth in both the Russian Federation and non-Russian Federation markets. Bishkek handled 970,000 international passengers in the first half of 2023, an increase of 42% compared to the same period in 2019, while Osh handled 794,000 international passengers, an increase of 88%. Total international traffic in the Kyrgyz Republic was up by over 60% in the first half of 2023 compared to 2019. Traffic in the smaller domestic market was up by 21% compared to 2019.

International seat capacity in the IATA summer 2023 season, which runs from the end of March to the end of October, is up 18% compared to summer of 2022 and 78% compared to summer of 2019 (based on OAG data). International traffic in the Kyrgyz Republic will likely grow by about 20% for the full year in 2023 and will

Figure 6: Bishkek Manas International Airport Annual Passenger Traffic, 2013–2022

Source: Author, using data from Manas International Airport OJCS.

Figure 7: Osh Airport Annual Passenger Traffic, 2013–2022

Source: Author, using data from Manas International Airport OJCS.

easily exceed 4 million for the first time. This will make the Kyrgyz Republic one of the fastest-growing markets in CAREC and globally for the third consecutive year.

Five new LCC routes were launched in summer of 2023, starting in June with Bishkek–Abu Dhabi, Bishkek–Ankara, and Bishek–Seoul. Osh-Jeddah was launched in late August 2023 and Bishkek-Jeddah in early October 2023. Abu Dhabi was launched by Wizz Air Abu Dhabi, Ankara by AnadoluJet, and Seoul by T'way Air, while both Jeddah routes are under flynas.

Nine LCCs are serving the Kyrgyz Republic market in summer of 2023 compared to seven in 2022. AnadoluJet is included among the seven as it already launched Bishkek–Antalya in 2022. The other six are Pegasus, flydubai, Jazeera, Air Arabia, and FlyArystan. SalamAir was serving the Kyrgyz Republic in Q1 2023 (Osh only as Bishkek–Muscat has not operated since 2022) but did not operate any services in summer of 2023.

Low-cost carriers came to Bishkek early

The first wave of LCC growth for Bishkek was in 2012 and 2013, leading to an LCC penetration rate of about 20% in 2014. LCCs now account for about 30% of international seat capacity in Bishkek, but the overall LCC penetration rate is lower than 2014 due to the lack of domestic LCC services.

There were only five scheduled LCC routes from Bishkek in the 2023 winter season: flydubai serving Dubai; Pegasus serving Istanbul Sabiha Gokcen and Antalya; Air Arabia serving Sharjah; and Jazeera serving Kuwait City. This increased to 11 in the 2023 summer season with the resumptions of Antalya from AnadoluJet and Astana from FlyArystan, as well as the launch of Abu Dhabi from Air Arabia Abu Dhabi, Ankara from AnadoluJet, Jeddah from flynas, and Seoul from T'way.

The first international LCC routes for Bishkek, Dubai, and Istanbul Sabiha Gokcen, are still the largest with each served once daily in the winter season and twice daily in the summer. For several years, these were the only regular LCC routes, and Pegasus and flydubai were the only foreign LCCs serving Bishkek.

Air Manas operated consistently from 2012 to 2019 with only Bishkek–Osh served throughout this period. Air Manas operated several other international routes, but these mainly were short-lived. Delhi, Moscow, and Urumqi were Air Manas' longest-lasting international routes, with Moscow served from 2014 to 2018,

Delhi from 2015 to 2018, and Urumqi from 2015 to 2018 (based on OAG schedules data). Delhi and Moscow were again served in 2021 and early 2022 prior to Air Manas' second suspension of services.

Air Arabia became the third foreign LCC in the Bishkek market when it launched services from Sharjah in 2019. Jazeera followed in 2020 and SalamAir in 2021. However, the SalamAir service was short-lived and has not operated since March 2022. Pegasus also added the Bishkek–Antalya route in late 2020.

Low-cost carriers came to Osh very recently

Osh has experienced a bigger surge in LCC penetration rate the last few years. Prior to the pandemic, Osh was not served by any LCC except for domestic services from Bishkek by Air Manas (which were suspended in 2019). Pegasus, Jazeera, and SalamAir all launched services to Osh in 2021, followed by Air Arabia and flydubai in 2022 and flynas in 2023. FlyArystan also briefly served Osh from Almaty during the pandemic although this operated as a charter service with most passengers connecting in Almaty to Russian Federation flights.

LCCs currently account for about 20% of total international capacity at Osh but they account for 100% of capacity in the non-Russian Federation market. Osh only had the Russian Federation and domestic services prior to the pandemic, and the Russian Federation still accounts for about 80% of Osh's international seat capacity.

Osh now has over 50% more Russian Federation seats than Bishkek as Kyrgyz authorities have been more liberal at approving additional Russian carrier flights to Osh despite objections from some of the Kyrgyz Republic carriers. Osh accounted for 56% of the Kyrgyz Republic–Russian Federation seats in 2022 compared to 40% for Bishkek with Issyk-Kul Airport accounting for the remaining 4%. In 2019, Osh accounted for 52% and Bishkek 48%, according to OAG schedules data.

The Osh region has a larger population than Bishkek and many Osh residents work in the Russian Federation. There is also a large and growing community of Osh residents now working in the GCC, which explains the recent growth in services from Middle Eastern LCCs. Osh's international passenger traffic increased by 170% from 2019 to 2022, driven by the four new LCC routes to the Middle East and the surge in Russian carrier flights. In 2023, there were five LCC routes to the Middle East with the addition of Jeddah, which was launched by flynas from August 2023. However, there are only four regular routes as SalamAir only operated Osh–Muscat in the first 3 months of the year with just one weekly frequency.

There is an opportunity to attract more LCCs at Osh as the market consists primarily of price-sensitive labor traffic. The Kyrgyz Republic should consider focusing on LCCs as it modernizes and expands Osh Airport, which is outdated and congested.

Osh is located next to the Uzbekistan border and competes for traffic with airports in Fergana and Namangan, which have also attracted several new LCC services during the pandemic. The Fergana Valley is essentially one big market straddling three countries with residents from the Kyrgyz Republic, Tajikistan, and Uzbekistan traditionally using the airport that has the lowest fare. The Kyrgyz Republic essentially needs to improve the airport at Osh and attract more LCC services to avoid losing passengers to the new airport that is expected to open within the next few years on the Uzbekistan side of the Fergana Valley.

Bishkek and Osh airports urgently need modernizing

Prior to the pandemic, the Kyrgyz government was considering a new airport for Osh as the existing airport relies on Uzbekistan airspace. However, a rehabilitation project for the existing project is now planned instead of a greenfield airport. The Osh Airport rehabilitation project includes a new modern passenger terminal to replace the existing outdated terminal that is now operating above capacity as well as a cargo terminal as Osh currently does not have any cargo facilities. There is no timeline yet for this project and any funding decision will likely only come after there is a decision for funding development of Manas Airport in Bishkek. The Kyrgyz government has been planning a PPP concession for Manas Airport for the last few years and could consider a PPP concession for Osh if a Manas concession is successfully awarded.

There is a pressing need to modernize and expand Manas Airport, which is congested and outdated. Under the long-delayed PPP process, an international airport investor would be selected to build and operate a new or expanded passenger terminal. If the PPP process does not go ahead, other funding options will need to be considered to ensure Manas has the capacity to support further growth.

Manas Airport is particularly congested during the early morning hours, resulting in very slow delivery of baggage and flight delays. The arrivals area, which now only has two baggage belts, needs to be expanded urgently. New equipment is urgently needed to speed up baggage delivery and improve efficiency levels to normal international standards.

The airport is now unable to meet LCC turnaround requirements of 30 minutes or less as it has old equipment and insufficient resources. LCCs are only offered turnaround times of 55 minutes, which is inefficient and goes against the LCC model, dissuading some airlines from launching or expanding in Bishkek. Manas Airport has been looking at acquiring new technology, which would improve efficiency and increase automation, but investing in new technology and equipment is not likely possible until after there is an outcome to the long-delayed PPP process.

If Manas is taken over by an international investor, the airport should be able to improve efficiency and service standards, including reduced turnaround times for LCCs. However, it is important that airport charges and fees are reasonable to facilitate LCC development. While Bishkek has a different traffic profile than Osh, with a stronger inbound segment and some business traffic, most passengers at Bishkek are also price sensitive. LCCs will therefore likely be needed to stimulate growth.

International airport charges in the Kyrgyz Republic are generally lower than airports in other Central Asian or CAREC countries. There have not been increases for several years and discounts are also provided for 1 year to incentivize new routes. However, charges and fees for international flights at both Bishkek and Osh are still high by international standards.

Catering, ground handling, and refueling services are also expensive. Airlines now need to negotiate separate contracts for these services as they are operated by separate subsidiaries under the airport company. This adds complexity and there is no competition for any of these services. There are also quality issues with the catering and ground handling operations.

LCCs have raised concerns about the cost of these services as well as quality issues for several years, including the inability of the ground handling provider to quickly turn around aircraft. LCCs also have raised concerns about rules which do not permit airlines to use their own equipment such as auxiliary power units or buses, which are needed to bring passengers to aircraft as there are limited aerobridges. These rules result in even higher costs, particularly for local LCCs that have the scale to invest in their own equipment and set up a self-handling operation.

The Kyrgyz government should consider adopting policies to ensure the airport service providers are not abusing their monopolies. The government should also consider abolishing a rule requiring airlines serve meals on flights over 3 hours. This is an archaic policy that particularly makes it difficult to attract LCCs from Asia or Europe, which the government is generally very keen on attracting. Selling rather than offering free meals is an important part of the LCC model.

Diversification of the aviation and tourism sectors is critical

The Kyrgyz Republic was an early mover in Central Asia in terms of adopting liberal aviation policies and attracting LCCs. Foreign airlines have generally been provided with unlimited access except the Russian Federation, which is still subject to bilateral negotiations. The Kyrgyz Republic formally announced an open skies policy in early 2019, providing unlimited access fifth freedom rights.

However, further policy adjustments are needed to fully unlock LCC growth opportunities. LCCs have a strong presence in the non-Russian Federation market but could become even stronger with the right policies and programs. This is critical as the Kyrgyz Republic needs to diversify and rely less on the Russian Federation from an aviation, tourism, and overall economic perspective.

Air Manas is the oldest low-cost carrier in Central Asia but its only aircraft, an Airbus A220, has been grounded since May 2022 as it is owned by a Russian leasing company (photo by Brendan Sobie).

Kyrgyz aviation and tourism authorities are eager to attract more LCCs from the Middle East as well as develop LCC links from Asia and the EU. In the Middle East, Saudi Arabia particularly has a lot of potential and low-fare stimulation can attract traffic in both directions (Saudi citizens visiting the Kyrgyz Republic for holiday and Kyrgyz citizens visiting Saudi Arabia for religious pilgrimage). The launch of services by flynas in Q3 2023 is just a start, and the Kyrgyz Republic could potentially be served by multiple LCCs from Saudi Arabia.

In Asia, the Republic of Korea has a lot of potential given the cultural ties between the two countries and the opportunity to develop the Republic of Korea as a source market for tourism. Korean LCCs operated charter flights to Bishkek during the pandemic and were discussing the possibility of regular services for a couple of years prior to the June 2023 launch from T'way. This is just a start as the new T'way service is initially only once per week and is operating more like a scheduled charter. There is potential to expand this service and possibly attract a second Korean LCC.

India, Pakistan, and the PRC are also potential growth markets, but demand is now impacted by visa requirements. The Kyrgyz Republic has had a relatively liberal visa policy for several years, introducing visa reforms before other Central Asian countries, and should consider extending its visa-free list to India, Pakistan, and the PRC.

Attracting an Indian LCC should be a priority. India's largest LCC, IndiGo, is launching services to four CAREC countries in the summer of 2023, but has not yet included Kyrgyz Republic in its Central Asia expansion. Service from a Pakistani LCC is also possible, while for the PRC market it is more feasible to attract more FSCs. Loong Air became the second airline from the PRC to serve the Kyrgyz Republic in March 2023, when it launched two weekly flights on the Bishkek–Xian route. China Southern operated three weekly flights on the Bishkek–Urumqi route in the summer of 2023, which is still down from the seven weekly flights it operated for most summer months in 2019.

Loong Air became only the sixth foreign full service non-Russian Federation airline to serve the Kyrgyz Republic market after Air Astana, China Southern, Hunnu Air, Turkish Airlines, and Uzbekistan Airways. AZAL Azerbaijan Airlines became the seventh in July 2023, when it launched one weekly flight on the Bishkek–Baku route. Qazaq Air became the eighth in early September 2023, when it started competing with Air Astana on the Bishkek-Almaty route with three weekly flights.

Bishkek–Baku is the eighth CAREC route from the Kyrgyz Republic after Bishkek to Almaty, Astana, Islamabad, Lahore, Tashkent, Ulaanbaatar, and Urumqi. However, only Almaty is served daily, and Ulaanbaatar is currently only served in the winter season. Baku will also likely be a seasonal or irregular route. At Osh, there are currently no CAREC routes and no foreign full-service airlines except the Russian Federation carriers.

Visitor numbers more than doubled in the decade prior to the pandemic, but Kazakhstan, the Russian Federation, and Uzbekistan dominate as source markets. The Russian Federation visitor numbers surged after the start of Russia's war in Ukraine and overall visitor numbers were back to pre-COVID levels in summer of 2022. However, it will take longer to rebuild other source markets including Europe.

Visitors from Europe and other long-haul markets such as Australia and North America typically combine the Kyrgyz Republic with Kazakhstan and Uzbekistan, and only stay in the Kyrgyz Republic for a few days. These visitors typically do not travel beyond Bishek and Issyk-Kul as the other regions are remote and—although they have significant tourism potential, particularly for ecotourism—require a much longer stay. Some European and Australian visitors also combine the Kyrgyz Republic with Tajikistan, but issues with the Kyrgyz Republic–Tajikistan border have impacted this market and tourism in the southwest region.

Recognizing that most long-haul tourists will continue to combine multiple Silk Road countries, the Kyrgyz Republic is keen to work more closely with neighboring countries and could benefit from CAREC support to facilitate joint tourism products and smoother border crossings. At the same time, there is potential to promote the Kyrgyz Republic as a single destination, resulting in longer average visits and more visitors in the remote regions. However, this is difficult to achieve without direct flights.

High airfares are another impediment identified by tourism authorities that could be resolved with more flights and competition on existing routes. Flights from Bishkek to the UAE and Türkiye, which are the main connection points for the rest of the world, are often higher than Almaty, resulting in tourists entering by land or skipping the Kyrgyz Republic entirely.

Europe is a priority market for tourism and aviation authorities as the launch of direct flights would attract more European tourists and longer average visits. The current connections via Istanbul and Dubai can be expensive and time-consuming.

Prior to the pandemic, airport and tourism authorities were negotiating a potential deal with Wizz Air, which would have resulted in a LCC service from Budapest. Wizz instead decided in 2023 to initially enter the Kyrgyz Republic market with a three times weekly service from its Abu Dhabi hub to Bishkek, and has been considering an Osh–Abu Dhabi service. A service from Budapest is not likely in the short term. The Kyrgyz Republic needs to beef up efforts to attract an EU carrier as a European route is critical in its ability to develop tourism and the overall economy. As Kyrgyz carriers are banned from serving the EU, the only option is attracting European carriers.

Aviation and tourism authorities should work together to align their strategies and come up with more attractive air service development programs. Discounts have helped attract new flights to Delhi, Islamabad, and Lahore by Aero Nomad, and to Ulaanbaatar by Hunnu Air. However, more significant and longer-term discounts should be considered. It is also important to ensure the costs of airport services are reasonable and in line with international LCC standards.

Plans for more international airports may be unrealistic

The Kyrgyz government should consider focusing on improving connectivity from Bishkek and Osh rather than investing in developing more international airports. There are plans to double the number of international airports from three to six, but the market is likely not big enough to support so many. It would be more prudent to focus limited resources on upgrading the two main gateways and attracting more airlines, particularly LCCs, to Bishkek and Osh.

The government is planning to develop new passenger and cargo terminals at Issyk-Kul Airport, but it is hard to justify this investment given the traffic patterns. While the current terminal is very small and can become congested on peak summer days, the facility is generally underutilized. Passenger traffic at Issyk-Kul Airport peaked at 111,000 in 2021, when there was an unusually strong labor market demand as workers returned to the Russian Federation as border restrictions eased. Traffic dropped by 18% in 2022 and the airport will not likely generate significantly more than 100,000 passengers per annum. The new passenger terminal now under construction at Issyk-Kul will increase capacity from 100 to 450 passengers per hour.

Tamchy attracts some Russian tourists in the summer, but this is a niche market and there are limited Russian Federation flights the rest of the year. Issyk-Kul Airport also has attracted some seasonal charters from Almaty and Tashkent, but these markets are limited as most visitors from Kazakhstan and Uzbekistan drive. The Tamchy area, where there are many lakeside hotels and resorts, is only a 3-hour drive from Bishkek. Many visitors to Issyk-Kul also visit Bishkek, making it easier to fly to Manas Airport.

The government is also planning to upgrade the airports at Batken and Isfana to support international services. However, local demand for international services in these regions is very limited. Even for domestic flights to Batken and Isfana, there is limited demand and very few frequencies (typically less than one per day). The focus should be on improving domestic connectivity with more frequencies, which would improve connectivity with international flights at Bishkek.

There are also plans to upgrade and reopen some of the five airports that currently do not have any services. The biggest and most ambitious of these projects is at Karakol Airport, which has not had flights for several years. Work has already begun at Karakol to extend and rehabilitate the runway and build a new passenger terminal. Airport authorities aim to reopen the airport by the end of 2024 and develop international services, including to the Russian Federation, Europe, and neighboring Central Asian countries.

Karokol is located on the opposite side of Issyk-Kul Lake than Tamchy, which is nearly 200 km away, and is much farther from Bishkek. Karakol Airport therefore serves a different market than Issyk-Kul Airport. There are aspirations to develop tourism infrastructure in the Karakol region and position it as a year-round destination with skiing and other winter sports. However, it is questionable whether there will be sufficient traffic to justify this investment, particularly given most future visitors to the Karakol area are likely to drive from Kazakhstan once a new road to Almaty opens.

The Kyrgyz Republic will need to rely on foreign airlines to serve new international airports, but attracting foreign airlines to new unknown markets will be very difficult. The existing local airlines are limited in their capabilities and are only interested in Bishkek and Osh.

The government has been looking at using Manas Airport to launch government owned carriers, which would be used to improve domestic connectivity and potentially launch international services from secondary airports including Issyk-Kul and Karakol. Manas International Airport OJSC announced in July 2023 the establishment of a new airline subsidiary, Asman Airlines, headed by the former director of Air KG (also known as Air Kyrgyzstan). Manas Airport and the government also have been considering resurrecting Air KG with the acquisition of regional aircraft.

Local airlines are small

Local airlines accounted for just 13% of international seat capacity in 2022. This included a 10% share for Avia Traffic, 2% for Aero Nomad, and less than 1% for Air Manas. There is potential for local airlines to grow in the international market, but the current environment is challenging.

Aero Nomad currently has the only non-Russian Federation passenger flights operated by Kyrgyz carriers, with several low frequency South Asia routes carrying mainly Indian and Pakistani students to schools in Bishkek. Most of Aero Nomad's capacity is on the Russian Federation routes. Aero Nomad operates four older-model all-economy A320s and is considered an FSC. Aero Nomad recently announced it will add in 2024 an A330-200, which would be the first passenger wide-body aircraft operated by a Kyrgyz carrier.

The Russian Federation routes, which have been profitable since the Russian invasion, will also continue to be Avia Traffic's primary focus, with services from both Bishkek and Osh. Avia Traffic is considering resuming services to India and Türkiye, but these will be limited and only pursued if it can expand its fleet. Avia Traffic currently operates four 737-300s and three A320s, which are 24 to 32 years old. It is considering purchasing newer second-hand aircraft, most likely 737-700s. All its aircraft are in all-economy configuration, but it is considered an FSC.

Avia Traffic uses partner airline Tez Jet to serve smaller domestic airports which cannot handle 737s or A320s. Tez Jet operates one McDonnell Douglas MD-83 and two BAE 146 regional jets, which are all over 25 years old and very inefficient, but there are no viable replacements. Avia Traffic/Tez Jet does not believe international services from smaller airports are viable and will instead focus on providing connections for the limited number of international passengers (mainly workers) from the smaller cities.

Tez Jet currently operates most domestic services in the Kyrgyz Republic. However, its limited schedule and the lack of interest in the domestic market from the other privately owned passenger carriers has led to the recent interest in the government to again use a government owned airline to develop the domestic market.

Prior to suspending services in May 2022, Air Manas was mainly serving non-Russian Federation markets. However, it was only operating one aircraft and had limited frequencies, focusing on niche leisure or charter routes. Destinations served by Air Manas in the 12 months after it resumed operations with the Airbus A220 included Antalya, Delhi, Jeddah, Medina, Moscow, Mumbai, and Sharm El Sheikh. Within CAREC, Air Manas also operated a few flights to Batumi, Shymkent, and Tashkent.

Air Manas is keen to focus on non-Russian Federation markets when it resumes operations, including India, Pakistan, Saudi Arabia, Thailand, and Türkiye. Air Manas plans to operate several international routes from Osh, which it believes is underserved, and Bishkek, but is not interested in Issyk-Kul. Air Manas is also not keen on the domestic market, although it flew the Bishkek-Osh route for several years, as the maximum domestic fare is below cost even as an LCC.

Air Manas took delivery of its first A220 in late April 2021 and was about to receive a second A220 when it suspended services on 15 May 2022. Both aircraft were sourced from a Russian leasing company and Air Manas has since been working on finding alternative sources for A220s. Securing other A220s has been challenging and a deal for two aircraft that were to be delivered in Q4 2022 fell through at the last second. Air Manas continues to look for A220s—as well as the possibility of acquiring its original A220 from the Russian owner and reactivating the aircraft—with the intention of resuming operations by the end of 2023.

Air Manas operated all-economy Boeing 737s prior to initially suspending operations in 2019. It also operated the A220 in all-economy configuration with 145 seats. Air Manas was the first airline in CAREC to operate the A220, a new aircraft type that entered service in 2016. Its business plan envisions growing the fleet to at least five A220s, which have the range to operate services to Southeast Asia and Europe (if the Kyrgyz Republic can get off the European Union Aviation Safety Agency [EASA] blacklist). Unlike some of the larger LCCs in CAREC, Air Manas has always followed a pure LCC model.

Foreign airlines generally have an advantage as they have scale and can offer connections beyond their hubs. Local airlines are also not able to serve the EU due to EASA's ban on all Kyrgyz carriers that has now been in place for several years. The Kyrgyz government has initiated a restructuring of its aviation sector aimed at meeting international standards, resulting in the establishment of an independent civil aviation agency in 2022. However, further reforms and investments are needed to be removed from the EASA blacklist.

While having a liberal policy permitting new airlines is sensible, the number of airlines registered in the Kyrgyz Republic has more than doubled following the launch of four new airlines in 2021. This has put pressure on oversight resources as the new civil aviation agency does not have sufficient staffing, including inspectors.

A few new privately owned airlines are planning to launch, having already submitted applications for Kyrgyz AOCs as the Kyrgyz Republic has become one of the most attractive countries to start an airline. Most of the new privately owned airlines are cargo airlines that operate primarily in other countries, with their aircraft only occasionally coming back to Bishkek. This provides little value but requires oversight resources the Kyrgyz Republic currently lacks, making it harder to implement the improvements needed to get off the EASA blacklist.

The reforms also have not gone far enough and several of the long-standing issues have not yet been resolved with the new structure. There is still resistance to change and a lack of initiative to tackle the fundamental issues which are holding back the development of the Kyrgyz aviation sector.

The Kyrgyz government should relook at the aviation sector to make sure the reforms required to meet international standards are implemented. The Kyrgyz government should also look at tightening regulations on establishing new airlines to ensure they meet international standards.

The Kyrgyz Republic should focus on creating an environment that is more supportive of the existing local airlines while also facilitating further expansion from foreign airlines, particularly LCCs. Resurrecting the former flag carrier or launching a new government owned carrier may not be necessary if the policies that are needed for privately owned airlines to flourish were in place.

A decade after Air Manas became the first local LCC in Central Asia, the operating environment for LCCs—and airlines, generally—is still not conducive. Facilitating expansion from both foreign and local airlines in the non-Russian Federation market is particularly important as the Kyrgyz Republic should strive to diversify and reduce its reliance on the Russian Federation and Russian carriers.

Recommendations for the Kyrgyz Republic

1. Consider adjusting aviation policies and introduce programs to facilitate LCC growth.
2. Adopt policies to ensure airport service providers are charging reasonable fees and meeting international quality standards.
3. Consider abolishing a rule requiring airlines serve meals on flights over 3 hours.
4. Modernize and expand Osh Airport with a focus on LCCs.
5. Proceed with the modernization and expansion of Manas Airport in Bishkek as quickly as possible while in the interim start investing in new equipment to improve efficiency levels and reduce aircraft turnaround times.
6. Focus on improving connectivity from Bishkek and Osh rather than invest in developing more international airports.
7. Tighten regulations on launching new airlines to ensure they meet international standards.
8. Consider further reforms for the aviation sector to ensure international standards are implemented and facilitate removal from the EASA blacklist.
9. Diversify its aviation and tourism sectors by developing new markets and reducing its reliance on the Russian Federation.
10. Consider extending its visa-free list to more countries—including India, Pakistan, and the PRC—to facilitate aviation and tourism growth.
11. Introduce programs with other CAREC countries to promote joint tourism products and facilitate border crossings for international visitors on multi-country itineraries.
12. Increase efforts to promote itself as a single destination, resulting in longer average stays, particularly from Europe and other long-haul markets.
13. Consider introducing new aviation and tourism strategies that are aligned, including joint programs for developing air services.

CASE STUDY 5
Mongolia and Eznis Airways

Mongolia is the smallest aviation market in CAREC with passenger traffic of only 1.5 million in 2019. Foreign LCCs only began serving Mongolia in 2016, and in 2019 the first Mongolian LCC, Eznis Airways, launched services. However, Eznis operated just one route prior to the pandemic and has not yet resumed scheduled services. LCCs accounted for only about 5% of scheduled seat capacity in 2019.

Mongolia's LCC penetration rate increased to about 8% in 2022, driven by the opening of the Ulaanbaatar–Seoul route to Korean LCCs. However, this was on a low base as international passenger traffic declined by 48% compared to 2019 levels. Passenger traffic on Ulaanbaatar–Seoul, Mongolia's largest international route, declined by a more modest 24% for the year. The decline was only 4% in the second half of 2022 as the new LCC competitors only secured approval to begin operating the route from middle of the year.

The two LCCs, Jeju Air and T'Way Air, operated a combined seven weekly flights between Ulaanbaatar and Seoul from July to September 2022. While this seems small, in the Mongolia context it is significant as during this 3-month period (Q3 2022), they accounted for 24% of Ulaanbaatar–Seoul seat capacity and 14% of total international seat capacity in Mongolia (based on OAG schedules data). Jeju had more frequencies, but T'way had more capacity, accounting for a 14% share of total capacity on the route compared to a 10% share for Jeju Air. T'way used 347-seat two-class A330-300s, an unusually high-capacity aircraft for the Mongolian market, while Jeju Air used 174-seat two-class 737–800s.

A third Korean LCC, Air Busan, also served the Mongolian market in 2022, operating two weekly frequencies from Busan to Ulaanbaatar in Q3 and one weekly frequency in Q4. Air Busan became the first LCC to serve Mongolia in June 2016, when it launched two weekly year-round flights from Busan to Ulaanbaatar. Summer of 2022 marked the first time Jeju Air and T'Way operated scheduled flights to Mongolia. However, Jeju operated a limited number of charter flights to Mongolia in 2017, 2018, and 2019 from several secondary cities in the Republic of Korea including Cheongju, Daegu, and Muan.

Korean LCCs lobbied for several years to serve the Seoul–Ulaanbaatar route but, until 2022, were only permitted to serve Ulaanbaatar from secondary Republic of Korea cities. The Seoul–Ulaanbaatar market was a duopoly until 2019 between MIAT Mongolian Airlines and Korean Air, two full-service flag carriers that have a long-standing codeshare partnership.

Asiana, another full-service airline that is now in the process of merging with Korean Air, was able to launch services on Ulaanbaatar–Seoul in summer of 2019 after the Mongolia–Republic of Korea air services agreement was extended to allow a second airline from each side. Mongolia elected at the time to give more frequencies to government-owned flag carrier MIAT Mongolian Airlines rather than designate a second Mongolian carrier despite requests for Ulaanbaatar–Seoul traffic rights from privately owned carriers, including Eznis.

In 2021, the Mongolia–Republic of Korea air services agreement was extended again with Mongolian authorities agreeing to open the Ulaanbaatar–Seoul route to more Korean carriers, including LCCs. The number of frequencies permitted from each side also increased by nine, but the additional frequencies could only be operated in the peak summer season (June through September). Therefore, Jeju Air and T'Way Air were only able to operate Ulaanbaatar–Seoul during the summer season in 2022.

On the Mongolian side, MIAT was awarded additional summer frequencies and designated Aero Mongolia as a second Mongolian carrier. However, MIAT was unable to expand its Ulaanbaatar–Seoul frequencies to 20 per week as permitted, as it was unable to secure approvals from Korean authorities. Aero Mongolia was also not able to secure approval from Korean authorities in time to launch Ulaanbaatar–Seoul services in summer of 2022 and had to postpone the launch.

Aero Mongolia, which is Mongolia's largest domestic carrier and oldest privately owned airline, has year-round Ulaanbaatar–Seoul rights for up to three weekly frequencies. It was finally able to launch these three weekly flights at the beginning of July 2023.

A third extension of the air services agreement with the Republic of Korea was forged in February 2023, resulting in more frequencies for all the existing competitors. The total number of weekly Ulaanbaatar–Seoul frequencies for each side for the summer season increased further, from 18 to 22, while there was also an increase this time for the off-peak season (October to May), from 9 to 12.

The Korean side allocated one additional summer season frequency to each Korean carrier, resulting in Jeju Air operating five weekly Seoul–Ulaanbaatar flights in summer of 2023, T'Way four flights, Korean Air eight flights, and Asiana five flights. The Korean side also allocated additional Busan–Ulaanbaatar frequencies to Air Busan and Jeju Air, enabling Air Busan to expand its Busan–Ulaanbaatar service to four weekly flights in summer of 2023, and Jeju Air to launch Busan–Ulaanbaatar service with three weekly flights in July 2023. Outside of the bilateral, T'Way launched Daegu–Ulaanbaatar service in late July 2023 with two weekly flights.

The Mongolia side allocated the additional frequencies to MIAT. While the Republic of Korea have now designated two Korean LCCs to operate the Seoul-Ulaanbaatar and Busan–Ulaanbaatar routes, Eznis has still not been able to secure a designation from Mongolian authorities. Eznis is keen to compete on Ulaanbaatar–Seoul, particularly now that Korean LCCs have been able to enter, as it the largest international route by far from Mongolia.

Eznis Airways is Mongolia's first low-cost carrier

Eznis only operated one scheduled service, Ulaanbaatar–Hong Kong, China prior to the pandemic. It also operated several charter services, including to secondary cities in the Republic of Korea and Viet Nam, after commencing operations as an LCC in June 2019 with one 737-700 in 149-seat all-economy configuration.

Eznis previously operated as an FSC, launching domestic services from 2006 and adding scheduled international services in 2009. However, the earlier iteration of Eznis ceased operations in 2014 and was subsequently sold to new owners who were keen to establish Mongolia's first LCC.

When it relaunched in 2019, Eznis followed an LCC model on scheduled flights, charging for checked baggage and seat assignments but offering a free small snack. This required educating the local population about the LCC model as LCCs are a relatively unknown concept in Mongolia. While Air Busan had been operating to Mongolia for 3 years prior to Eznis' launch, Air Busan carried predominantly Korean tourists, who are familiar with the LCC model as the Korean market has been served by several local LCCs for several years. Eznis has mainly carried Mongolian residents.

Eznis was gaining some traction in building awareness of the LCC model in Mongolia prior to the pandemic. However, it only operated about 180 scheduled flights—all to or from Hong Kong, China—before suspending flights in early February 2020 (based on OAG schedules data). Eznis was never able to launch any other scheduled route prior to the beginning of the pandemic as it took longer than initially expected to secure traffic rights for other routes.

Eznis has not yet resumed scheduled operations (as of September 2023), but still aims to restart scheduled flights. In addition to resuming Hong Kong, China, Eznis is keen to launch several other routes although once again securing traffic rights could be a challenge.

Eznis initially operated three weekly flights to Hong Kong, China from July to October 2019 and reduced the schedule to two weekly flights from November 2019 until suspending the route at the beginning of February 2020 due to the pandemic. Eznis competed on the route with MIAT, which operated four to seven weekly flights to Hong Kong, China prior to the pandemic. MIAT resumed service to Hong Kong, China in late 2022 and in 2023 is operating two to seven weekly flights (depending on the time of year) on the Ulaanbaatar–Hong Kong, China route.

Eznis did succeed at stimulating demand and growing the Ulaanbaatar–Hong Kong, China market in the 8 months it operated the route (June 2019 to January 2020). During this 8-month period, 68,000 passengers were carried on the Ulaanbaatar–Hong Kong, China route (by both Eznis and MIAT), according to National Statistics Office of Mongolia data. This represents a 32% increase compared to the 51,000 passengers carried on the Ulaanbaatar–Hong Kong, China route for the same 8 months the prior year (June 2018 to January 2019) despite protests in Hong Kong, China, impacting demand for most of this period. The increase peaked at 50% in December 2019 following the end of the protests.

While the volume of passengers is small, this highlights the impact an LCC can have even on a relatively small route. Prior to the pandemic, Ulaanbaatar–Hong Kong, China was the fourth-largest international route from Mongolia, but with less than 100,000 annual passengers. The Seoul route is about four times larger and the Beijing route more than twice. Moscow was third largest and only slightly ahead of Hong Kong, China in 2019. Tokyo was fifth largest in 2019 and Busan, the only route served by LCCs in 2019, was sixth largest (Table 28).

Beijing and other PRC routes had very little traffic in 2022 as the PRC did not reopen borders and remove quarantine requirements until early 2023. The Mongolia–PRC market overall had 313,000 passengers

Table 28: Top 10 International Routes from Mongolia Based on Passenger Traffic

Rank	Route	2019	2022	Recovery Rate
1.	Ulaanbaatar–Seoul	388,000	293,000	76%
2.	Ulaanbaatar–Beijing	214,000	13,000	1%
3.	Ulaanbaatar–Moscow	95,000	3,000	3%
4.	Ulaanbaatar–Hong Kong, China	89,000	3,000	3%
5.	Ulaanbaatar–Tokyo	79,000	49,000	62%
6.	Ulaanbaatar–Busan	65,000	19,000	29%
7.	Ulaanbaatar–Erenhot	51,000	0	0%
8.	Ulaanbaatar–Istanbul	41,000[a]	109,000	262%
9.	Ulaanbaatar–Berlin	17,000	0	0%
10.	Ulaanbaatar–Hohhot	16,000	3,000	19%
N/A	Ulaanbaatar–Frankfurt	11,000	49,000	465%
N/A	Ulaanbaatar–Almaty	0	12,000	N/A
N/A	Ulaanbaatar–Ulan-Ude	8,000	10,000	138,000
N/A	Ulaanbaatar–Antalya	0	7,000	N/A
N/A	Ulaanbaatar–Bishkek	N/A	7,000	N/A
Others		44,000	42,000	95%
	TOTAL	**1,118,000**	**619,000**	**52%**

[a] Ulaanbaatar–Istanbul was served with a one-stop service via Bishkek in 2019.
Notes: Ranking based on 2019 traffic, but routes that were in the top 10 in 2022 and were not in the top 10 in 2019 are included. Annual passenger traffic has been rounded to the nearest thousand.
Source: Author, based on data from National Statistics Office of Mongolia.

in 2019, accounting for 26% of total Mongolia international traffic. In 2022, there were only 10,000 passengers in the Mongolia–PRC market, accounting for less than 2% of total traffic. Prior to the pandemic, there were seven Mongolia–PRC routes including Baotou, Beijing, Guangzhou, Hailar, Hohhot, Manzhouli, and Tianjin. Baotou, Erenhot, Hailar (Hulunbuir), Hohhot, and Manzhouli are in Inner Mongolia, which is part of CAREC.

Traffic on the Ulaanbaatar–Hong Kong, China route dropped 97% as travel restrictions in Hong Kong, China only started to ease in the last few months of 2022, prompting MIAT to resume the route in November.

Moscow also had very little traffic in 2022 as services were suspended in March 2022 due to Russia's war in Ukraine. However, much shorter routes to Irkutsk and Ulan-Ude in the Siberia region of the Russian Federation continued to operate. Overall Mongolia–Russian Federation traffic declined by 85% in 2022 compared to 2019 levels.

Mongolia's air transport market gradually recovers

When excluding the PRC, the Russian Federation, and Hong Kong, China markets, international traffic declined by only 12% in 2022 compared to 2019 levels. There was an increase in two markets, Germany and Türkiye, and most of the other markets came close to fully recovering in the second half of the year after a weak first half. Total international passenger traffic in Mongolia recovered by 63% in the second half of 2022 (compared to the second half of 2019) and by 104% when excluding the PRC, the Russian Federation, and Hong Kong, China. In the first half of 2022, these recovery figures were only 48% and 63%, respectively.

There has been further recovery in 2023 driven by the reopening of the PRC market and the resumption of growth in other markets. Monthly international passenger traffic in Mongolia was higher than 2019 levels for the first time in January 2023. In the first half of 2023, there were 472,000 international passengers, an increase of 10% compared to the first half of 2019.

Figure 8: Mongolia International Passenger Traffic, 2009–2022

Source: Author, based on data from National Statistics Office of Mongolia.

International seat capacity for summer of 2023 is about 10% higher than summer of 2019. Therefore, for the full year in 2023, Mongolia should be able to exceed the 1.2 million international passengers from 2019. Mongolia's international market grew by 50% in the 3 years prior to the pandemic (2016 and 2019) and increased fivefold in the 10 years prior (2009 to 2019). However, the pandemic essentially set back the market by 3-4 years (Figure 8).

While the overall market will see relatively modest growth in 2023, the Mongolia–Republic of Korea market will far exceed 2019 levels in 2023. Scheduled seat capacity in this key market was about 50% higher in summer of 2023 due to additional frequencies permitted under the extended Mongolia–Republic of Korea agreement. Further growth in the Mongolia–Türkiye and Mongolia–Germany markets are also likely in 2023.

The Ulaanbaatar–Frankfurt route grew from only 11,000 passengers in 2019 to 49,000 in 2022. MIAT now operates two to six weekly flights to Frankfurt, with six operating during the peak months of June, July, August, and September. Prior to the pandemic, MIAT only operated seasonal flights to Frankfurt with three frequencies in the peak summer months.

While Frankfurt has expanded significantly, MIAT has stopped serving Berlin. Prior to the pandemic, MIAT operated one weekly nonstop wide-body flight to Berlin in the peak summer months and served Berlin year-round with two to three weekly narrow-body flights that operated via Moscow (although most of the Moscow–Berlin passengers were local Russian Federation–Germany passengers rather than Mongolia–Germany passengers). Overall, Mongolia–Germany passenger traffic increased by 26% in 2022 compared to 2019 levels, while Mongolia–Türkiye traffic nearly tripled.

There has been rapid expansion in the Mongolia–Türkiye market

During the pandemic, Türkiye became a popular route for Mongolian travelers. Istanbul is popular for both leisure and business travelers as business ties with Türkiye increased due to the border restrictions with the PRC. Other destinations in Türkiye, including Antalya, also became popular for leisure travel. In addition, Istanbul has emerged as the main transit point for Mongolia–Europe traffic, both for Mongolians heading to Europe and European visitors heading to Mongolia.

Ulaanbaatar–Istanbul was Mongolia's eighth-largest international route in 2019, when it was only served with three weekly narrow-body Turkish Airlines flights that stopped in Bishkek prior to continuing to Istanbul. In 2022, Ulaanbaatar–Istanbul became Mongolia's second-largest international route in 2022 with over 100,000 passengers (based on National Statistics Office of Mongolia data).

Turkish Airlines initially launched nonstop flights on the Ulaanbaatar–Istanbul route in January 2020 following a long battle to secure sufficient traffic rights from Mongolian authorities to support a nonstop wide-body service. MIAT launched Ulaanbaatar–Istanbul in April 2022 and both airlines operated three weekly flights on the route in the summer of 2022. This resulted in full utilization of the capacity entitlements under the Mongolia–Türkiye air service agreement that had been expanded in 2019 from only 500 to a still modest 850 weekly seats (equivalent to three weekly flights) for both sides.

Mongolia and Türkiye agreed to a further expansion of their air services agreement in December 2022, permitting daily flights on the Ulaanbaatar–Istanbul route from each side and increasing the number of flights permitted to other destinations in Türkiye, including Antalya. At the signing ceremony between the two countries, Turkish Airlines and MIAT Mongolian Airlines also signed a codeshare partnership agreement.

Turkish Airlines increased Ulaanbaatar flights to four weekly flights from late March 2023. For now, MIAT plans to maintain a schedule of three weekly flights but could potentially add frequencies in the future.

Some privately owned Mongolian carriers are also now seeking Ulaanbaatar–Istanbul traffic rights, although it could be hard to persuade Mongolian authorities to designate a second airline. Eznis is interested in launching Istanbul, Prague, and Busan, as well as resuming Hong Kong, China. Prague and Busan should be more feasible from a traffic rights perspective as

Prague is not served by any airline, while Busan traffic rights were increased under the most recent expansion of the Mongolia–Republic of Korea air services agreement.

Eznis Airways is keen to expand

Eznis already has traffic rights for Chengdu and Macau, China which were secured in 2019 along with Hong Kong, China. However, Chengdu and Macau, China are small unserved markets that may not be viable. It is generally easier to secure traffic rights for unserved markets, while Mongolian authorities have been reluctant to open most existing routes to LCC competition to avoid impacting MIAT. However, the unserved routes are usually too small to justify launching even with LCC stimulation.

Prague could be an exception as there are about 13,000 Mongolian citizens working in Czech Republic, making it the third-largest Mongolian expatriate community after the United States (US) and the Republic of Korea. However, it is a long high-risk route that could be hard to sustain year-round given most Mongolians living overseas only return for visits during the summer, which is also the time of year Mongolia attracts more visitors.

Prague, which has never been served nonstop from Ulaanbaatar by any airline, and Istanbul, would be served with newly acquired Airbus A330 aircraft. Eznis only operated 737s until late 2022, when it added an A330-200. It is also now looking at adding a larger A330-300.

Eznis was only operating one aircraft prior to the pandemic, but was planning to lease a second 737 in spring 2020, which it cancelled after the pandemic hit. At the beginning of the pandemic, Eznis briefly operated its only 737 on cargo flights for DHL before sending the aircraft to Africa, where it spent most of the pandemic operating wet-lease contracts for other airlines. In 2021, Eznis added a second 737-700, which was also initially operated in Africa as part of a wet-lease contract for another airline. One of the 737-700s was brought back to Mongolia in late 2022 and was used in early 2023 for passenger charter flights from Mongolia, but in summer of 2023 Eznis was again only operating wet-lease flights from other countries.

The A330-200 that was added in late 2022 cannot be operated on passenger flights from Mongolia as it is 23 years old and Mongolia does not permit airlines to use such old aircraft on passenger flights. Eznis initially leased the A330-200 with the intention of wet leasing the aircraft to cargo customers, including cargo flights from Mongolia, but subsequently used the aircraft for wet-lease passenger services from other countries. Eznis also has been looking at establishing an air cargo business in Mongolia by building an air cargo warehouse at Ulaanbaatar's new airport and potentially acquiring full freighters.

While Eznis is keen on the cargo segment of the market, it is still interested in operating as a scheduled passenger airline and following the LCC model. Eznis is planning to add a third 737, this time a higher-capacity 737-800s, which seats 189 passengers in all-economy configuration. Eznis aims to eventually have a fleet of four 737s—two 737-700s and two 737-800s.

The additional 737s and the A330-300 would be used to expand its passenger operation although even if it resumes scheduled services under the LCC model, it plans to continue to offer wet lease and charter services which do not fall under the LCC model. Mongolia is a very seasonal market with much stronger demand during the summer and having a wet-lease business in other countries can provide a counterbalance as other countries have a high season during different times of the year. For example, one or two aircraft may be wet leased out year-round, but during off-peak months for travel in Mongolia another two aircraft could be operated in other countries under wet-lease or charter arrangements.

Eznis also plans to grow its aircraft maintenance business by constructing a wide-body hangar at the new Ulaanbaatar airport and pursuing work for third-party customers. Eznis already has a narrow-body hangar at the old airport and completed in late 2022 its first heavy maintenance check on a 737. It is now seeking US Federal Aviation Administration (FAA) certification, which would enable it to start pursuing aircraft maintenance work from third-party customers (other airlines or leasing companies). MIAT already has a large maintenance operation at the old airport that does significant third-party work, but LCCs do not typically do maintenance work for other airlines. Most LCCs also do not have in-house maintenance capabilities and typically outsource heavy maintenance checks and only do their own line or light maintenance.

Hunnu has scheduled flights from Ulaanbaatar to four domestic and five international destinations, including the CAREC destinations of Almaty, Bishkek, Hailar, and Manzhouli (photo by Brendan Sobie).

Pursuing such a wide mix of businesses (cargo, wet lease, and maintenance) is unusual for an LCC as LCCs typically want to focus entirely on the core business as this facilitates a lower cost structure. However, Mongolia is an unusual market as it is very small, making it very difficult to achieve the economies of scale an LCC usually needs to succeed. There is also an unusually large number of local airlines in Mongolia given the size of the market, which make it even more difficult to establish a successful LCC operation, particularly how difficult it is for new Mongolian carriers to secure scheduled passenger route rights.

There are now five local airlines in Mongolia

In addition to Eznis, there are three other privately owned passenger airlines in Mongolia that follow the FSC model— Aero Mongolia, Hunnu Air, and Mongolia Airways. All have been trying to secure traffic rights on routes that historically have only been served by MIAT. Prior to the pandemic all Mongolian carriers combined carried only 1.1 million passengers— 700,000 international passengers and 400,000 domestic passengers (includes both scheduled and charter traffic). These are hardly sufficient volumes to justify five airlines, even factoring in potential opportunities to wet lease aircraft outside Mongolia, a business Eznis and Mongolia Airways are particularly keen to pursue.

Mongolia Airways is the latest start-up, launching in 2019 with a 737-300 freighter. The company is very ambitious and since added a Fokker 50, A320, and A330. Mongolia Airways also now has three AOCs— one for cargo, operating as Mongolia Airways Cargo and used initially to operate the 737 freighter; a second for turboprop aircraft and helicopters that has been used since 2021 for domestic passenger charters and general aviation flights, including a pilot training academy; and a third which was secured in 2022 and is expected to be used for scheduled passenger flights with the newly acquired A320 and A330.

During the pandemic, Mongolia Airways had very limited passenger flights using the Fokker 50, and no cargo flights as the 737-300F that was added in 2019 was grounded. It has been allowed to use the Fokker 50 on charters despite the government rule from early 2019 banning old aircraft.

A much larger operation for Mongolia Airways is expected using a second 737-300F, which was added to the cargo airline AOC in early 2023, as well as the A320 and A330, which were added to the passenger airline AOC in late 2022. However, as of September 2023, Mongolia Airways had not yet launched any scheduled flights and was operating the A320 on a wet-lease contract in another market. If Mongolia Airways succeeds at launching scheduled passenger flights, it could put significant pressure on the three airlines that are already in this segment of the market (Aero Mongolia, Hunnu, and MIAT), as well as Eznis, assuming Eznis succeeds at resuming scheduled passenger flights.

After MIAT, Aero Mongolia is the largest and most established of these airlines. Aero Mongolia became Mongolia's first private airline in 2003, when it launched domestic services with Fokker 50s, filling a void left by MIAT which subsequently phased out turboprop aircraft and stopped operating scheduled domestic services to focus on the international market. Mongolia for many years relied entirely on private sector airlines, which, until 2003, were not permitted to provide domestic connectivity, while continuing to fund a flag carrier to provide international connectivity. This only changed at the end of June 2023, when MIAT resumed scheduled domestic flights.

Aero Mongolia was followed by Eznis, which became Mongolia's second private airline in 2006, and Hunnu in 2012. Eznis and Hunnu both initially used turboprop aircraft in the domestic market. All three private airlines were also able to operate short international routes to the PRC and the Russian Federation using turboprop aircraft. Over time, all three airlines added jets, which were used to expand in the international market beyond short turboprop flights to Inner Mongolia and Siberia. However, until recently, the private airlines were confined to smaller international routes not served by MIAT, as MIAT was able to maintain exclusive rights to the main routes.

As of early September 2023, Aero Mongolia was operating one Airbus A319 in the international market and was expecting a second A319 to be delivered shortly. Hunnu was operating one Embraer E190 and was expecting a second E190 to be delivered shortly.

Aero Mongolia's A319 is in 141-seat all economy configuration, while Hunnu's E190 is in 98-seat two-class configuration. MIAT operates larger aircraft, including three 737-700s, one 737 MAX 8, one 767-300 and one 787-9. The 737s all are in two-class configuration with 12 business class seats, but the total number of seats varies with two aircraft at 162 seats, one at 168 and one at 174. The 767-300 and 787-9 are also in two-class configuration with 252 and 292 total seats respectively. In 2022, MIAT also added its first freighter, a 757-200F.

Aero Mongolia added the A319 in 2021 and used the type to launch services to Tokyo Narita in January 2022. This represented the first time Aero Mongolia was able to launch a MIAT route. In 2022, Aero Mongolia also used the A319 to operate charter flights, including to Antalya, Bangkok, and Ha Noi, with Antalya operating with a fuel stop in Kazakhstan. Ha Noi was launched as a scheduled route in early 2023.

Aero Mongolia, at the beginning of July 2023, launched flights to Seoul, representing the second time it has competed with MIAT on an international route. It also currently (as of summer 2023) uses the A319 to operate scheduled flights to Ha Noi, Hohhot, and Tokyo. Aero Mongolia was already operating scheduled flights to Hohhot and Tianjin prior to the pandemic using Embraer ERJ-145s, a 50-seat all-economy regional jet which Aero Mongolia has also used for domestic services since 2018. Tianjin was initially launched in late 2019 using newly awarded traffic rights, while Hohhot had been served for several years, initially with Fokker 50s, prior to both routes being suspended during most of the pandemic. On the Ulaanbaatar-Hohhot route Aero Mongolia competes against Air China, which resumed its service in early August 2023.

Aero Mongolia also uses the ERJ-145 fleet for two international routes, Irkutsk and Novosibirsk. Irkutsk has been served for several years, initially with Fokker 50s, while Novosibirsk was launched in late 2022.

Aero Mongolia added ERJ-145s in 2018 and phased out Fokker 50s in early 2019 to comply with a new government regulation banning older aircraft. It initially operated two ERJ-145s but has been down to just one since summer 2022 as the second aircraft has been grounded for maintenance issues. Aero Mongolia has been aiming to reactivate the second ERJ-145, but it also has been considering potential replacements for the ERJ-145s as these aircraft have been unreliable and expensive to operate as they are not fuel efficient.

Aero Mongolia intends to schedule its flights from Seoul to connect with domestic flights to popular tourist destinations. Korean tourists visiting Mongolia in the summer months typically opt to holiday in remote destinations such as Khovsgol Lake or the Gobi Desert. Aero Mongolia has prior experience selling in the Korean market, having served the secondary Korean city of Cheongju several years ago when it was operating Fokker 100 regional jets.

The Tokyo route so far has catered mainly to Mongolian travelers, particularly students and business passengers. The route initially struggled as it was difficult for the first several months of 2022 to travel to Japan and secure a visa, but demand improved later in the year as Japan eased travel restrictions. Mongolia is hoping to start again attracting more Japanese tourists, which should improve inbound demand.

Aero Mongolia plans to continue with the FSC model, believing it is difficult to have an LCC model in Mongolia given the small size of the market does not allow any airline to achieve significant scale, and the need to have multiple aircraft types. Aero Mongolia does not charge extra for checked baggage and offers passengers on the Seoul and Tokyo routes a free hot meal. However, it does not have a business class product and its economy fare is usually priced lower than MIAT.

Aero Mongolia has been working to upgrade its reservation and distribution systems to improve sales in overseas markets, which is critical if it is to succeed at further growing its international operation as the outbound Mongolia market is limited. However, Aero Mongolia has a relatively cautious approach to international expansion. Aero Mongolia is interested in gradually expanding its fleet of A320 family aircraft, but only if market conditions are suitable and if it can secure more international traffic rights from Mongolian authorities.

Hunnu also has a relatively cautious approach to international expansion, and expansion in general as it is no longer focusing on the domestic market. Hunnu stopped operating domestic scheduled services in 2021 and returned two ATR 72-500s, which had been primarily used for domestic services, in 2022. This left Hunnu with only one aircraft, an Embraer E190 which had been added in 2019 to support international expansion. Hunnu also operated Fokker 50s until early 2019, when, like Aero Mongolia, it was forced by the government to phase out the type.

Hunnu several years ago experimented with the LCC model, charging for bags on domestic flights. However, the experiment was unsuccessful and Hunnu does not believe the LCC model can work in Mongolia given passenger expectations and the small size of the market. Hunnu is now considered an FSC and its E190 has a small business class cabin with six seats.

Hunnu currently uses the E190 to operate scheduled flights to Almaty and Bishkek, as well as charter services. Almaty and Bishkek were both launched in March 2022 and are generally served with two weekly flights (although in 2023, Bishkek was only being served during the winter season). Hunnu plans to mainly focus on the charter market, including charter flights to the Philippines, Thailand, and the UAE, as it expands its E190 fleet to two aircraft.

Hunnu also resumed flights to Ulaan-Ude in the Russian Federation in summer of 2022 after taking delivery of an ATR 42-500. It also now uses the ATR 42-500 on services to Hailar and Manzhouli in Inner Mongolia and on some domestic services. In summer of 2023, Hunnu was again operating four domestic routes using both the ATR 42 and the E190. But Hunnu is focused primarily on the international market.

Hunnu plans to proceed cautiously in expanding its fleet and is focused on niche opportunities with smaller aircraft rather than joining the other Mongolian carriers in operating larger aircraft. It has no intention of operating larger jets, having learned a difficult lesson several years ago when it briefly operated two A319s. Hunnu is also not keen on following other private airlines in developing cargo or wet-lease businesses as it believes Mongolia does not have sufficient personnel to support this kind of expansion. It is particularly concerned about the availability of pilots and mechanics as other Mongolian carriers expand and operate aircraft overseas.

Prior to the pandemic, Hunnu served three points in Inner Mongolia (Erenhot, Hailar, and Manzhouli) with ATR 72s. Hunnu is keen to expand its Inner Mongolia network and launch longer routes into the PRC with the E190. Hunnu has traffic rights for Beijing Daxing and Harbin, which it intends to launch.

Hunnu is interested in developing Ulaanbaatar as a niche regional hub connecting the PRC and the Russian Federation. This plan was developed prior to the pandemic and is still a long-term ambition, but it could be difficult to implement in the short term.

Hunnu is also looking at further developing its network in Central Asia, which is an underserved niche market that so far that no other Mongolian carrier has served. Hunnu is looking at adding Tashkent, but is waiting for Mongolia and Uzbekistan to forge an air services agreement as the two countries have historically not had any agreement.

MIAT is also now looking at potentially launching services to Tashkent. Mongolia should consider accelerating talks with Uzbekistan and other CAREC countries to facilitate intra-CAREC connectivity. There is potential to develop tourism and air services, but this is only possible with supportive policies and programs.

The Almaty and Bishkek routes have done relatively well, catering mainly to Mongolians. So far, around 70% of the traffic on these flights are Mongolians, while the remaining 30% of passengers are from Central Asia or other countries. Some of the traffic transits beyond Bishkek and Almaty to destinations such as Türkiye.

The Almaty and Bishkek routes and particularly the Ulan-Ude service have carried transit passengers who connect at Ulaanbaatar, particularly to Seoul. This traffic self-connects in Mongolia with passengers clearing immigration and rechecking in for their next flight as Hunnu does not yet have any interlines with other airlines. Hunnu is interested in potentially partnering other airlines, including MIAT.

As Hunnu plans to focus on smaller niche routes, it does not overlap much with MIAT. Under a partnership arrangement, Hunnu could feed MIAT flights with passengers connecting from Hunnu's intra-CAREC flights (Central Asia and Inner Mongolia) to MIAT's flights to the Republic of Korea, Japan, and, in the future, the US. A partnership would help both airlines as well as Mongolia's aspirations to develop the new Ulaanbaatar airport as hub.

MIAT has ambitious plan to launch US services in 2024 and pursue transit traffic

MIAT is planning to launch services to the US in 2024. Chicago, San Francisco, and Seattle have been evaluated as potential US gateways, with San Francisco the most likely initial US destination. Mongolia completed in early 2023 an air services agreement with the US, which was required to facilitate US flights as the two countries never had an agreement previously. Mongolian aviation authorities are now working on securing a category 1 safety rating from the US FAA, which is also needed before any Mongolian carrier can launch scheduled services to the US.

Launching US services is an ambitious plan and requires major investment from both MIAT and the Mongolian government. The government is very keen to launch US flights and has been driving this project. Upgrading security infrastructure and safety standards to comply with US regulations can be very expensive as other CAREC countries such as Azerbaijan and Uzbekistan have previously experienced. MIAT also needs to expand its wide-body fleet to support US flights. Once operations can finally start, a significant investment is required to market services and to cover operating losses, which are likely to be significant for at least the first few years.

The airline is now planning to lease three Boeing 787s over the next 2 years to support the new US flights and other expansion. It has already committed to leasing two 787-9s, including one which was delivered in August 2023 and one which is expected to be delivered in Q1 2024. MIAT, historically, has had two wide-body aircraft but for 2 years had just one, a Boeing 767-300ER, after returning one of its two 767s in 2021.

MIAT wet leased an Airbus A330-300 in summer of 2022 to help operate its summer schedule, and wet leased a 767-300ER for part of the summer of 2023 season due to a delay in the delivery of its first 787. The second 787 is needed to support the launch of US flights. The third 787 is tentatively planned for 2025 and would be used to phase out the 767 from passenger service. The 767 could be converted to a freighter and potentially replace the 757 freighter that was added in 2022.

MIAT's aspirations to launch US flights with 787s predate the pandemic. In 2019, it signed a lease deal for a new 787-9 that was initially slated to be delivered in 2021. However, in 2022, MIAT exercised its right to cancel this deal due to delivery delays and decided to instead pursue leases on smaller 787-8s. After a deal for second hand 787-8s fell through in late 2022, it switched back to the 787-9 although this is a large aircraft for the Mongolian market which could prove challenging to fill.

The launch of US services and the acquisition of 787-9s represent a major high-risk investment that is somewhat surprising given the government's current financial situation and the size of the Mongolia–US market. There is limited traffic between the two countries (less than 50 passengers per day on average) and the traffic is spread across several US cities.

There are about 20,000 Mongolians living in the US, but there are no cities in the US with more than 3,000 Mongolians. MIAT will therefore need to rely on US domestic airlines to feed its flights, regardless of which US airport it serves. However, securing a partnership with a US airline will be very difficult given MIAT's tiny size. Without any partnerships, a lot of the traffic traveling between Mongolia and the US will likely continue to fly via Seoul.

The inbound market is also small as Mongolia is a relatively unknown destination for American tourists. There were also only 20,000 US visitors to Mongolia in 2019. This dropped to 9,000 in 2022 although it should recover in 2023 or 2024.

Mongolia is hoping to attract significantly more US visitors once direct flights are launched. However, this will require a major marketing effort and it will be difficult to achieve rapid inbound growth. Feed from US domestic carriers will also be crucial as otherwise most of the inbound traffic will continue to fly to Mongolia via Seoul.

Almost all visitors to Mongolia arrive in the summer months and most Mongolians living overseas also return home for visits in the summer. Therefore, MIAT will have to rely very heavily on transit passengers during the non-summer months to make the new US flights viable. However, it will be challenging for MIAT to attract this transit traffic given its limited network. This type of traffic is also generally low yielding and MIAT will particularly have to price aggressively as it does not have a strong brand overseas and some passengers may be reluctant to transfer in Ulaanbaatar.

The Mongolian government should reconsider its strategy of pursuing US flights, given these flights are likely to be highly unprofitable and require significant investment to launch as well as maintain. It would be sensible for MIAT to continue bolstering partnerships with foreign airlines to serve the US and other markets. MIAT already works with Korean Air and Japan Airlines to serve the US, with most Mongolia–US traffic now flying through Seoul.

The Mongolian government is keen to privatize MIAT through a possible initial public offering. This is sensible as it would facilitate liberalization of the aviation sector and enable the government to focus limited funds on other areas. However, US flights will likely make MIAT less attractive to potential investors. A more conservative and realistic strategy for MIAT should be considered as this would make the desired initial public offering or privatization more feasible.

MIAT's new ambitious strategy includes launching US flights as well as several new routes in Asia such as Ho Chi Minh, Shanghai, and Singapore. The new Asia routes are needed to help feed the US flights and are part of a strategy that involves concentrating more on sixth freedom transit traffic.

MIAT could also consider launching services to India, which is particularly attractive if MIAT launches San Francisco as there is significant traffic between San Francisco and India. This would also help Mongolia develop India as a source market. There were less than

3,000 Indian visitors to Mongolia in 2019, but there could be significant growth if there is a direct flight and if Mongolia adds India to its visa-free list.

MIAT does not currently serve India, and in Southeast Asia only currently serves Thailand. Both Bangkok and Phuket are currently served with 737s in the winter season, but these flights could be extended into a year-round service to help feed US flights.

New Central Asia services including Tashkent are also being considered to help feed the US flights. Central Asia routes would be operated by Embraer E170 regional jets that MIAT is now considering acquiring for new domestic services, but could also be used on international flights to Central Asia and secondary destinations in the PRC and the Republic of Korea.

Attracting transit traffic, which is necessary to support the US flights, would help position Ulaanbaatar as hub, which is another desire of the government. However, this traffic will likely not be profitable.

MIAT's new strategy also includes focusing more on cargo, which makes sense given the opportunities in the cargo sector. However, this also requires a heavy reliance on transit cargo, which can also be a very competitive and low-yielding segment. Some of the transit cargo will be carried on the 787 passenger flights and supplemented by cargo flights using the 757 freighter.

Most of the new Asia routes could be served with the 737 fleet, while the new 787 fleet could be used for the US, Istanbul, and Frankfurt. MIAT currently operates three 737-800s and one 737 MAX 8. MIAT initially ordered two 737 MAX 8s in 2017 but subsequently cancelled the second aircraft. It is now considering again ordering a second 737 MAX 8 to support expansion of Asia routes.

In addition to operating winter season flights to Thailand, MIAT currently uses the 737 on year-round services to Beijing; Busan; Guangzhou; Seoul; Tokyo; and Hong Kong, China, as well as summer-only flights to Osaka. Moscow was also served with the 737 prior to the pandemic but has not yet resumed due to Russia's war in Ukraine.

Wide-body aircraft are also used for some of the Seoul flights, which is by far MIAT's largest route but has been impacted by the opening of the route to Korean LCCs from summer of 2022. MIAT accounted for 32% of seat capacity on the Ulaanbaatar–Seoul route in Q3 2022, compared to a 50% share in Q3 2019 (based on OAG schedules data). Mongolian carriers regained some market share in summer 2023 but Korean carriers again accounted for a majority of capacity.

In July 2023, MIAT's seat capacity share on the Ulaanbaatar–Seoul route was 39%, while Aero Mongolia accounted for 4% and Korean carriers 57%. Both MIAT and Aero Mongolia had issues securing approvals from Korean authorities in summer of 2022, and Aero Mongolia again had issues in 2023 resulting in a delay to its launch of flights to Seoul. Mongolian authorities should work with Korean authorities to ensure Mongolian carriers are able to operate all frequencies to avoid a repeat of the unlevel playing field that resulted in 2022.

The Republic of Korea is a critical market for Mongolian carriers as it the most popular destination for Mongolian travelers with strong student, business, leisure, and ethnic traffic. Outbound traffic from Mongolia to the Republic of Korea was 77% recovered in 2022, consisting of 75,000 travelers.

Türkiye has become the second-largest outbound aviation market, consisting of 32,000 travelers in 2022 compared to only 7,000 in 2019. Japan is third largest with 22,000 travelers in 2022 (80% recovered), followed by the US with 13,000 (83% recovered) and Germany with 12,000 (120% recovered). Thailand was also fully recovered but with a modest 8,000 Mongolian travelers in 2022.

Tourism is slow to recover but is a priority

The Republic of Korea is also the largest inbound aviation market (Korean tourists visiting Mongolia). However, it was only 53% recovered in 2022—despite all the new LCC capacity—with 55,000 Korean visitors. The inbound Korean market is very seasonal with most visitors arriving in the summer while the outbound market is more year-round. In Q3 2022, there were

35,000 Korean visitors, representing a recovery rate of 65% compared to Q3 2019.

The Mongolian government decided to open the Ulaanbaatar–Seoul route to LCCs in summer of 2022 with the objective of accelerating a recovery in Mongolia's battered tourism sector, which is important to the overall economy. However, Korean tourists did not return as fast as anticipated, impacting load factors. In Q3 2022, seat capacity on the Ulaanbaatar–Seoul route was 5% higher than Q3 2019, but passenger numbers were down 10% due to the 35% drop in Korean visitor numbers. The average load factor on Ulaanbaatar–Seoul flights was about 77% in Q3 2022 compared to nearly 90% in Q32019.

Japanese visitors did not return despite the Ulaanbaatar–Tokyo route opening to a second Mongolian carrier. There were only slightly over 6,000 Japanese visitors in 2022 compared to over 24,000 in 2022.

Mongolia also struggled to attract tourists from Europe in 2022 despite MIAT increasing nonstop flights to Europe. In 2022, there were only 4,000 visitors from Germany, which is Mongolia's largest Western European source market, compared to nearly 13,000 in 2019. French visitor numbers dropped from 11,000 to 3,000, while both Dutch and Italian visitor numbers declined from about 4,000 to 1,000. An overwhelming majority of passengers on the new Istanbul and Frankfurt flights were Mongolians.

Overall, Mongolia visitor numbers were only at 47% of 2019 levels in 2022. Visitors from the Russian Federation were at 107% of 2019 levels as Ulaanbaatar became a popular destination after the start of the Russian invasion, particularly for shopping. However, most of these visitors crossed by land from cities in nearby Siberia.

Prior to the pandemic, the Russian Federation was the second-largest source market for Mongolia after the PRC. Most visitors from the PRC cross by land although there is also a significant number of visitors that arrive by air. There were only 14,000 PRC visitors in 2022 as borders remained closed, compared to 208,000 in 2019.

Mongolia is keen to fully recover its tourism sector and resume tourism growth as soon as possible given its importance to the overall economy. Tourism has become a priority sector, and this has driven a desire to liberalize the aviation sector as more air services are needed to achieve tourism growth targets. The new emphasis on tourism also has led to relaxation of Mongolia's visa policy.

In January 2023, Mongolia added 23 countries to the visa-free list, expanding the total number of countries or territories that are exempt from visas to 60. The 23 countries that were added include 21 European countries as well as Australia and New Zealand. Surprisingly, visas were still required from all of the EU, except Germany, which impacted the ability of Mongolia to attract more European tourists. Adding virtually all of Europe, as well as Australia and New Zealand, is a sensible and long-overdue move.

Mongolia should consider adding these 23 countries to the visa-free list permanently as the decision in early 2023 only applies to 2023, 2024, and 2025. Mongolia should also consider further extending the visa-free list. India and the PRC still require visas but are important growth markets for Mongolia's tourism sector. In CAREC, Azerbaijan, Georgia, Pakistan, Tajikistan, and Turkmenistan are not visa-free. While these are small source markets, they have potential and Mongolia should consider adopting a visa-free policy for all CAREC countries in order to help facilitate improved connectivity and economic ties with other CAREC countries.

The number of airlines and aircraft may not be sustainable

Overall, the outbound market is larger than the inbound market and has so far recovered much faster, driving the resumption of growth in international passenger numbers in the first half of 2023. While there is potential to grow international tourism, the outbound market is likely to remain significantly larger as it is less seasonal. There are more outbound travelers in the summer than in the winter, but while there are very few visitors in the winter, the outbound travel continues as Mongolian residents look to escape the cold weather.

However, the outbound segment is also not that large given the relatively small size of the local population. While attracting transit traffic can help grow the overall market, the transit segment will likely be small and used mainly to help balance out the seasonality by attracting transit passengers (at a very low yield) during the off-peak months. Combined, the three segments of the market realistically do not justify five airlines.

Realistically, each international route can only support one or two Mongolian carriers. Even with Seoul, the market is not that large when factoring in a lot of the traffic transits beyond Seoul, which gives MIAT an advantage as it is the only Mongolian carrier that has partnerships with Korean carriers (as well as any foreign carriers).

Over the last 4 years, the number of local airlines has increased from three to five and the number of commercial aircraft registered in Mongolia has nearly doubled. While this indicates airlines are bullish on growth prospects, it is likely too much capacity given the small size of the market. Adding so many aircraft on the Mongolian registry in a short period also puts pressure on the Civil Aviation Authority of Mongolia (CAAM).

Mongolia has limited aviation resources, including aircraft inspectors, and could struggle to manage such a large fleet. Even with some of these aircraft operating overseas on wet-lease contracts, they need to be managed by Mongolian authorities as they are operating under the Mongolian registry. The pressure on CAAM, created by the rapid increase in the number of AOCs and aircraft, is particularly a concern as Mongolia is now in the process of securing a Category 1 safety rating from the US FAA.

CAAM needs more staff but has funding issues due to a significant reduction in overflight revenues the last 3 years because of the pandemic and Russia's war in Ukraine. The Russian invasion initially had an even bigger impact on overflight revenues, which are used to fund Mongolia's aviation authority, than the pandemic as airlines that stopped overflying the Russian Federation also stopped overflying Mongolia. The Mongolian government needs to make sure CAAM is sufficiently funded to manage the expansion in the local fleet and ensure international standards are met.

Aviation staffing is another potential concern as there is a limited pool of pilots, aircraft mechanics, and other aviation professionals in Mongolia. It takes time to recruit and train staff in these technical areas. As airlines add aircraft, the risk is that there are not enough workers with sufficient experience, which has safety and operational implications.

Mongolia should consider putting in place measures that tighten the process of adding aircraft and launching new airlines. While opening the airline sector to new entrants is beneficial, Mongolia should consider the potential ramifications of having more aircraft and more airlines than what is commercially viable.

Mongolia has limited domestic market consisting mainly of mining charter flights

Mongolian carriers combined flew only 1.14 million passengers in 2019, including 710,000 in the international market and 430,000 in the domestic market. Their traffic dropped to only 380,000 in 2020 and 150,000 in 2021 due to the pandemic before recovering 61% in 2022 to 690,000. International traffic was 50% recovered in 2022 with 356,000 passengers carried by Mongolian carriers, while domestic traffic was 77% recovered with 334,000 passengers. However, in the first half of 2023 international traffic was 112% recovered with 229,000 passengers carried by Mongolian carriers, while domestic traffic was 95% recovered with 188,000 passengers.

Mongolia's domestic market consists mainly of charter flights arranged by Rio Tinto to its Oyu Tolgoi mine. Most of Mongolia's airlines operate regular charters between Ulaanbaatar and Oyu Tolgoi Airport, which is owned and operated by Rio Tinto. Oyu Tolgoi traffic has fully recovered while scheduled traffic to government-owned domestic airports, which are operated by the Airports Authority of Mongolia, has declined significantly.

About 290,000 passengers were carried on the Ulaanbaatar–Oyu Tolgoi route in 2022, an increase of 6% compared to 2019. While most of these passengers are Mongolian citizens who live in Ulaanbaatar and work at the mine, there are also a significant volume of foreigners who work at the mine and use the domestic charters to connect with international flights at Ulaanbaatar.

The Ulaanbaatar–Oyu Tolgoi route accounted for 87% of all domestic passenger traffic in Mongolia in 2022 and 64% in 2019. There are about 10 regional airports in Mongolia with scheduled domestic flights, but some of these airports are not served year-round and most have very limited service (Table 29).

Khovd and Ulgii in western Mongolia are the largest of the government-owned domestic airports, both handling 24,000 passengers in 2019. Traffic at Khovd was at 46% of 2019 levels in 2022, while traffic at Ulgii was at only 41% of 2019 levels. Murun was the third-largest regional airport in 2019 with 17,000 passengers, but its traffic was at only 19% of 2019 levels in 2022.

Almost all the traffic at Murun consists of international tourists heading to nearby Lake Khovsgol in the summer. Korean tourists are the main source market for Lake Khovsgol but, as highlighted earlier in this section, the number of Korean tourists was significantly lower in summer of 2022 compared to summer of 2019. Improvements in the road between Ulaanbaatar and Murun also has impacted the demand for flights to Murun.

Dalanzadgad is another domestic airport that relies heavily on tourism as it is the gateway to the Gobi Desert. There were only 2,000 passengers on the Dalanzadgad–Ulaanbaatar route in 2022, which represents a recovery of only 15% compared to 2019 levels.

Khovd, Ulgii, and other airports in western Mongolia such as Ulaangoom do not rely significantly on tourism, which is relatively undeveloped in the western Mongolia although has a lot of potential. There is more local traffic at airports in western Mongolia as this region is very remote and far from Ulaanbaatar. There is also mining traffic in western Mongolia, which generally uses the scheduled flights although charters are

Table 29: Top 10 Domestic Routes in Mongolia Based on Passenger Traffic

Rank	Airport	2019	2022	Recovery Rate
1	Ulaanbaatar–Oyu Tolgoi	275,000	291,000	106%
2	Oyu Tolgoi–Dalanzadgad	27,000	0	N/A
3	Ulaanbaatar–Ulgii	24,000	10,000	42%
4	Ulaanbaatar–Khovd	24,000	11,000	46%
5	Ulaanbaatar–Murun	17,000	3,000	19%
6	Ulaanbaatar–Ulaangoom	15,000	1,000	10%
7	Ulaanbaatar–Ovoot	15,000	0	N/A
8	Ulaanbaatar–Dalanzadgad	13,000	2,000	15%
9	Ulaanbaatar–Altai	11,000	1,000	9%
10	Ulaanbaatar–Choibalsan	6,000	<1,000	2%
N/A	Ulaanbaatar–Tavan Tolgoi	0	7,000	N/A
N/A	Ulaanbaatar–Uliasti	3,000	5,000	149,000
	Others	2,000	1,000	N/A
	Total	433,000	334,000	77%

N/A = not applicable.
Notes: Ranking based on 2019 traffic, but routes that are in the top 10 in 2022 but were not in the top 10 in 2019 are included. There was no traffic between Oyu Tolgoi and Dalanzadgad in 2022; prior to 2022, there were charter flights on this route to shuttle mine workers who live in Dalanzadgad. Annual passenger traffic has been rounded to the nearest thousand.
Source: Author, based on data from National Statistics Office of Mongolia.

sometimes needed to shuttle workers. The airports in western Mongolia are all under the Airport Authority of Mongolia, while Oyu Tolgoi and Tavan Tolgoi are private airports serving mines in southern Mongolia.

A full recovery of international tourism is needed to support a full restoration of scheduled domestic traffic. International tourists frequently fly when traveling around Mongolia, while domestic tourists typically drive. Domestic flights are relatively expensive, and became more expensive in 2022 due to higher fuel prices, making them unaffordable for many families.

Families in Ulaanbaatar also prefer to drive when taking a domestic holiday and to have access to a car when they reach their destination as there are generally no car rental facilities at the domestic airports. Some individuals fly, particularly residents from smaller communities, heading to Ulaanbaatar for medical reasons, but this is a small segment. Government employees used to account for a large share of scheduled domestic passengers but during and since the pandemic, this type of travel has declined significantly due to budget cuts implemented by the government. However, government traffic will likely increase following the resumption of domestic flights from MIAT.

While the resurgence in government traffic and return of international tourists will lead to some additional traffic, the outlook on Mongolia's scheduled domestic air transport market is challenging. The charter market is an exception and the Ulaanbaatar–Oyu Tolgoi route will continue to be an important revenue generator for Mongolian carriers.

MIAT is the largest operator of the Ulaanbaatar–Oyu Tolgoi route, operating several 737 flights per day, but was not interested in the scheduled domestic market for many years. MIAT exited scheduled domestic services in 2008 and only private airlines, starting with Aero Mongolia, served the scheduled domestic market until the end of June 2023, when MIAT resumed scheduled flights following a shift in government policy.

MIAT is now operating two to three weekly flights on eight domestic routes using a wet-leased Bombardier CRJ200, and plans to operate these routes on its own once it acquires a regional jet. While the new domestic flights facilitate domestic travel, the government's decision to subsidize a new MIAT domestic operation is controversial as it creates an unlevel playing field with private carriers. Aero Mongolia and Hunnu Air are now competing with MIAT on all their domestic routes but are struggling as they are unable to match MIAT's subsidized fares, which are priced well below cost. It will be difficult for them to maintain domestic services year-round unless they start receiving the same subsidies.

Aero Mongolia and Hunnu both currently operate four domestic routes. Eznis is not interested in operating scheduled domestic services but is looking at launching charters on the Ulaanbaatar–Oyu Tolgoi route. Mongolia Airways also only has been operating charter flights in the domestic market since commencing operations in 2021.

The government for several years wanted the private airlines to operate more scheduled domestic flights and to reduce domestic airfares as this would improve access to smaller communities and facilitate tourism. However, the government did not provide any subsidies. The cost of operating domestic flights in Mongolia is very high and, without any subsidies, it is difficult for airlines to offer a low enough fare to stimulate demand. The LCC model is not an option for Mongolia's domestic market as size of the market is very small, even when factoring in potential growth under a lower-fare environment.

Mongolia should revisit its domestic aviation policy and consider new initiatives to reduce the cost of domestic flights. Trying to pressure domestic airlines to reduce fares without providing support, either from a financial or policy perspective, was unfair as the airlines operating in the domestic market were private companies.

Launching a subsidy scheme for domestic flights is not unusual in countries with remote communities where domestic connectivity is critical and most of the population cannot afford air travel. However, there are usually competitions to select airlines to operate under public service obligation schemes, and Mongolian should relook at how it can provide subsidized domestic services without creating an unlevel playing field.

Mongolia would benefit from new airport strategy and policies

Mongolia should also consider adopting a new domestic airport strategy to facilitate development of the domestic air transport market. Airport costs at Ulaanbaatar's new airport are too high to support growth in domestic flights, and domestic airlines are not able to use Ulaanbaatar's old airport, which have much cheaper costs. A potential new domestic airport strategy should look at options for reducing costs at Ulaanbaatar by reopening the old airport for domestic flights or introducing programs to reduce the cost of the new airport.

Ulaanbaatar's old airport continues to handle general aviation, including VIP flights, and host aircraft maintenance facilities, but the concession agreement for the new airport does not allow the old airport to handle commercial passenger or cargo flights.

Mongolian carriers have been advocating the old airport reopen for cargo and domestic passenger flights, which is sensible and should be considered although will be difficult to negotiate.

A new airport strategy should also look at new options for funding and expanding regional airports, which along with Ulaanbaatar's old airport are still under the Airport Authority of Mongolia. There are opportunities to grow traffic at domestic airports, but none of the airports are likely to reach traffic levels where they can be operated without government funding or subsidies or be able to attract any international flights. Mongolia is keen to upgrade or expand several regional airports and for some airports such as Murun, there are plans to add an international designation. However, attracting international flights to Murun or other secondary airports would be challenging. The potential volume of traffic, both domestic and international, is also likely insufficient to justify private sector investment.

MIAT Mongolian Airlines launched a new domestic operation, MIAT Regional, in July 2023 with eight routes using a Bombardier CRJ200 regional jet, marking the first time MIAT has had scheduled domestic services since 2008 (photo by MIAT).

Domestic flights and domestic airports will continue to be critical in providing access to remote areas for both residents and international tourists. However, strategies and policies are needed to ensure sufficient funding. As Mongolia revisits its domestic air transport strategy, it should start factoring in environmental and sustainability considerations. New technology such as small electric aircraft could be a game changer and facilitate tourism, including ecotourism, but support from both a financial and policy perspective will be required.

Mongolia also should revisit its strategy for the international market, particularly its airport strategy. High fees and charges at Ulaanbaatar's new airport are not only an issue impeding domestic growth; it is a major impediment to international growth, including LCC growth.

International passenger facility charges, which are added to all tickets, more than tripled when flights shifted to the new airport. Landing, aircraft parking, and ground handling fees, which the airlines pay directly, also increased significantly. The costs to rent offices and maintenance hangars are also much higher at the new airport, and airlines have incurred additional costs to transport crew to the new airport as it is much further from the city than the old airport. Refueling costs are also very high compared to other international airports. There is no competition for refueling and most other airport services, resulting in monopolies that in some cases are not being properly regulated.

The Mongolian government should consider policies to facilitate a reduction in fees and charges at the new airport. Aviation and airport authorities should also look at discounts and initiatives to support new routes. There are no discounts for new routes, which is common at other international airports, and some airlines are reluctant to expand due to airport-related cost issues. Mongolia needs to resolve this issue to meet long-term growth targets for both the aviation and tourism sectors. It will also be hard to develop transit traffic unless charges for airport-related services are reduced and become more competitive with other hub airports. Providing a more attractive operating environment for both local and foreign airlines is critical.

Mongolian carriers are eager to expand but under the current policies and fee structures, it will be very challenging for any significant expansion to be sustainable. It will also be difficult to attract more foreign airlines which are needed to improve international connectivity and increase competition, facilitating lower fares. For several years, Mongolia was only served by foreign airlines from four countries—the PRC, the Republic of Korea, the Russian Federation, and Türkiye. Foreign airlines flew only 482,000 passengers to or from Mongolia in 2019, accounting for 41% of the total international market. The foreign airline share was 42% in 2022 with 263,000 passengers carried.

Mongolia has liberalized to some extent over the last few years by permitting more flights from the Republic of Korea and Türkiye. However, access is still a major impediment, both for foreign- and privately owned local airlines, which can only be resolved with further liberalization or an open skies policy.

Pursuing further liberalization is feasible but tackling the airport cost issue will be challenging as the new international airport is operated by new private sector joint venture company under a 15-year concession agreement. The cost of canceling the concession agreement, which has been very unpopular with all the local airlines, would be steep. However, the Mongolian government should at least look at possible alternatives for operating and funding the new airport, including potential expansion.

New investment is required as the new airport's initial facilities are small. Both the passenger and cargo terminals are already congested during peak periods. In summer of 2022, there were operational issues and delays, including long wait times for delivery of bags, during peak morning hours. While the airport is relatively quiet most of the day and during the non-summer months, the size of the passenger terminal and number of gates are already insufficient for peak periods.

The government needs to start planning for the next phase of development to ensure the capacity is in place for future growth. As expansion options are examined with the joint venture company operating the new airport, it is critical that fees and costs to airlines are not increased further.

Mongolia's air transport market will never be that big, but has the potential to grow rapidly from the current small base. This growth could come from a combination of full-service airlines and LCCs. However, this growth cannot be achieved without the right policies and infrastructure. LCCs particularly will struggle to grow beyond its current very small presence in the Mongolian market without liberalization and supportive programs or policies.

Recommendations for Mongolia

1. Consider revisiting its domestic aviation policy and consider new initiatives to reduce the cost of domestic flights.
2. Consider reopening the Ulaanbaatar's domestic airport to scheduled domestic flights.
3. Find new options for funding and expanding regional airports.
4. Look at environmental and sustainability considerations in developing domestic air transport, including new technologies such as small electric aircraft.
5. Consider policies to facilitate a reduction in fees and charges at the new airport and look at introducing programs to incentivize the launch of new routes.
6. Adopt a new aviation strategy that provides a more favorable environment for airlines and aligns with its aspirations for tourism and air hub development.
7. Look at possible alternatives for operating and funding the new Ulaanbaatar airport, including potential expansion.
8. Plan for the next phase of development of the new Ulaanbaatar airport as it is already congested during peak periods.
9. Facilitate partnerships between MIAT and private airlines to improve the long-term viability of its airline sector and help Ulaanbaatar achieve its aspirations to become a hub airport.
10. Reconsider its strategy of pursuing US flights given the massive investment required to launch these flights and maintain them given their poor financial prospects.
11. Put in place measures that tighten the process of adding aircraft and launching new airlines.
12. Consider investing in training of aviation personnel, including mechanics and pilots, to ensure there is sufficient supply as airlines expand.
13. Look for new options to fund its aviation authority and ensure it is sufficiently staffed and has the resources to properly regulate local airlines as it expands despite the reduction in overflight revenues.
14. Consider further visa liberalization by extending the visa-free list to include all CAREC countries and India, as well as by making permanent the temporary extension of the visa-free list to include 21 European countries, Australia, and New Zealand.

CASE STUDY 6
Uzbekistan and Uzbekistan Express

Uzbekistan has experienced very rapid growth in LCC traffic in a very short period, driven by the launch of Uzbekistan Express and foreign LCC expansion. Further rapid growth is expected as more local LCCs launch and as foreign LCCs expand further with both benefiting from continued liberalization.

Uzbekistan started to liberalize its aviation sector less than 2 years prior to the pandemic with major reforms and new policies. The first phase of liberalization, which included separating Uzbekistan Airports from Uzbekistan Airlines in 2018 and ending the vertical structure that was still left from the Soviet era, led to rapid growth in passenger traffic. Liberalization has enabled a much healthier level of competition with a much larger group of foreign airlines now serving Uzbekistan, and the launch of privately owned airlines.

International passenger traffic in Uzbekistan increased by over 50% from 2017 to 2019. There was a full recovery in 2022 with traffic again above 2019 levels. International passenger traffic in 2023 will likely exceed 30% of 2019 levels.

There has been a significant increase in the LCC penetration rate, from a base of literally zero only 4 years ago. Flydubai became the first LCC to serve Uzbekistan in March 2019, when it launched services to Tashkent. LCCs accounted for a meager 1% of scheduled seat capacity in Uzbekistan 2019, with flydubai the only LCC. The LCC share of international seat capacity grew to 16% in 2022, including a 10% share for Uzbekistan Express and a 6% share for nine foreign LCCs. Overall, international seat capacity was 6% higher in 2022 compared to 2019, with the surge in LCC capacity offsetting an 8% decline in FSC capacity.

The international LCC penetration rate in Uzbekistan could reach 25% in 2023, which is remarkable given there was only one LCC route in the entire Uzbekistan market prior to the pandemic. In early 2023, LCCs already accounted for over 20% of international seat capacity in Uzbekistan. The foreign LCC share of the market reached 12% in January 2023, including a 4% share for market leader flydubai, while Uzbekistan Express' share was 11%.

Uzbekistan Express was Uzbekistan's first local low-cost carrier

Uzbekistan Express commenced operations in September 2021, becoming Uzbekistan's first local LCC. Uzbekistan Express currently links nine cities in Uzbekistan with Moscow Domodedovo Airport (based on its schedule for summer of 2023). It also serves several secondary cities in the Russian Federation from Tashkent and Namangan. In summer of 2023, Uzbekistan Express was operating 24 routes from nine cities in Uzbekistan to 12 destinations in the Russian Federation. It is not currently operating domestic services or to any country other than the Russian Federation.

Uzbekistan Express is similar to Buta Airways and FlyArystan in that it is a brand rather than a separate airline, using the AOC and IATA flight code of its parent. Uzbekistan Express has a fleet of four A320s that were transferred from parent Uzbekistan Airways and retrofitted into a 174-seat all-economy configuration.

Most of Uzbekistan Express' routes were also transferred from Uzbekistan Airways, which established the LCC brand to compete more effectively against Russian carriers on routes that consist mainly of price-sensitive labor traffic and have very little business class demand.

Uzbekistan Airways still carries more passengers to the Russian Federation than Uzbekistan Express, but most of Uzbekistan Airways' Russian Federation capacity are on the core Tashkent to Moscow and Saint Petersburg routes, which have premium demand.

The Russian Federation is the largest market for the Uzbekistan Airways Group, accounting for nearly 50% of its international seat capacity, and has generated strong profits since the start of Russia's war in Ukraine. There has been a large influx of Russian visitors to Uzbekistan, and the Uzbekistan Airways Group has also benefited from a large increase in transit traffic from the Russian Federation to Europe, which is high yielding due to the suspension of nonstop flights. Russian carriers have also benefited from the strong demand for Russian Federation–Uzbekistan services. Overall, Russian Federation–Uzbekistan capacity was above pre-COVID-19 levels in 2022 although the increase was roughly equal to the overall increase in capacity.

The Russian Federation accounted for about 52% of total international seat capacity in Uzbekistan in both 2019 and 2022. The Russian Federation share of total international seat capacity has declined slightly in 2023, but still accounted for a 44% share in summer of 2023. Uzbekistan–Russian Federation capacity was up almost 20% in summer of 2023 compared to summer 2019 levels, while overall Uzbekistan international seat capacity was up by almost 50% (according to OAG data).

Uzbekistan Express' share of the Uzbekistan–Russian Federation market is now about 23% with the full-service Uzbekistan Airways brand accounting for another 34%, giving the Uzbekistan Airways Group about a 57% share (based on OAG schedules for summer of 2023).

The LCC penetration rate in the Uzbekistan–Russian Federation market is about 25%. The only other LCCs in this market are Centrum Air, a new Uzbekistan-based LCC, and Aeroflot LCC subsidiary Pobeda. While Pobeda is the Russian Federation's only LCC, several Russian carriers are aggressive competitors in the Uzbekistan market, with particularly low fares prior to the Russian invasion. Uzbekistan Airways' decision prior to the pandemic to launch an LCC brand was primarily a response to low-fare competition from Russian carriers.

Foreign low-cost carriers expand rapidly, driving growth at several airports

As of the beginning of 2023, there were about 40 LCC routes in Uzbekistan, including about 25 Russian Federation routes from Uzbekistan Express (Table 30). While foreign airlines operate less than 40% of these routes, they accounted for over half of the LCC capacity in Uzbekistan as none of the Uzbekistan Express routes are served with more than four weekly frequencies. All top six LCC routes in Uzbekistan are operated by foreign airlines. Only four of the routes are served daily (at least seven frequencies per week).

Of the 13 foreign LCC routes that were operated in January 2023, 8 were launched within the previous 5 months (August 2022 to January 2023). This includes Namangan to Dubai, Kuwait, Muscat, and Sharjah; Tashkent to Abu Dhabi and Cairo; and Samarkand to Abu Dhabi and Dubai.

Another four foreign LCC routes have since been launched or relaunched, including Samarkand–Almaty (FlyArystan, twice per week resumed in March); Samarkand–Kuwait (Jazeera, twice per week launched in March); Tashkent–Ankara (AnadoluJet, once per week launched in April); and Tashkent–Astana (FlyArystan, twice per week launched in July). Flynas also has upgraded its Tashkent service to nonstop, eliminating the fuel stop in Baku.

The first scheduled LCC service to Asia was launched in September 2023, when India's IndiGo began four weekly flights on the Tashkent–Delhi route. Viet Nam's VietJet Air began serving Tashkent in late 2022 but so far has only operated charters (all the routes listed on Table 30 are scheduled services).

Uzbekistan Express has not added any new routes in 2023. Centrum Air has launched several routes since beginning operations in February 2023 but initially operated charters rather than scheduled services.

Namangan, Tashkent, and Samarkand are currently the only airports with foreign LCCs, although Pobeda briefly served Bukhara from Moscow in 2022. Uzbekistan Express is currently the only LCC with scheduled

Table 30: Low-Cost Carrier Routes in Uzbekistan Ranked by Weekly Frequency, January 2023

Route	Weekly Frequency	Airline
Tashkent–Kuwait	Up to 13	Jazeera Airways
Samarkand–Dubai	7	flydubai
Tashkent–Jeddah	7	flynas
Tashkent–Dubai	7	flydubai
Namangan–Kuwait	6	Jazeera Airways
Tashkent–Abu Dhabi	5	Air Arabia/Wizz Air
Bukhara–Moscow	4	Uzbekistan Express
Namangan–Dubai	4	flydubai
Namangan–Moscow	4	Uzbekistan Express
Samarkand–Moscow	4	Uzbekistan Express
Tashkent–Moscow	4	Uzbekistan Express
Tashkent–Sharjah	4	Air Arabia
Tashkent–Sochi	4	Uzbekistan Express
Fergana–Moscow	3	Uzbekistan Express
Namangan–Sharjah	3	Air Arabia
Samarkand–Abu Dhabi	3	Wizz Air
Urgench–Moscow	3	Uzbekistan Express
Namangan–Sochi	2	Uzbekistan Express
Tashkent–Kazan	2	Uzbekistan Express
Tashkent–Yekaterinburg	2	Uzbekistan Express
Fergana–Kazan	1	Uzbekistan Express
Karshi–Moscow	1	Uzbekistan Express
Namangan–Irkutsk	1	Uzbekistan Express
Namangan–Krasnoyarsk	1	Uzbekistan Express
Namangan–Muscat	1	SalamAir
Namangan–Omsk	1	Uzbekistan Express
Namangan–Orenburg	1	Uzbekistan Express
Namangan–Perm	1	Uzbekistan Express
Namangan–Samara	1	Uzbekistan Express
Namangan–Ufa	1	Uzbekistan Express
Namangan–Yekaterinburg	1	Uzbekistan Express
Navoi–Moscow	1	Uzbekistan Express
Nukus–Moscow	1	Uzbekistan Express
Tashkent–Krasnoyarsk	1	Uzbekistan Express
Tashkent–Mineralnye Vody	1	Uzbekistan Express
Tashkent–Muscat	1	SalamAir
Tashkent–Sharm El Sheik	1	flyEgypt
Tashkent–Ufa	1	Uzbekistan Express

Notes: Tashkent–Jeddah had a fuel stop in Baku (there are no fifth freedom rights to pick up or drop off passengers in Baku). Tashkent–Abu Dhabi is operated by both Air Arabia Abu Dhabi and Wizz Air Abu Dhabi. Tashkent–Sharm El Sheikh is operated on a Cairo–Tashkent–Sharm El Sheikh routing. Charter routes such as Tashkent–Cam Ranh, which was launched by VietJet in December 2022, are excluded.

Source: Author, based on data from OAG and other sources.

international services at Bukhara as well as Fergana, Karshi, Navoi, Nukus, and Urgench. However, it has only four or fewer flights per week at all seven of these airports.

Centrum Air has operated limited flights to Bukhara, Termez, and Urgench (in July 2023, it was operating one weekly flight from each airport to Moscow). Termez is not served by Uzbekistan Express.

Namangan and Tashkent are the two main hubs for Uzbekistan Express and have several foreign LCC routes. Namangan is a small airport, handling only about 300,000 passengers per annum, but has emerged as a major LCC airport with 15 LCC routes. It is currently served by four Middle Eastern LCCs and Uzbekistan Express, which has 11 routes to the Russian Federation. The frequencies are low—none of the 15 LCC routes are served daily and 12 are served with three or fewer flights per week. All four of the Middle East routes are also not served year-round. However, LCCs dominate, accounting for over 90% of international seat capacity on an annual basis. Kutaisi in Georgia is the only airport in CAREC with a higher LCC penetration rate than Namangan.

Samarkand is a much larger airport and is the second-largest city in Uzbekistan, but has only five LCC routes. Four of these routes launched in 2022 with FlyArystan commencing Almaty in March 2022, followed by Uzbekistan Express commencing Moscow in April, flydubai commencing Dubai in September, and Wizz Air Abu Dhabi commencing Abu Dhabi in December. The fifth route, a service from Kuwait from Jazeera Airways, launched in March 2023. FlyArystan suspended Almaty–Samarkand in September 2022 but relaunched the route in March 2023 with two weekly flights. Aeroflot LCC subsidiary Pobeda also began serving the Samarkand–Moscow route in April 2023 (Pobeda is operating to Samarkand from Moscow Vnukovo, while Uzbekistan Express links Samarkand with Moscow Domodedovo). Of Samarkand's five LCC routes, only three are currently operating year-round (Abu Dhabi, Dubai, and Moscow).

The LCC share of international seat capacity at Samarkand is about 30% on an annual basis. The Russian Federation dominates the Samarkand market with about 10 routes.

Tashkent has a lower LCC penetration rate (about 15%), but has twice as much LCC capacity as Namangan and more than three times as much LCC capacity as Samarkand. Tashkent is Uzbekistan Express' main base, but the LCC has almost as much capacity at Namangan and its market share at Namangan is much higher. Uzbekistan Express accounts for almost 70% of international seat capacity at Namangan, but only 5% at Tashkent (based on OAG schedules data for summer of 2023).

Foreign LCCs still have a relatively small presence at Tashkent. In summer of 2023, there were only six non-Russian Federation routes with regular LCC services (Abu Dhabi, Astana, Dubai, Jeddah, Kuwait, and Sharjah). There were several routes (including Ankara, Muscat, and Sharm El Sheikh) with very limited LCC services.

High airport costs and Tashkent access issues can dissuade LCCs

Tashkent would be able to attract more LCCs under a more liberal regime. Uzbekistan's open skies policy, which was adopted in 2019, only applies to secondary airports and excludes Tashkent. Several foreign airlines (both LCCs and FSCs) have continued to struggle to secure traffic rights to enter the Tashkent market or add frequencies to existing services.

High airport costs and charges at Tashkent also often dissuade potential new airlines, particularly LCCs. Ground handling and refueling costs are also very high. Some costs, charges and fees are higher for foreign airlines than local airlines, creating an unlevel playing field and further impacting the ability to attract airlines.

Uzbekistan Airports has been more proactive at developing new routes at Tashkent and has reduced some charges or fees since it was split from Uzbekistan Airways. It also has been working on creating separate companies for cargo handling and refueling, which should facilitate lower fees and charges in these key areas. However, there has not yet been a significant change to the airport's fee structure and airport charges in Uzbekistan are still much higher than international norms. Handling and refueling costs also remain high, due in part to aging equipment from the Soviet era that is expensive to maintain and is inefficient.

Uzbekistan Airports is now investing heavily in new ground handling equipment and modernizing airports, which should result in efficiency improvements. Airport and aviation authorities are confident costs will come down over time, but for airlines the changes are not occurring fast enough—or at all—and they are concerned about the continued lack of competition for services. Foreign airlines are attracted to the Tashkent market but often are dissuaded by the high costs, while new privately owned local airlines believe high costs and charges—and a lack of competition for services such as handling and refueling—pose a major impediment and risk. Uzbekistan Airways is also not happy with airport charges and ground handling fees. It took years for the flag carrier to complete its first contract with Uzbekistan Airports following their split; a deal was finally concluded in May 2022 with the airline believing the charges were too high although it is still paying less than other airlines.

For foreign airlines, there are also still access issues. Several foreign airlines have launched services to Tashkent over the last few years, but at least a few foreign airlines have still not succeeded at entering the market.

Uzbekistan is still reluctant to adopt open skies at Tashkent as it wants to provide an opportunity for local airlines to beef up their international operations without a flood of foreign airline capacity impacting their ability to survive. While over the years the reluctance to adopt an open skies policy was aimed at protecting Uzbekistan Airways, the current reluctance is more aimed at helping new airlines, which have launched recently or are now in the process of launching as the government has opened the local airline sector to new entrants and is encouraging private sector investment.

Samarkand Airport opened a modern new terminal in 2022 with ample capacity for growth and featuring the first business-class lounge and first duty-free shop outside Tashkent (photo by Brendan Sobie).

Uzbekistan has air service agreements with more than 50 countries and is working on new agreements to facilitate the launch of new services. For example, a new agreement with Hungary is planned, which would facilitate the potential launch of services from Budapest by Wizz Air. However, Uzbekistan has only one open skies agreement, with the US. No foreign airline has fifth freedom rights and there are no foreign airline bases (which requires seventh freedom rights) in Uzbekistan. There have been several requests for fifth freedom rights at Tashkent, but the government has denied these. While the open skies policy for secondary airports technically allows fifth freedom rights at all other airports, there has been no interest so far and there is no mechanism yet to award these rights.

Access is not an issue at other airports in Uzbekistan due to the more liberal policy providing unlimited third and fourth freedoms outside Tashkent. However, high airport fees and charges are also a major issue at secondary airports. Fees and charges are the same at all airports in Uzbekistan—and much higher than international norms—although demand is strongest at Tashkent.

Secondary airports typically have lower fees and charges than primary airports. Uzbekistan should reconsider its policies and programs to make sure its fees and charges at secondary airports, which it is keen to develop, are more reasonable.

Samarkand is Uzbekistan's first public-private partnership airport

Even Samarkand Airport has maintained the same fee structure and has not been offering discounts to new entrants since becoming the first public-private partnership (PPP) airport in Uzbekistan. Air Marakanda, a new joint venture company between Uzbekistan Airport and private sector investors, won Uzbekistan's first airport PPP contract in 2021, and took over management of the airport when a new passenger terminal opened in early 2022.

Air Marakanda was able attract several new foreign airlines in 2022 and early 2023, including AZAL Azerbaijan Airlines, FlyArystan, flydubai, Jazeera, and Wizz Air Abu Dhabi. While these route development successes are noteworthy, the AZAL, FlyArystan, and Jazeera services have not operated consistently, with all three suspended during the peak summer months of 2023. Air Marakanda needs to become more aggressive by offering discounts and other schemes to fully leverage Samarkand's potential.

Samarkand's new modern terminal has capacity to handle 2 million passenger per annum and 1,000 passengers per hour. But the airport is currently operating at less than half its capacity with about 500,000 passengers handled in 2022. Most flights are in the early morning or night, leaving several hours during the day where the new asset is not utilized or has just one flight.

Samarkand is a United Nations Educational, Scientific and Cultural Organization (UNESCO) heritage site and an increasingly popular tourist destination with potential to generate over 1 million passengers within the next couple of years, and over 2 million passengers within the next several years. LCCs should be a major component of the airport's strategy given the Samarkand market consist mainly of price-sensitive travelers. Several more LCC routes to the Middle East are feasible, particularly to Saudi Arabia. There is also an opportunity to attract LCCs from Europe and Asia with the right policies and programs.

Samarkand Airport is keen to reduce its reliance on the Russian Federation. However, as most of Samarkand's non-Russian Federation markets consist primarily of inbound tourists, it needs to be competitive with tourist destinations in other countries. The airport now provides an attractive entry point for tourists entering Uzbekistan given its modern terminal and its location near the center of historic city that serves as a gateway to the Silk Road. Samarkand Airport amenities include the first immigration e-gates in Uzbekistan, as well as the second duty-free shop and the second lounge after Tashkent Airport. Prior to the opening of the new terminal Samarkand Airport had very basic amenities, which is still the case with all other airports in secondary cities.

Air Marakanda has been working on boosting non-aeronautical revenues, which were virtually zero in the old terminal and now account for about 20% of total revenues. This should help the airport offer more competitive charges and fees but so far it has not offered any discounts. Samarkand will need to become more aggressive to achieve its ambitious growth targets and fully utilize its new terminal. It needs to be particularly aggressive at attracting LCCs during daytime hours, when the airport is now generally empty.

Tashkent will benefit from new terminal and, eventually, a new airport

Samarkand is currently the only airport in Uzbekistan that does not have infrastructure constraints, giving it an advantage. However, this is about to change as Uzbekistan has a massive airport modernization and program that includes $1 billion in upgrades to existing airports by 2024.

Tashkent's current terminal is outdated and congested. Uzbekistan Airports is in the process of expanding and modernizing the current passenger terminal, increasing capacity to 12 million passenger per annum and up to 2,400 passengers per hour.

A new much larger airport is also planned for outside Tashkent which would open by 2030, at which point the existing airport could again be at capacity. Tashkent needs a new airport as the existing airport is near the center of the city and does not have the space to expand further.

Tashkent Airport handled about 5 million passengers in 2022, while all of Uzbekistan's airports handled nearly 8 million passengers, with both figures higher than 2019. Uzbekistan Airports expects average annual growth of 17% over the next several years, with traffic exceeding 9 million passengers in 2023. Uzbekistan is aggressively investing in airport capacity, confident of very rapid growth over the long term driven by both local and in future more transit traffic, which currently only accounts for about 10% of total traffic.

Tashkent will need to become more aggressive at attracting new routes and airlines once the new infrastructure comes online. It would be sensible to focus on LCCs with both the near-term expansion of the existing airport and the development of the new airport. An LCC terminal could be considered for the new airport and potentially the old airport by repurposing some of the existing space.

Silk Avia launched services in April 2023, operating an initial fleet of three ATR 72-600s on domestic routes (photo courtesy of ATR).

A new airport is planned for Fergana Valley under a public-private partnership

There are also infrastructure constraints in the Fergana Valley, which Uzbekistan Airports aims to resolve by developing a new airport. Uzbekistan Airports expects the new airports in Fergana Valley and Tashkent will cost a combined $2.5 billion to develop. It plans to pursue PPP options for both airports with a tender process that is slated to begin in late-2023.

The new Fergana Valley Airport is slated to open by 2026 and replace the existing airports at Andijan, Fergana, and Namangan, which are all located within 100 km of each other and have outdated infrastructure. It would also be sensible for Uzbekistan Airports to consider an LCC terminal for the new Fergana Valley Airport given the Fergana market consists mainly of price-sensitive labor traffic. While the Fergana Valley is not a popular tourist destination, it has a large population. Andijan, Fergana, and Namangan are all among the six largest cities in Uzbekistan.

There are many Uzbeks from the Fergana Valley that work abroad, particularly in the Russian Federation and the Middle East. This segment of the market has driven the recent LCC expansion at Namangan. While technically Andijan and Fergana airports also are under the open skies policy, Uzbekistan Airports has focused the LCC growth in Fergana Valley at Namangan due to constraints at Andijan and Fergana. Andijan has particularly poor infrastructure and, prior to its temporary closure in April 2023, was only served by Uzbekistan Airways with flights to Moscow and Tashkent.

Fergana Airport is bigger but also has limited infrastructure and is congested. It is currently served by several Russian carriers and Turkish Airlines. AZAL Azerbaijan Airlines launched a weekly service from Baku in December 2022, but this service was suspended in May 2023. Baku was the only link in 2023 between the Fergana Valley and other CAREC countries although there were temporarily services from Namangan to Almaty in 2022 that were operated by FlyArystan, SCAT, and Uzbekistan Express, taking advantage of demand for flights during a period the land border was still closed or had limitations.

Uzbekistan Express developed its Fergana Valley mini-hub at Namangan due to congestion at Fergana and the poor condition of the infrastructure at Andijan. Uzbekistan Express does not serve Andijan and is currently (based on summer 2023 schedules) only operating one international routes (Moscow) from Fergana.

Namangan could experience further LCC expansion until the opening of the new Fergana Valley Airport. But there are also infrastructure constraints at Namangan and the high charges could dissuade some LCCs.

The new Fergana Valley Airport represents an opportunity for Uzbekistan to develop LCCs in a region that has massive LCC potential. In addition to serving the Uzbek population in the Fergana Valley, the new airport can also attract passengers from nearby communities in the Kyrgyz Republic and Tajikistan, which are relatively underserved and have growth potential particularly with LCC stimulation. Uzbekistan Airports expects the new airport in the Fergana Valley will have a catchment area of 15 million, which would represent the largest airport catchment area in Central Asia and is an indication of how populated the Fergana Valley is compared to other parts of Central Asia.

As it looks at PPP options for the Fergana Valley, Uzbekistan Airports should look at bringing in international airport investors with LCC experience. While over the last year Namangan and Samarkand have had some success at attracting LCCs, a more LCC-focused strategy will be needed to fully leverage the LCC potential of the Fergana Valley and Samarkand markets. So far, what has been achieved is essentially the low-hanging fruit. As these markets were so underserved it was feasible to attract some LCCs despite high airports costs. However, there is a limit to how much traffic can be generated under the current high-cost regime.

Bukhara and Urgench will benefit from airport public-private partnerships

International airport investors with LCC experience could also help develop other markets, including Bukhara and Urgench. These two airports are next on the Uzbekistan Airports list for PPP, with a tender process that is slated to start in 2023. Uzbekistan was considering combining the management of both airports in a single contract, but is now planning two separate tenders to encourage competition. Each airport is small with less than 400,000 passengers per annum, but has significant growth potential which could attract private sector investment.

New terminals for Bukhara and Urgench are planned as part of the PPP tender, following the model that was initially used for Samarkand. Bukhara and Urgench have similar, albeit smaller markets as Samarkand. All three airports are popular tourist destinations along the Silk Road. Uzbekistan Airports plans to focus Bukhara and Urgench on the inbound tourist segment and recognizes LCCs will drive most of their future growth.

The privatization and expansion of the airports at Bukhara, Samarkand, and Urgench are important components of an overall push in Uzbekistan to significantly boost international tourism. Tourism authorities are targeting nearly 12 million international visitors in 2027, up from nearly 7 million prior to the pandemic (including visitors by land). Visitor numbers recovered in the second half of 2022, driven by a large increase from the Russian Federation, but were still down for the overall year due to a weaker first half. Overall visitor numbers are expected to return to 2019 levels in 2023.

Visa reform has led to rapid growth in tourism but further reform is needed

Visitor numbers more than tripled from 2016 to 2019, driven by visa reform and facilitated by aviation reform as airline capacity increased significantly from key source markets. Uzbekistan now has about 100 countries on its visa-free list, with e-visas available for more than 50 additional countries. It is important for Uzbekistan to continue to liberalize its visa policy by providing visa-free entry for countries where e-visas are now required and countries that still require paper-based visa.

E-visas dissuade some travelers as they have a small cost and can be tedious, while markets with paper-based visas are very hard to develop. Pakistan is an example of a country that is not on either the visa-free or e-visa list.

This is impacting demand and dissuading airlines from serving this key intra-CAREC market. Uzbekistan Airways served Lahore prior to the pandemic but is not currently operating any flights to Pakistan as it believes this market, which consists mainly of inbound travelers, cannot be commercially viable without a change in the visa regime. Pakistan could become a major source market for Uzbekistan given their cultural and religious ties. There are several potential Uzbekistan–Pakistan routes, including from Samarkand, Bukhara, and Urgench, but these are only possible with the right policies.

While visas continue to be an impediment in some source markets such as Pakistan, the biggest barrier to visitor growth identified by tourism authorities are insufficient airline competition and capacity, which is contributing to high fares. Tourism authorities are particularly concerned about airfares, which are higher than competing destinations, making it hard to attract visitors. The high fares are due in part to the lack of competition and airline capacity, but tourism authorities also believe high airport costs are contributing to the high fares.

Tourism authorities have been pushing to reduce airport costs and have submitted several proposals aimed at facilitating lower costs and airfares. For example, they have been proposing the elimination of a 14% tax on aviation fuel.

Tourism authorities have also been working with aviation and airport authorities to attract foreign airlines. Uzbekistan has held several conferences to try to address the issues impeding tourism growth. All these efforts need to be stepped up for Uzbekistan to meet its tourism and aviation goals.

There are several potential new source markets that can be tapped with the right programs, policies, and initiatives. Southeast Asia is a market of particular interest and authorities are keen to attract scheduled services from Southeast Asian carriers. Malaysia Airlines and VietJet Air, an LCC from Viet Nam, have operated some charter flights to Uzbekistan over the last year. Batik Air Malaysia planned to launch flights to Tashkent by the end of 2023, although this is also more like a charter service with agents pre-committing to almost all the seats.

Attracting more scheduled services from European carriers is also a priority, including LOT Polish Airlines, which launched a charter service in March 2023 and is planning to launch scheduled services to Tashkent in February 2024.

A large portion of international visitors enter by land and Uzbekistan also has a fast-growing domestic tourism sector, which now consists of about 10 million visitors per year. However, international visitors entering by air account for the largest portion for visitor spend and growth in this segment is crucial for the economy, particularly in regions such as Samarkand, Buhkhara, and Urgench/Khiva.

International visitors accounted for about 30% of international passenger traffic in Uzbekistan prior to the pandemic and this could reach or even exceed 50% over the next several years given the strong interest globally in Uzbekistan as a destination. Uzbekistan has noticed the success of Georgia, which had the fastest aviation and tourism growth in CAREC in the decade prior to the pandemic. Uzbekistan is well placed to become the fastest-growing aviation and tourism market in CAREC in the post-pandemic era.

Most international tourists now enter Uzbekistan at Tashkent, but there is potential to attract more tourists to enter at Bukhara, Samarkand, and Urgench given these are the most popular destinations. Urgench has been able to attract some European visitors as part of a stopover program from Uzbekistan Airways, which in the summer season routes some of its European flights via Urgench on a one-way basis. In summer of 2023, it operated some flights to Urgench from Milan and Paris. These flights enable visitors to start or end their Uzbekistan holiday at Khiva, which is more convenient than having to fly out of Tashkent at both the ends of the holiday given Urgench's location in western Uzbekistan. However, this traffic is limited and there is an opportunity for Urgench to attract more regular flights to and from Europe.

Urgench also has an opportunity to attract more flights within CAREC following the launch in January 2023 of a weekly service from Baku, its first CAREC link, by AZAL Azerbaijan Airlines. This route did not operate in June and July but resumed in early August 2023.

Except for the seasonal one-way Europe flights and the one weekly flight from Baku, Urgench is only currently linked with Istanbul and several Russian Federation destinations. Bukhara also has a limited network, with international flights only to the Russian Federation and Istanbul. Similar to Urgench, Bukhara has the potential to attract flights from Europe, the GCC, and CAREC.

Bukhara is a UNESCO heritage site, while Urgench is the gateway to Khiva, another UNESCO heritage site. Tourists visiting Uzbekistan often combine Bukhara, Khiva, and Samarkand. There is now a high speed train connecting Bhukhara with Samarkand as well as Samarkand with Tashkent. An extension of this train line from Bhukahra to Khiva/Urgench is slated to open in 2024, reducing travel time from Bukhara to Khiva to 3 hours. The train already connects Tashkent with Samarkand in 2 hours, and Samarkand with Bukhara in 1.5 hours. The airports at Bukhara, Urgench, and Samarkand will therefore essentially compete for the same international tourist traffic. Uzbekistan is hoping this competition will be beneficial to consumers and the tourism sector.

There is also an airport at Navoi, located between Bukhara and Samarkand. Navoi currently has limited passenger services to Moscow and Tashkent. It would be sensible to close Navoi's outdated passenger terminal and focus this airport on cargo as it already has the largest cargo terminal in Uzbekistan.

There are 11 airports in Uzbekistan that have scheduled services in 2023: Andizhan, Bukhara, Fergana, Karshi, Namangan, Navoi, Nukus, Samarkand, Urgench, Tashkent, and Termez. All these airports have both domestic and international flights. For all the airports, except Samarkand, the current condition of the infrastructure is poor (Andizhan Airport, which serves the city of Andijan, has been temporarily closed since April 2023).

Consolidation of the portfolio and focusing on fewer airports with new modern terminals is sensible. The closure of the passenger terminals at Andizhan, Fergana, Navoi, and Namangan would still leave nine airports with commercial passenger flights when factoring in the new Fergana Valley Airport and Muynak, an airport that was recently reopened after a modernization and renovation project and is expected to start attracting regularly scheduled services.

Muynak is the gateway to the Aral Sea, a remote region in the far western region of Uzbekistan with tourism potential. The government has been investing in improving the tourism infrastructure in the Aral Sea region as well as other remote areas such as Zaamin, a remote mountainous region in the east. Road and hotel construction is occurring at a fast pace throughout the country to facilitate tourism growth. While there has and will continue to be significant road access improvements, the government believes domestic aviation also needs to be developed given the large size of the country.

Domestic market captures new attention with the launch of Silk Avia

Muynak and several of Uzbekistan's smaller airports could experience a surge in domestic traffic as new local airlines launch services. There are several new airlines in Uzbekistan that have recently launched or are now planning to launch services, following a mix of models. One of the new airlines, Silk Avia, is focusing on domestic services using turboprop aircraft. Other proposed new airlines are intending to operate a mix of domestic and international services using jet aircraft.

Until the launch of Silk Avia in April 2023, domestic services were predominantly operated by Uzbekistan Airways. However, the flag carrier has not been focusing on the domestic market in recent years, particularly since phasing out turboprop aircraft in 2018. Uzbekistan Airways has since operated a low-frequency domestic schedule using larger aircraft that are more suitable for international flights. Most of its domestic flights are geared around its international schedule and used to reposition aircraft to support an international flight at a secondary airport, often at a time that is not convenient for most domestic travelers. Uzbekistan Airways' domestic schedule is therefore irregular, with different flight times depending on the day and often in the early hours of the morning.

Uzbekistan Express, Centrum Air, Panaroma Airways, and Qanot Sharq Airlines also have operated a small number of domestic flights that are generally used to reposition aircraft to a secondary airport for an international flight. (Uzbekistan Express and Panorama Airways did not have any domestic services in their summer 2023 schedule, but operated a limited number of domestic flights earlier in the year.)

Uzbekistan Airports decided in 2021 to establish Silk Avia as it believes there is an opportunity to drive significant domestic growth across its airport portfolio by providing more frequent domestic flights and more domestic routes. Silk Avia commenced operations in late April 2023 following a regional LCC model. In its first month of operation, Silk Avia launched flights to eight airports across Uzbekistan and operated 10 routes using an initial fleet of three 70-seat ATR 72-600 turboprops. As of July 2023, Silk Avia was operating 12 routes with a total of 31 weekly return flights.

Silk Avia has ambitions to operate around 40 domestic routes and has announced plans to add another five ATR 72-600s as well as two smaller ATR 42-600s. It expects to receive two of the additional ATR 72-600s in Q4 2023.

Uzbekistan Airports expects Silk Avia to operate a high-frequency bus-like service with 10 or more daily flights on the main routes. The high-frequency schedule will facilitate same-day business trips, which has not been possible previously because of Uzbekistan Airways' limited domestic schedule. In its first few months of operations, Silk Avia also had a low-frequency schedule with a less than daily service on all routes due to its small initial fleet, but more frequencies are expected across all its routes as it expands its fleet.

A high-frequency domestic schedule will also support tourism by providing more options for international visitors to travel around Uzbekistan and stimulate domestic tourists to travel more often. Domestic and international tourism is expected to continue growing rapidly over the next several years, but domestic connectivity is a major obstacle due to the current small number of domestic flights and the lack of available seats on the high-speed train network.

Silk Avia's planned network includes all Uzbekistan airports, and includes trunk routes from Tashkent as well as about 30 point-to-point routes bypassing Tashkent. The airline is based in Tashkent and plans to have aircraft based at both Tashkent and Samarkand, where several point-to-point routes not previously served will be launched.

Currently in Uzbekistan, there are nine domestic trunk routes from Tashkent and only a few point-to-point domestic routes bypassing Tashkent. Prior to Silk Avia's launch, only five of these routes were served daily and none were served with more than two daily flights. Prior to launching Silk Avia, Uzbekistan Airports believed demand for domestic air travel in Uzbekistan was four times higher than capacity, and demand will grow significantly with the right schedule. Domestic traffic in Uzbekistan is currently about 1 million passengers per annum.

Uzbekistan Airways has been eager for several years to drop domestic services entirely as they are unprofitable. It was originally intending to stick with an all-jet fleet and let Silk Avia focus on smaller aircraft and the domestic market. However, Uzbekistan Airways announced in June 2023 the acquisition of at least two and up to four Let L-410 turboprops, which have only 19 seats. The first L-410 was delivered in July 2023 and a second aircraft was delivered in August 2023. Uzbekistan Airways is initially using the L-410 to operate routes that it also serves with A320s, including Tashkent to Fergana and Samarkand. However, it is planning to use the new type to launch domestic services to smaller airports that do not currently have any commercial service, including Shakhrisabz, Zaamin and Zarafshan.

Domestic airfares are very low and are regulated by the government. There are opportunities to stimulate domestic growth, particularly with smaller and more efficient aircraft. An LCC model makes sense for Uzbekistan's domestic market as domestic travelers are very price sensitive. However, it will be very difficult for any airline in Uzbekistan to be profitable in the domestic market given the low fares airlines are now required to offer on all domestic routes. It is unlikely Uzbekistan will stop regulating domestic fares as it views domestic air transport as a social service. Even if airfare regulations are dropped and airlines can charge domestic airfares that would be sufficient to cover their costs, this would likely result in a drop in demand as domestic travelers are very price sensitive.

For example, the one-way airfare from Tashkent and Nukus or Urgench is now only about $35. Without any subsidy, the fare would need to more than double and perhaps triple, which Uzbekistan authorities believe would be unaffordable for most local travelers. The government has expanded the domestic airfare subsidy program to support Silk Avia. While Uzbekistan Airports expects Silk Avia can be profitable once its fleet size reaches six aircraft, it seems unlikely that profitability can be achieved without government subsidies. The new Uzbekistan Airways small turboprop operation will also require significant subsidies.

Competition with trains is intensifying

Trains compete on virtually all the domestic routes in Uzbekistan and train services are continuing to improve, resulting in shorter travel times. Some of the domestic air routes from Tashkent already compete with trains that take only a few hours, with tickets that are very cheap. Train competition will increase as Uzbekistan's electric high-speed train network expands and as more trains are acquired. Uzbekistan may need to rethink its domestic aviation strategy, particularly given the increased global focus on sustainability, which is leading many countries to reduce or even eliminate domestic flights.

As mentioned earlier in this section, Uzbekistan is now working on an extension of the high-speed line from Bukhara to Urgench that is slated to open in 2024. Uzbekistan also recently announced plans to further extend the line from Urgench to Nukus. This will result in Tashkent–Urgench train times reducing from 14 to 6 hours, and Tashkent–Nukus from 16 to 7 hours. These are now the two biggest domestic air routes in Uzbekistan, with an average of two return flights per day on each route. While some passengers will continue to fly, it could be hard to stimulate growth given the availability of faster trains.

Table 31: Domestic routes in Uzbekistan Ranked by Weekly Frequency (Prior to Silk Avia Launch)

Route	Frequency	Airline	Train Time
Tashkent–Urgench	14	Uzbekistan Airways	6 hours
Tashkent–Nukus	13	Uzbekistan Airways	7 hours
Tashkent–Bukhara	9	Uzbekistan Airways, Qanot Sharq[a]	4 hours
Tashkent–Fergana	9	Uzbekistan Airways, Uzbekistan Express[a] Qanot Sharq[a]	5 hours
Tashkent–Termez	8	Uzbekistan Airways	14 hours
Tashkent–Samarkand	5	Uzbekistan Airways, Qanot Sharq[a]	2 hours
Tashkent–Andizhan	2	Uzbekistan Airways	6 hours
Tashkent–Karshi	2	Uzbekistan Airways	3 hours
Tashkent–Namangan	2	Uzbekistan Airways	5 hours
Andizhan–Samarkand	2	Uzbekistan Airways	N/A
Bukhara–Namangan	2	Uzbekistan Airways	N/A
Fergana–Urgench	2	Uzbekistan Airways	N/A
Fergana–Samarkand	2	Uzbekistan Airways	N/A
Namangan–Samarkand	2	Uzbekistan Airways	N/A

N/A = not applicable.
[a] Qanot Sharq and Uzbekistan Express had just one weekly frequency, with Uzbekistan Airways operating the other flights.
Notes: Frequency of flights based on January 2023 schedule. Train times are approximate. Train time for Nukus and Urgench based on completion of high-speed train line.
Source: Author, based on OAG schedules data.

Silk Avia is also now operating most of the routes mentioned on Table 31 but with less than daily frequencies. In July 2023, Silk Avia was serving Tashkent–Termez with five weekly flights; Tashkent–Bukhara and Tashkent–Samarkand with four weekly flights; Tashkent–Karshi, Tashkent–Nukus, and Tashkent–Fergana with three weekly flights; and Tashkent–Namangan and Tashkent–Urgench with two weekly nonstop flights (with several one-stop flights to Urgench available via Bukhara and Samarkand). Silk Avia had not yet launched services to Andizhan as Andizhan was temporarily closed for renovation a few weeks prior to Silk Avia commencing operations.

Point-to-point domestic routes could offer more potential as the train network is Tashkent focused. However, how much demand there will be for point-to-point routes that have never been served previously is unclear.

It is questionable whether there will be sufficient domestic demand overall to support a domestic-focused airline such as Silk Avia. Silk Avia plans to initially serve only the domestic market and while some regional international services are possible at a later stage, the focus will be on the domestic market as the number of international routes will be limited due to the range of the ATR (SilkAvia so far has operated some international charter flights).

Several new local airlines have launched recently or are planning to launch

The establishment of Silk Avia was also controversial as it is owned by Uzbekistan Airports and therefore contradicts the reforms from a few years ago which resulted in Uzbekistan Airways separating from

Uzbekistan Airports. A second airport-owned airline, Air Samarkand, is also planning to launch services in 2023.

The owners of Samarkand Airport plan to use Air Samarkand to expand and diversify Samarkand's international network, reducing the airport's reliance on the Russian Federation. The airline was initially also branded Air Marakanda, but the owners subsequently decided to have the Air Marakanda brand for the airport company and use a separate brand, Air Samarkand, for the airline.

Airports in most countries are not allowed to own airlines as it is a conflict of interest. The launch of Silk Avia by a government company also sends the wrong message to the private sector, which is being encouraged to establish new airlines.

Uzbekistan Airports decided to invest in a domestic airline as Uzbekistan Airways was not interested in domestic expansion and it did not believe any of the new privately owned airlines would have a significant domestic operation. However, some privately owned airlines have expressed interest in the domestic market and Uzbekistan Airways also now seems to have a renewed domestic interest following its acquisition of small turboprop aircraft.

Uzbekistan Airports is keen to sell Silk Avia to private investors in future and has already been in talks with potential private sector investors. However, it is prepared to take all the risk in the initial phase as it saw this as the only option for developing the domestic market, which it believes is critical for the development of Uzbekistan's airports and the overall economy, particularly the tourism sector.

Uzbekistan's first privately owned airline, Qanot Sharq, is not interested in the domestic market. Qanot Sharq launched in 2021 and currently operates 10 international and 3 domestic international routes (as of summer of 2023) with a fleet of four A320 family aircraft. The three domestic routes are only operated once per week and are used to reposition aircraft, which are all based in Tashkent, to support international services from Bukhara, Fergana, and Samarkand. These are the only airports in Uzbekistan that Qanot Shark currently serves, with Tashkent accounting for about 50% of its capacity (based on summer 2023 schedules).

Air Samarkand also plans to focus on the international market. It has ambitions to operate 14 international routes, all from Samarkand, with a fleet of several A320s and, potentially, A330s. Saudi Arabia and the Republic of Korea are two of the target markets along with several potential countries in Europe and Southeast Asia. Istanbul is also possible as the current Samarkand–Istanbul flights, which are operated by Turkish Airlines, Qanot Sharq and Uzbekistan Airways, are often full.

However, other private sector start-up airlines have more of a domestic focus. Some are concerned with the launch of another government-owned airline and believe the government subsidy scheme that has been expanded to support Silk Avia should have instead been offered on a tender basis to private airlines. Some of Uzbekistan's private airlines would also like the opportunity to bid for subsidized domestic services to smaller communities that will be operated by Uzbekistan Airways with its new fleet of up to four L-410 turboprops.

Overall, Uzbekistan could see the launch of up to five new scheduled airlines in 2023. This is a significant development given that there were only three airlines operating scheduled commercial flights in 2022—Qanot Sharq, Uzbekistan Airways, and Uzbekistan Express—and in some respects only two given that Uzbekistan Express operates as a brand using the Uzbekistan Airways AOC.

The first of the new airlines, Panorama Airways, began operating charter flights in late December 2022. It initially operated domestic and Russian Federation charter flights, but in summer of 2023 was operating charters to Israel and Saudi Arabia. As of September 2023, Panorama was still a very small airline operating just one 144-seat A320. However, it has expansion plans and is expected to begin operating scheduled flights in both the domestic and international markets in 2023. The Republic of Korea and the UAE are part of Panorama's network plan, In addition to Israel, the Russian Federation, and Saudi Arabia.

Panorama has a full-service product while the other two new start-ups, Centrum Air and Silk Avia, operate under an LCC model with higher-density aircraft. Another new airline, Humo Air, also plans to follow the LCC model, potentially resulting in four local LCCs competing in the Uzbekistan market by the end of 2023, when also including Uzbekistan Express.

Centrum Air began operating charter flights in February 2023 using A320s and 737s wet leased from a foreign airline. It began operating three A320s on its own in summer of 2023 and has plans for expanding its fleet.

Centrum Air made bold statements after receiving its first aircraft, claiming it will have 20 aircraft by the end of 2023 and 100 aircraft by the end of 2026, which would make it by far the largest airline in Uzbekistan. However, little is known about its network, business model, or business plan.

As of September 2023, two of Centrum's initial fleet of three A320s were operating from Kuwait on a wet-lease contract for Jazeera Airways, while the third aircraft was operating low-frequency services from five Uzbekistan airports. Routes operated in summer of 2023 included Bukhara, Termez, and Urgench to Moscow, as well Tashkent to Novosibirsk. Non-Russian Federation routes have so far included Tashkent to Almaty in Kazakhstan, Issyk-Kul in the Kyrgyz Republic, Hurghada and Sharm El Sheikh in Egypt, Ras Al Khaimah in the UAE, and Tbilisi in Georgia. The non-Russian Federation flights are generally sold as charters.

Centrum Air was also operating limited domestic flights in summer 2023, primarily to reposition aircraft for international flights from secondary cities. Centrum Air is part of the same company and shares an AOC with cargo airline My Freighter, which took delivery of its first aircraft, a 747-200F, in late 2022.

Humo Air is also planning to add narrow-body jets (A320s of 737s) in single-class high-density configuration to support the launch of scheduled services. Humo was initially established in 2020 and so far has only been operating Antonov An-2s, a very small single-engine aircraft that it uses for agriculture, cargo, and 12-seat passenger flights. Humo started as a government-owned entity but in late 2022 secured a foreign investor to support its new business plan, which includes upgrading its AOC to support regular flights and larger aircraft. However, it appears the deal with the foreign investor was not completed and Humo's future is now uncertain.

Humo has been working on starting a scheduled passenger airline since 2018, when it became the first company to be selected under Uzbekistan's new liberal aviation policy that ended Uzbekistan Airways' monopoly. Humo initially planned to add ATR 72s in 2020 as part of a domestic LCC business plan, but scrapped the acquisition of six ATRs and delayed the establishment of a scheduled airline due to the pandemic.

Qanot Sharq also applied to launch a passenger airline soon after the new policy opening the market to new entrants was adopted in 2018. In 2021, Qanot Sharq overtook Humo to become the second airline after Uzbekistan Airways to successfully launch commercial passenger flights.

Qanot Sharq originally launched in 2003 as a cargo airline operating Ilyushin Il-76 freighters. The company also started a passenger charter business at about the same time and was always interested at operating passenger aircraft. However, it was only permitted to offer charters using passenger aircraft operated by other airlines. Qanot Sharq stopped operating freighters in 2010 and did not have an active AOC for several years, but finally was able to pursue a passenger airline AOC following the policy change in 2018.

Qanot Sharq is considered a full-service airline as it provides free meals and checked baggage. However, all its aircraft are in single-class high-density configuration like an LCC. Qanot Sharq is a low-fare competitor and provides a product with similar fares as Uzbekistan Express.

Qanot Sharq started with two 174-seat A320s when it commenced services in August 2021. Two 240-seat A321LRs were added in late 2022. While it is now only offering passenger services, it has been considering A330 freighters.

Qanot Sharq started with charter services to the Russian Federation and the UAE. It was able to upgrade its Russian Federation services to scheduled services in early 2022. It currently only serves two Russian destinations, Moscow and Saint Petersburg, and has struggled to secure additional Uzbekistan–Russian Federation traffic rights.

Qanot Sharq currently also operates services to Hungary, Israel, Saudi Arabia, Thailand, Türkiye, and Viet Nam, and is keen to further diversify its network. All its non-Russian Federation routes are low frequency (three weekly flights or less), and most are seasonal charters. Most of its non-Russian Federation routes are from Tashkent, although it did launch a thrice weekly service to Istanbul from Samarkand in May 2023 and has been operating some of its Tel Aviv flights via Samarkand.

It is aiming to launch services to Europe with the A321LR, a new longer-range variant of the A321neo that has the range to reach Western Europe from Tashkent. Qanot Sharq has operated a small number of ad hoc charter flights to Bulgaria, Cyprus, and Greece (as well as Egypt), but has not yet operated to Western Europe.

Air Samarkand also plans to start with two all-economy 180-seat A320s, following a full-service leisure airline model. However, it could potentially introduce business class with future A320s and possible A330s.

The opening up of Uzbekistan's airline sector to new entrants is sensible, as having a competitive market will lead to more capacity and lower fares. This will benefit Uzbekistan's economy, particularly the tourism sector, which has ambitious growth targets that cannot be achieved without more airline capacity and lower fares.

However, the launch of several airlines in a short period of time will put pressure on the aviation regulator, who will need more resources to effectively manage several AOCs. There will also likely be personnel constraints at airlines as it will take time to train enough pilots and mechanics to support the rapid expansion of Uzbekistan's airline sector. There is a concern some of the start-ups lack the experience to effectively manage airlines and will struggle to hire pilots and technical staff.

Uzbekistan has extensive aviation experience and a lot of well-qualified aviation people, but it does have enough experienced people to support a large surge in the number of airlines and aircraft. Uzbekistan should consider measures to ensure the rate of expansion of local airlines is reasonable from an operational, personnel, and oversight perspective.

Uzbekistan Airways Group—and Uzbekistan, in general—would benefit from a new strategy

The launch of several new airlines will also put pressure on Uzbekistan Airways, which has been preparing for possible privatization. Uzbekistan Airways has a bright outlook and is resuming expansion but would benefit from a clear strategy, particularly for its LCC operation.

The decision to establish an LCC was sensible as Uzbekistan Airways was struggling to compete against foreign airlines on many routes and recognized low fare competition would intensify further as the market continues to liberalize. However, Uzbekistan Express needs to follow a purer LCC model to compete effectively against foreign LCCs as well as new local independent LCCs.

Uzbekistan Express does not have a typical LCC product as it offers free checked baggage, snacks, and drinks. All its revenues are generated from airfare as it does not sell any ancillary products, which are a major revenue generator for most LCCs.

Uzbekistan Express initially offered 15 kg for checked baggage, but there was an outcry from many passengers, and it responded by increasing the checked baggage allowance to 23 kg, matching what Uzbekistan Airways provides. There were also complaints about not providing hot meals.

Any market that is new to LCC often have these issues. LCCs need to be firm about their business model and educate passengers about it. As more foreign LCCs serve Uzbekistan and as more local LCCs launch, inevitably there will be a transition to purer LCC models, which are needed to lower fares. For example, Silk Avia is trying to follow a pure LCC model and charge passengers for all extra items, including checked baggage and water. Uzbekistan Airports believes this is the only way to make an LCC work and that local passengers will get used to not having any amenities.

Silk Avia is only operating short domestic flights, but passengers should become more aware of what the LCC model means on longer international flights as local privately owned LCCs launch international services. These airlines will be starting from scratch and are not under a full-service parent, giving them a potential advantage.

Uzbekistan Express now relies on Uzbekistan Airways for all functions, including sales and marketing, and uses Uzbekistan Airways crew. Many Uzbekistan Express passengers also connect to Uzbekistan Airways. Uzbekistan Airways should consider spinning off Uzbekistan Express as its own company with its own AOC. By negotiating its own contracts and having its own employees—rather than relying on legacy contracts and staff from the parent company— Uzbekistan Express should be able to lower its unit costs.

An independent Uzbekistan Express could also potentially establish crew bases in secondary cities, particularly in Namangan given its large operation there. A Namangan crew base would be more efficient than the current setup where all crew members are based in Tashkent and often stay at hotels in Namangan. Most LCCs do not lay over crews, as they operate schedules that ensure their crews fly a return trip between their base and a destination within crew duty time limits. Uzbekistan Express is not able to do this and frequently needs to overnight crew at secondary cities in Uzbekistan or Moscow as about two-thirds of Uzbekistan Express' flights are not from Tashkent.

Uzbekistan Express currently has unit costs (cost per available seat kilometer) about 20% less than that of Uzbekistan Airways. This cost gap is entirely driven by operating higher-density aircraft. As it does not follow other elements of the LCC model, its unit costs are significantly higher than foreign LCCs.

Uzbekistan Express will also benefit from a larger fleet, which would generate economies of scale and support a lower cost structure. With a larger fleet and a pure LCC model, Uzbekistan Express would be able to compete in other markets aside from the Russian Federation. The Middle East is particularly a strong potential market for Uzbekistan Express given this market consists primarily of price-sensitive travelers, including Uzbek citizens working in the Middle East, and as it faces growing LCC competition.

Uzbekistan Express could also be used on regional international routes to other CAREC countries. It briefly served Kazakhstan with services from Namangan to Almaty, Nukus to Aktau and Aktobe, and Urgench to Aktau. None of these services operated more than 6 months and have operated since June 2022.

Uzbekistan Express is keen to grow further in the Russian Federation, where there has been strong demand since the start of Russia's war in Ukraine. However, securing approvals from Russian authorities has been difficult, including a plan to nearly double the number of Russian Federation flights from Namangan.

As Uzbekistan Airways modernizes and expands its own fleet, it expects to transfer more aircraft to Uzbekistan Express, enabling expansion of the LCC. Uzbekistan Airways still operates five dual-class A320ceos, having so far only retrofitted and transferred four of its A320ceos to Uzbekistan Express. Uzbekistan Express will likely take over these five aircraft over the next few years as Uzbekistan Airways takes delivery of newer A320neos.

Uzbekistan Airways already operates six A320neos and five A321neoLRs (as of September 2023). The A321neoLR were all delivered in 2022 and are now used on long-haul routes to East Asia and Europe. Three A320neos were delivered in June, July and August 2023, following delivery of the first three in 2019 and 2020. Uzbekistan Airways announced in January 2023 orders for an additional eight A320neos as well as four A321neos.

The new order with Airbus will enable Uzbekistan Airways to phase out aging 757s and 767s as well as continue to grow its full-service operation. More 787s are also planned and A350s are under consideration, facilitating full-service wide-body growth. Uzbekistan Airways currently operates six 787-8s, which were delivered in 2016 to 2019.

Uzbekistan Airways' traffic has been above pre-COVID-19 traffic levels since May 2022, driven in part by load factors that have been about 10 percentage points higher than pre-pandemic levels. Uzbekistan Airways Group carried over 4 million passengers in 2022 and expects 10% growth per annum over the next several years. These figures include both Uzbekistan Airways and Uzbekistan Express.

In summer of 2023, the group had restored virtually its entire network, and international seat capacity was up about 20% compared to summer 2019 levels. Seat capacity was roughly flat in summer of 2022 compared to 2019, but traffic was higher due to the higher load factors. The group was serving about 45 international destinations in summer of 2023, roughly matching the number of destinations from 2019 with a few adjustments.

While overall traffic levels for the group are now at historic highs, as a brand Uzbekistan Airways has only slightly more traffic than before the pandemic due to the launch of Uzbekistan Express. The group's market share also has declined as Uzbekistan's overall market has grown faster. Even as it resumes expansion, Uzbekistan Airways Group will likely see its market share further decline given the rapid expansion of foreign airlines, particularly LCCs, as well as the launch of several new local airlines.

The Uzbekistan market can clearly support more capacity and benefit from more competition. However, capacity could increase faster than demand, impacting yields and profitability.

It is important for Uzbekistan to reduce costs in areas such as ground handling, in-flight catering, and refueling. While Uzbekistan has restructured, ending Uzbekistan Airways' control of several services including ground handling, all airlines are now impacted by monopolistic providers. Uzbekistan needs a more competitive aviation service provider sector to facilitate further growth. A lower-cost environment is not only critical for LCCs but all airlines, particularly given that several new local airlines have now entered the market.

Uzbekistan can achieve rapid passenger growth, but it needs to provide an environment in which both the flag carrier and several independent airlines are able

Tashkent Airport will be modernized and expanded to support rapid growth, including from Uzbekistan Airways, which is one of the largest airlines in CAREC (photo by Brendan Sobie).

to thrive. It should consider adopting a new aviation strategy that continues down the liberalization path while also putting in place policies that enable sustainable growth. Uzbekistan also needs to accelerate airport infrastructure investments to support the anticipated growth while reviewing airport policies to ensure sufficient competition and a lower cost base for airlines.

Uzbekistan has made remarkable progress in reforming its aviation sector, becoming a model for liberalization that other CAREC countries can learn from. It is now at a critical juncture that, with the right decisions, strategies and investments could result in a prolonged period of rapid air transport growth with profound implications on tourism and the overall economy.

Recommendations for Uzbekistan

1. Continue liberalizing and consider a more open policy for Tashkent that provides full access without restrictions.

2. Adjust its policy for secondary airports by making access to these airports more meaningful, and introduce a pricing structure which recognizes that secondary airports should be cheaper.

3. Consider forging open skies agreements with several countries, including other CAREC countries, and start providing fifth and seventh freedom rights.

4. Consider revisiting its domestic air transport strategy to ensure domestic expansion is commercially viable and environmentally sustainable.

5. Continue to encourage new competitors and private sector investment in the airline sector, but adjust policies to ensure the number of new entrants is realistic given the size of its market, and the availability of staff and oversight resources.

6. Reconsider policies that allow airports to own airlines, to ensure potential conflicts of interest are avoided.

7. Adjust its dual-brand strategy by separating Uzbekistan Express, following a purer LCC model and accelerating expansion.

8. Invest in expanding and modernizing airports, but make sure airport charges and fees are reasonable.

9. Relook at policies for airport service providers to ensure there is more competition and more reasonable prices.

10. Align better its aviation and tourism strategies and consider new joint programs for incentivizing the launch of new routes and attracting more airlines, particularly LCCs.

11. Consider adjusting its pricing structure at Samarkand Airport to facilitate development of air services and tourism, and to increase utilization of its new terminal, particularly during daytime hours.

12. Focus on LCCs and bring in international LCC expertise as it considers PPP options for Bukhara and Urgench airports.

Low-Cost Carrier Opportunities, Air Transport Liberalization, and Post-Pandemic Recovery in CAREC

Rapid growth of low-cost carriers (LCC) would help members of the Central Asia Regional Economic Cooperation (CAREC) Program improve connectivity and increase tourism. LCCs generate significant economic benefits as lower fares make air travel more affordable, stimulating demand in both domestic and international markets. However, LCCs cannot thrive without a supportive regulatory environment. Several CAREC countries have adopted more liberal aviation policies, facilitating the recent wave of LCC growth. This study finds that further liberalization is needed for further growth and for LCCs to reach their full potential in the CAREC region.

About the Central Asia Regional Economic Cooperation Program

The Central Asia Regional Economic Cooperation (CAREC) Program is a partnership of 11 member countries and development partners working together to promote development through cooperation, leading to accelerated economic growth and poverty reduction. It is guided by the overarching vision of "Good Neighbors, Good Partners, and Good Prospects." CAREC countries include: Afghanistan, Azerbaijan, the People's Republic of China, Georgia, Kazakhstan, the Kyrgyz Republic, Mongolia, Pakistan, Tajikistan, Turkmenistan, and Uzbekistan.

About the Asian Development Bank

ADB is committed to achieving a prosperous, inclusive, resilient, and sustainable Asia and the Pacific, while sustaining its efforts to eradicate extreme poverty. Established in 1966, it is owned by 68 members —49 from the region. Its main instruments for helping its developing member countries are policy dialogue, loans, equity investments, guarantees, grants, and technical assistance.

CAREC SECRETARIAT
www.carecprogram.org

ASIAN DEVELOPMENT BANK
6 ADB Avenue, Mandaluyong City
1550 Metro Manila, Philippines
www.adb.org